Ajax

BRUCE PERENS' OPEN SOURCE SERIES

www.prenhallprofessional.com/perens

Bruce Perens' Open Source Series is a definitive series of books on Linux and open source technologies, written by many of the world's leading open source professionals. It is also a voice for up-and-coming open source authors. Each book in the series is published under the Open Publication License (www.opencontent.org), an open source compatible book license, which means that electronic versions will be made available at no cost after the books have been in print for six months.

Ajax

Creating Web Pages with Asynchronous JavaScript and XML

Edmond Woychowsky

Upper Saddle River, NJ • Boston • Indianapolis • San Francisco
New York • Toronto • Montreal • London • Munich • Paris • Madrid
Cape Town • Sydney • Tokyo • Singapore • Mexico City

Many of the designations used by manufacturers and sellers to distinguish their products are claimed as trademarks. Where those designations appear in this book, and the publisher was aware of a trademark claim, the designations have been printed with initial capital letters or in all capitals.

The author and publisher have taken care in the preparation of this book, but make no expressed or implied warranty of any kind and assume no responsibility for errors or omissions. No liability is assumed for incidental or consequential damages in connection with or arising out of the use of the information or programs contained herein.

The publisher offers excellent discounts on this book when ordered in quantity for bulk purchases or special sales, which may include electronic versions and/or custom covers and content particular to your business, training goals, marketing focus, and branding interests. For more information, please contact:

U.S. Corporate and Government Sales
(800) 382-3419
corpsales@pearsontechgroup.com

For sales outside the United States, please contact:

International Sales
international@pearsoned.com

 This Book Is Safari Enabled

The Safari, Enabled icon on the cover of your favorite technology book means the book is available through Safari Bookshelf. When you buy this book, you get free access to the online edition for 45 days. Safari Bookshelf is an electronic reference library that lets you easily search thousands of technical books, find code samples, download chapters, and access technical information whenever and wherever you need it.

- To gain 45-day Safari Enabled access to this book:

- Go to http://www.prenhallprofessional.com/safarienabled

- Complete the brief registration form

- Enter the coupon code WZM8-GZEL-ZTEE-4IL7-W2R5

If you have difficulty registering on Safari Bookshelf or accessing the online edition, please e-mail customer-service@safaribooksonline.com.

Visit us on the Web: www.prenhallprofessional.com

Library of Congress Cataloging-in-Publication Data:

Woychowsky, Edmond.

Ajax : creating Web pages with asynchronous JavaScript and XML / Edmond Woychowsky.

p. cm.

ISBN 0-13-227267-9 (pbk. : alk. paper) 1. Web sites—Design—Computer programs. 2. Ajax (Web site development technology) 3. JavaScript (Computer program language) 4. XML (Document markup language) I. Title.

TK5105.8885.A52W69 2006

006.7'86—dc22

2006017743

ISBN 0-13-227267-9

Text printed in the United States on recycled paper at R. R. Donnelley in Crawfordsville, Indiana.
First printing, August 2006

This book is dedicated to my wife, Mary Ann, and my children, Benjamin and Crista. Without their constant support, the book that you hold in your hands would definitely not exist.

Contents

About the Author

A graduate of Middlesex Country College and Penn State, Edmond Woychowsky began his professional life at Bell Labs as a dinosaur writing recursive assembly-language programs for use in their DOSS order entry system. Throughout his career, Ed has worked in the banking, insurance, pharmaceutical, and manufacturing industries, slowly sprouting feathers and evolving into a web developer. He is best known for his often unique articles on the TechRepublic website, as well as his ability to explain how Muenchian grouping works in small words. Currently, he can be found working in New Jersey as a consultant, applying both Ajax and XSLT to problems in often bizarre ways and looking forward to his next meal.

Preface

The purpose of the book that you hold in your hands, *Ajax: Creating Web Pages with Asynchronous JavaScript and XML,* is simply to show you the fundamentals of developing Ajax applications.

WHAT THIS BOOK IS ABOUT

For the last several years, there has been a quiet revolution taking place in web application development. In fact, it was so quiet that until February 2005, this revolution didn't have a name, even among the revolutionaries themselves. Actually, beyond the odd mention of phrases such as `XMLHttpRequest` object, *XML,* or *SOAP,* developers didn't really talk about it much at all, probably out of some fear of being burned for meddling in unnatural forces. But now that the cat is out of the bag, there is no reason not to show how Ajax works.

Because I am a member of the "we learn by doing" cult (no Kool Aid required), you'll find more code examples than you can shake a stick at. So this is the book for those people who enjoyed the labs more than the lectures. If *enjoyed* is the wrong word, feel free to substitute the words "learned more from."

Until around 2005, the "we learn by doing" group of developers was obscured by the belief that a piece of paper called a certification meant more than hands-on knowledge. I suppose that, in a way, it did. Unfortunately, when jobs became fewer and farther between, developers began to collect certifications the way that Imelda Marcos collected shoes. Encyclopedic knowledge might have helped in getting interviews and subsequent jobs, but it really didn't help very much in keeping those jobs. However, now that the pendulum has begun to swing in the other direction, it is starting to become more important to actually know a subject than to be certified in it. This leads to the question of "Why learn Ajax?"

The answer to that question can be either short and sweet or as rich and varied as the concept of Ajax itself. Let's start with the first answer because it looks good on the resumé. We all know that when something looks good on the resumé, it helps to keep us in the manner in which we have become accustomed, living indoors and eating regularly. Couple this with the knowledge of actually having hands-on knowledge, and the odds of keeping the job are greatly increased.

The rich and varied answer is that, to parrot half of the people writing about web development trends, Ajax is the wave of the future. Of course, this leads to the statement, "I heard the same thing about DHTML, and nobody has talked about that for five years." Yes, some of the same things were said about DHTML, but this time it is different.

The difference is that, this time, the technology has evolved naturally instead of being sprung upon the world just so developers could play buzzword bingo with their resumés. This time, there are actual working examples beyond the pixie dust following our mouse pointers around. This time, the companies using these techniques are real companies, with histories extending beyond last Thursday. This time, things are done with a reason beyond the "it's cool" factor.

WHAT YOU NEED TO KNOW BEFORE READING THIS BOOK

This book assumes a basic understanding of web-development techniques beyond the WYSIWYG drag and drop that is the current standard. It isn't necessary to have hand-coded HTML; it is only necessary to know that HTML exists. This book will hopefully fill in the gaps so that the basics of what goes where can be performed.

Beyond my disdain for the drag-and-drop method of web development, there is a logical reason for the need to know something about HTML—basically, we're going to be modifying the HTML document after it is loaded in the browser. Nothing really outrageous will be done to the document—merely taking elements out, putting elements in, and modifying elements in place.

For those unfamiliar with JavaScript, it isn't a problem; I've taken care to explain it in some depth because there is nothing worse than needing a second book to help understand the first book. Thinking about it now, of course, I missed a wonderful opportunity to write a companion JavaScript volume. Doh!

If you're unfamiliar with XML, don't be put off by the fact that Ajax is short hand Asynchronous JavaScript and XML because what you need to know is in here, too. The same is also true of XSLT, which is a language used to transform XML into other forms. Think of Hogwarts, and you get the concept.

In this book, the evolution (or, if you prefer, intelligent design) of Ajax is described from the beginning of web development through the Dynamic HTML, right up to Asynchronous JavaScript and XML. Because this book describes a somewhat newer technique of web development, using a recent vintage web browser such as Firefox or Flock is a good idea. You also need an Internet connection.

HOW THIS BOOK IS LAID OUT

Here is a short summary of this book's chapters:

+ Chapter 1, "Types of Web Pages," provides a basic overview of the various ways that web pages have been coded since the inception of the Web. The history of web development is covered beginning with static web pages through dynamic web pages. In addition, the various technologies used in web development are discussed. The chapter closes with a discussion on browsers and the browser war.

+ Chapter 2, "Introducing Ajax," introduces Ajax with an account of what happened when I demonstrated my first Ajax application. The concepts behind Ajax are described and then are introduced in a step-by-step manner, from the first primordial Ajax relatives to the current evolution.

+ Chapter 3, "HTML/XHTML," describes some of the unmentioned basic building blocks of Ajax, HTML/XHTML, and Cascading Style Sheets.

+ Chapter 4, "JavaScript," serves as an overview of JavaScript, including data types, variables, and operators. Also covered are flow-control statements, recursive functions, constructors, and event handlers.

+ Chapter 5, "Ajax Using HTML and JavaScript," describes one of the earlier ancestors of Ajax. Essentially, this is how to fake it using stone knives and bear skins. Although the technique described is somewhat old-fashioned, it demonstrates, to a degree, how processing flows in an Ajax application. In addition, the "dark art" of communicating information between frames is covered. Additionally, in an effort to appease those who believe that this is all old hat, the subject of stored procedures in MySQL is covered.

+ Chapter 6, "XML," covers XML, particularly the parts that come into play when dealing with Ajax. Elements, attributes and entities, oh my; the various means of describing content, Document Type Definitions, and Schema are covered. Also included are cross-browser XML data islands.

+ Chapter 7, "XMLHttpRequest," dissects the `XMLHttpRequest` object by describing its various properties and methods. Interested in making it synchronous instead of asynchronous? You'll find the answer in this chapter. In addition, both web services and SOAP are discussed in this chapter.

+ Chapter 8, "Ajax Using XML and XMLHttpRequest," covers what some might consider pure Ajax, with special attention paid to the `XMLHttpRequest` object that makes the whole thing work. Additionally, various back ends are discussed, ranging from PHP to C#. Also covered are two of the more popular communication protocols: RPC and SOAP.

+ Chapter 9, "XPath," covers XPath in detail. Starting with the basics of what is often considered XSLT's flunky, this chapter describes just how to locate information contained in an XML document. Included in this chapter is a detailed description of XPath axis, which is at least worth a look.

+ Chapter 10, "XSLT," goes into some detail about the scary subject of XSLT and how it can be fit into a cross-browser Ajax application. Starting with the basics and progressing to the more advanced possibilities, an attempt is made to demystify XSLT.

+ Chapter 11, "Ajax Using XSLT," takes the material covered in the first four chapters the next logical step with the introduction of XSLT. Until relatively recently, this was typically considered a bad idea. However, with some care, this is no longer the case. XSLT is one of those tools that can further enhance the site visitor's experience.

+ Chapter 12, "Better Living Through Code Reuse," introduces a home-grown client-side JavaScript library that is used throughout the examples shown in this book. Although this library doesn't necessarily have to be used, the examples provide an annotated look at what goes on behind the scenes with most of the Ajax libraries currently in existence.

+ Chapter 13, "Traveling with Ruby on Rails," is a gentle introduction to the open source Ruby on Rails framework. Beginning with where to obtain the various components and their installation, the chapter shows how to start the WEBrick web server. Following those examples, a simple page that accesses a MySQL database is demonstrated.

+ Chapter 14, "Traveling Farther with Ruby," looks a little deeper into Ruby on Rails, with the introduction of a simple Ajax application that uses the built-in Rails JavaScript library.

+ Chapter 15, "The Essential Cross-Browser HTML DOM," describes the dark and mysterious realm of the cross-browser HTML Document Object Model. Another unmentioned part of Ajax, the HTML DOM is essentially how the various parts of an HTML or XHTML document are accessed. This is what makes the "only update part of a document" feature of Ajax work.

+ Chapter 16, "Other Items of Interest," describes some of the resources available via the World Wide Web. These resources range from pre-written Ajax-capable JavaScript libraries to some of the numerous browsers available for your personal computer.

CONVENTIONS USED IN THIS BOOK

Listings, code snippets, and code in the text in this book are in monospaced font. This means that the code could be typed in the manner shown using your editor of choice, and the result would appear as follows:

```
if(enemy = 'troll')
    runaway();
```

Acknowledgments

Even though this book is essentially "my" book, it has been influenced in many ways (all of them good) by multiple individuals. Because the roles that each of these individuals played in the creative process were very significant, I would like to take the time to thank as many of them as I can remember here.

Mary Ann Woychowsky, for understanding my "zoning out" when writing and for asking, "I guess the book is finished, right?" after catching me playing Morrowind when I should have been writing. Benjamin Woychowsky, for asking, "Shouldn't you be writing?" whenever I played a computer game. Crista Woychowsky, for disappearing with entire seasons of *Star Gate SG-1,* after catching me watching them when I should have been writing.

My mother, Nan Gerling, for sharing her love of reading and keeping me in reading materials.

Eric Garulay, of Prentice Hall, for marketing this book and putting me in touch with Catherine Nolan. Catherine Nolan, of Prentice Hall, for believing in this book and for her assistance in getting started with a book. Bruce Perens, for his belief that because I use Firefox, I had not tread too far down the path that leads to the dark side. Denise Mickelson, of Prentice Hall, for making sure that I kept sending in chapters. Chris Zahn, of Prentice Hall, for his editing, for answering my often bizarre questions, and for his knowledge of things in general. Thanks to George Nedeff for managing the editorial and production workflow and Heather Fox for keeping this project in the loop and on track. Any errors remaining are solely my own.

I would like to thank the late Jack Chalker for his assistance with what to look for in writing contracts and for essentially talking me through the process using words that I could understand. Also for his writing a number of science-fiction novels that have influenced the way that I look upon the world. After all, in the end, everything is about how we look upon the world.

Dossy Shiobara, for answering several bizarre questions concerning MySQL.

Richard Behrens, for his assistance in formulating my thoughts.

Joan Susski, for making sure that I didn't go totally off the deep end when developing many of the techniques used in this book.

Premkumar Ekkaladevi, who was instrumental in deciding just how far to push the technology.

Jon (Jack) Foreman, for explaining to me that I can't know everything.

David Sarisohn, who years ago gave a very understandable reason for why code shouldn't be obscure.

Finally, to Francis Burke, Shirley Tainow, Thomas Dunn, Marion Sackrowitz, Frances Mundock, Barbara Hershey, Beverly Simon, Paul Bhatia, Joseph Muller, Rick Good, Jane Liefert, Joan Litt, Albert Nicolai, and Bill Ricker for teaching me how to learn.

CHAPTER 1

Types of Web Pages

While I was in college, sometime during the Pliocene, I took a science fiction class. The interesting thing about this class is that one student didn't realize until midterms that it wasn't a physiology class. I bring this up only because if you've picked up this book expecting Corinthian helmets and hoplites, which, incidentally, have one-third less fat than regular hops (useful information for Hydras on a diet), this is the wrong book.

According to legend, the Web was originally created by Tim Berners-Lee to distribute documents of a technical nature. Think of it as the late-twentieth-century version of leaving a note on the refrigerator describing how to preheat the oven, put the casserole in, make a salad, and serve it after 1 hour. As you can well imagine, posting this kind of information on a computer network has a much farther reach than posting it on a single refrigerator.

The existence of the World Wide Web hit all of us suddenly, like a summer thunderstorm, from clear skies to cracks of lightning in what felt like 15 minutes. All of a sudden all the friends and relatives who thought I was a little strange for having a computer were calling Gateway and Dell or were in a store getting a Toshiba or Compaq. It was as if they were all suddenly afflicted with some illness that made them say words like *bits, bytes,* and *baud.* Instead of strutting around comparing the size of their sailboats, they were all strutting comparing the size of their hard disks.

In just over a decade of existence, the World Wide Web has transformed dramatically from its humble beginnings on a single server stuck on a desk in an out-of-the-way office. In the first few years, the growth of the World Wide Web resembled Fibonacci numbers. If you're unfamiliar with Fibonacci numbers, they are a mathematical representation of the increase in the numbers of immortal bunnies in a garden with no predators. Assume an infinite supply of carrots and, well, you get the idea—it was that kind of growth. Unfortunately, growth at that rate cannot be maintained forever; eventually, that many bunnies are bound to attract something with a taste for hasenpfeffer.

My opinion of this situation is that, contrary to popular belief, the end of growth in leaps and bounds is not the beginning of the end; it is merely the end of the beginning. Change is good, change is inevitable, and change rarely comes without pain.

Speaking of change, Ajax is a bit of a change from the earlier types of web pages, be they static HTML or Dynamic HTML/DHTML. The interesting thing is that all types of web pages rely upon essentially the same ingredients: HTML, JavaScript, CSS, and sometimes XML. In this chapter, I take our discussion a little beyond those simple ingredients, though, to consider the only two additional factors that can affect the end result: the browser and the web server.

1.1 STATIC WEB PAGES

Static web pages are the original type (and for what seemed like about 10 minutes the only type) of web pages. When dealing with the distribution of technical documents, there aren't very many changes to the original document. What you actually see more of is a couple of technical documents getting together, settling down, and producing litter after litter of little technical documents. However, the technical documents didn't have this fertile landscape completely to themselves for very long.

If you've ever traveled anywhere in the United States by automobile, you might be familiar with one of the staples of the driving vacation: the travel brochure. Often describing places like Endless Caverns, Natural Bridge, Mystic Aquarium, or Roadside America, they're a staple of the American landscape. Designed to catch attention and draw the traveler in to spend some cash, they've been around seemingly forever.

The web equivalent, sometimes referred to as brochure-ware, also is designed to draw in the virtual traveler. This type of website is usually used to inform the visitor about subjects as varied as places to visit, cooking, children, or my nephew Nick and niece Ashley's 2002 visit to Walt Disney World. This is actually a great medium for information that is relatively unchanging.

Allow me to digress for a little computer history lesson. Back in the old days when dinosaurs—eh, mainframes—ruled computing, there were pseudo-conversational systems that faked some of the functionality seen in web applications. These applications essentially displayed a form on what was called a dumb terminal. It was called a dumb terminal because it had no real processing power of its own. The user then filled out the form and hit a program function key, which transferred the input data to the mainframe. The mainframe processed the data, based upon content and the specific program function key, and the results, if any, were displayed on the user's dumb terminal. End of history lesson.

Static web pages offer the same functionality as those monster computers of old, in much the same way. The only real changes are form "buttons" instead of program function keys, the presence of a mouse, and the price tags for the equipment involved. Well, maybe that isn't entirely true; a dumb terminal will set you back about as much as one of today's off-the-shelf computers. The real difference lies in the price difference between a web server and a mainframe: thousands of dollars vs. millions of dollars. Those dinosaurs didn't come cheap.

1.2   DYNAMIC WEB PAGES

Static web pages have three major problems. The first is that they're boring. Think of it as visiting the park down the road on vacation every year. Unless that park is Yellowstone, or there's lots of alcohol involved, it's going to get old very quickly.

The second problem is that, unlike a dumb terminal, a personal computer has processing power of its own. Some, in fact, have more processing power than the web servers that they are communicating with. Why not take advantage of this processing power? It won't cost the server anything to utilize this essentially free resource.

The final problem with static web pages is that all validation is performed by the server. This means that if a user enters a telephone number as (999)999-9999 instead of 999-999-9999, it is up to the server to catch the error and inform the user of the correct format. So the user is forced to endure the entire cycle in which the form is sent to the server, which finds the error and then sends the whole page back to the web browser. And unless the web developer took care to retain the information already entered, the user is forced to re-enter everything. I don't know about you, but this wouldn't give me the warm fuzzes about a website.

For all of these reasons and the "wouldn't it be cool?" factor, a technique called Dynamic Hypertext Markup Language, or DHMTL, was created. Even at first glance, it was obvious that there was a vast difference between static web pages and pages that employed DHTML techniques. The first of these differences is that things happened on dynamic web pages.

There were events. No, not events like the grand opening of the Wal-Mart Super Center down the road—browser events. When the mouse pointer was moved around the page, things happened, and not just the pointer changing from an arrow to a hand and back again. Real things happened. Hyperlinks changed color; menus dropped down.

As incredible as all of this seemed, the biggest difference came when working with HTML forms. Much of the validation was performed on the client side, right on the browser (which is what *client side* means, but I was going for the effect here). The fact was that the user no longer had to wait for the entire unload/reload cycle to discover that some moron web developer wants dashes separating the parts of a date instead of forward slashes. This was a real improvement.

In fact, on some websites, techniques were used to prevent the user from entering characters that weren't allowed. If a numeric value is expected in an input box, well, try as you might, only the numeric keys and the decimal point will work; if an integer is expected, users don't even get the decimal point.

Of course, it wasn't long before DHTML was taken to the extreme. On some pages the mouse pointer turned into a magic wand, trailing pixie dust like flies behind a garbage truck. Other web pages seemed to nearly explode whenever the mouse pointer moved because of the sheer number of drop-down menus, rollovers, and assorted "features." Basically, too much of a good thing makes it no longer a good thing.

However, as they say on television, "How'd they do that?"

The quick answer is "Very carefully," but if we we're concerned with quick answers, we would all be millionaires from using a Magic Eight Ball for investment decisions. Of course, this doesn't seem to be working for my broker, so I could be wrong.

The way DHTML works is through a mixture of HTML, Cascading Style Sheets, and JavaScript. Also, as the cooking shows demonstrate, it is all in how the ingredients are put together instead of the fact that they are put together. For example, quite a few people like chicken and chocolate, but with the exception of *mole,* how many dishes are there that combine the two?

1.2.1   HTML

Yeah, Hypertext Markup Language was what made static web pages work, but just because the web pages were static doesn't mean that HTML was static. Time moved forward, as time usually does, and new capabilities and features were added. Some were, well, not removed, but deprecated, which means that they're still there, but only for compatibility purposes. These deprecated features, however, were more than made up for by the addition of the new features.

The big question is, who decides which features stay, which are deprecated, and which are added? The answer is that all of these decisions are made by the World Wide Web Consortium, which, in secret midnight meetings, dances around a bonfire, drinks mead, and listens to Jethro Tull CDs. Alright, the truth is that committees meet periodically in a conference room and discuss modifications to HTML. However, my explanation accounts for the existence of the marquee tag better than the official explanation.

The World Wide Web Consortium is the governing body that issues "Recommendations" concerning the more technical aspects of the Web. Starting with Hypertext Markup Language version 1.0 and moving through the more current version 4.01 and XHTML version 1.1, the World Wide Web Consortium attempts to keep things standard among the various web browser developers. Theoretically, the end result of these "Recommendations" is that all web browsers behave identically on any specific website, but as I explain later, there are degrees of compliance and interpretation. In addition, there are plenty of nonstandard extensions by browser developers, who, in the hopes of getting a leg up on the competition, continue to add "features" until their browser resembles a Swiss Army knife more than a web browser.

1.2.2 CSS

The problem with HTML is that it was never intended to deal with anything beyond the structure of a page. Unfortunately, early on, somebody new to HTML asked the question, "Hey, how do I make text bold?" and the pure structural language called HTML was polluted by presentation. The end result of this was documents with more HTML than text. Mostly consisting of b tags, i tags, and the dreaded font tags, these documents were a nightmare if it became necessary to make a change.

Cascading Style Sheets, Level 1, are an attempt to bring this situation back under control by providing a way to avoid the b, i, and font tags. Instead, presentation could be dealt with on a per-tag basis, which makes coding somewhat like being a Roman emperor: "The text in the anchor tags amuses me—make it bold and Tahoma!"

Cascading Style Sheets work by associating style rules to the elements of an HTML document. These rules can be applied to single tags, tags of a specific type, or developer-specified tags. This eliminates the need to code tags within tags until the page is so bloated that it is nearly impossible to follow; instead, a CSS is specified on the page level or tag level to describe the style for the entire page.

Just in case you're wondering, the *cascading* part of Cascading Style Sheets comes into play when there is more than one style sheet with rules that can be applied to a specific tag. The specific style sheet rule that is applied depends exactly on how the applicable Cascading Style Sheet is defined. The problem, for me, at least, is remembering cascade sequence. One method of keeping the cascade straight is equating it to something else, something a bit more familiar, as in the winning hands of poker. In poker, the winning hands, from high to low, are:

1. Royal flush
2. Straight flush
3. Four of a kind
4. Full house
5. Flush

With Cascading Style Sheets, the "winning" hands are as follows:

1. Inline CSS defined in the element's `style` attribute
2. Internal CSS defined using the `style` tag
3. External CSS defined using the `style` tag
4. External CSS defined using the `link` tag
5. The default built into the web browser

As with poker, when there is a winning hand, any other hands are all for naught.

1.2.3 JavaScript

JavaScript is a lightweight, interpreted, object-based programming language that has become the standard client-side scripting language. Based upon the C programming language of Kernighan and Richie fame, JavaScript is how all of those neat and nifty little client-side tricks work. Whether it is event trapping, validation, or whatever, nine times out of ten, JavaScript is the man behind the curtain pulling the levers to make things happen.

Even though JavaScript is widespread doesn't mean that there isn't a lot of confusion about JavaScript. Take, for example, the name; originally called LiveScript, the name was changed to cash in on some of the press that Java was getting early on. To confuse things further, Microsoft sometimes refers to its implementation as JScript, while in Europe, the name ECMAScript is used to refer to JavaScript. I, for one, believe that all of these aliases are designed to hide a gangster past or something along those lines.

Seriously, most of the client-side logic on the Web is coded in JavaScript. This doesn't mean that JavaScript is innately superior to VBScript, Perl, or even Java itself; it is only because JavaScript is built into practically every browser currently available. This means that visitors to websites that use JavaScript, as opposed to any of the alternatives, can jump right into shopping or whatever without waiting for a download to complete.

1.3 WEB BROWSERS

Without a web browser, though, web pages are rather useless. The majority of people wandering around the Internet wouldn't fully appreciate them. Yes, there is the indentation, but without a browser, there is no scripting or pictures. A lot can be said about web browsers; after all, they color our web browsing experience nearly as much as the pages we visit. The decision to use a specific web browser probably says a great deal about who each of us is as an individual. Unfortunately, I'm not aware of any study along those lines. I, for one, would like to see what would be said about somebody still running Internet Explorer version 2 on a 100-MHz Pentium with Windows 95. But come to think of it, that describes some of the employees on my last consulting assignment.

Nevertheless, a web browser is our window (note the small w) to the World Wide Web, and, as with windows, quite a few choices are available to us. However, instead of having names like "double hung" and "casements," web browsers have names like "Firefox" and "Opera." And just as with window styles, web browsers go in and out of fashion. For example, think for a moment: How many houses in your neighborhood have arrow slits for windows? However, unlike the majority of windows that either work or do not work, an added factor must be taken into account when considering web browsers: They are not stagnant. Even though their evolution has slowed somewhat compared to a few years ago, web browsers are still evolving.

In some ways, this evolution parallels the evolution that has taken place in the natural world, with the better adapted supplanting those that don't quite fit in as well. Of course, just as in the natural world, there are hangers-on from earlier ages. Sometimes these holdovers exist in isolated communities, and sometimes they're lone individuals living among us unnoticed.

However, unlike in the natural world, evolution in web browsers is driven by an intelligence, or, at least, I'd like to think so. Behind every feature there are individuals who decide what features to include and how to implement those features. Because of this, web browsers can be both very similar to and very different from one another. Let's now take the opportunity to explore some of those similarities and differences.

1.3.1   Microsoft Internet Explorer

Love it or hate it, there is no denying that Microsoft Internet Explorer is currently the most used web browser. In fact, according to one website that measures browser statistics, Internet Explorer comes in both first and third. Huh? Sounds a little like the 1960s version of *The Love Bug,* doesn't it? This incredible feat can be attributed to the estimated 5 percent of people who are still running some incarnation of version 5, which can be versions 5.0, 5.01, or 5.5—your guess is as good as mine.

Although I can't tell you exactly which version of Microsoft Internet Explorer they might be running, I can give several possible reasons for living in the past. The first of these is simple inertia; a body at rest tends to stay at rest. Upgrades take time, and there is always the possibility of something going wrong, so why run the risk of causing problems?

Another possibility is the old "if it ain't broke, why fix it?" reason. Of course, there are different tolerances for "ain't broke." For example, I knew a professor in college who had a car that lost a quart of oil every 50 miles. For him, 50 miles fell within the boundaries of his "ain't broke" tolerance. Unfortunately, the car had other tolerances when someone borrowed the car and forgot about the leak.

The third possible reason for still running some flavor of Microsoft Internet Explorer version 5 is that the machine simply doesn't have the resources for version 6. I know that this can happen; I've seen it with my own eyes. In fact, it was quite some time before Mary Ann, my wife, let me near her computer or its replacement.

I can think of one final reason for running version 5 of Internet Explorer: the sheer size of the download for version 6. When last I looked, it was more than 100MB. This is tolerable with DSL or cable, but with a dial-up connection, it would finish up around the same time that the sun is a burnt-out cinder.

Now let's look at the users of Internet Explorer as a whole, all of the more recent versions, be they 5.0, 5.01, 5.5, or even 6.0. Why do these individuals use a web browser that, according to many, is several years out-of-date? Well, the fact that it came with the computer might have a little to do with it.

The average user has problems setting the clock on the VCR; do you really think that users are ready to install what could be considered a part of the computer's operating system? Some of them know their limitations, and a computer represents a substantial amount of money. They are more likely to give themselves a haircut using a bowl and scissors than to risk "breaking" the computer. After all, Internet Explorer version 6 isn't so bad; it does work, after all.

From a developer's perspective, Internet Explorer also isn't too bad. Yes, it is dated and a little flakey, but that's nothing that we haven't been able to deal with in the past. We're developers; we have powers like Super(insert appropriate gender here). Just beware of the deviations from standards, the developer's version of Kryptonite.

1.3.2 Mozilla-Based Browsers (Netscape, Mozilla, and Firefox)

Before going any further, allow me to come clean. I use Firefox whenever I can, and before Firefox, I used Mozilla, so I'm a wee bit biased. Just in case you've only recently come out of the Y2K shelter, Firefox is an open-source browser that is the descendant of the Netscape Navigator that you remember from before going into the shelter.

Netscape was the original Godzilla—eh, Mozilla—web browser, which, in its day, had a market share equally as impressive as Microsoft Internet Explorer's. In fact, it could be considered more impressive if you consider that, before 1998, Netscape wasn't free. Unfortunately, without the advantage of being bundled to an operating system, Netscape lost ground and Internet Explorer has kept nibbling away until the present day.

The Mozilla browser was the first attempt at an open-source browser, which, unfortunately, never achieved the popularity of the original browser. There is, however, an interesting side note: Version 7 of Netscape was created using Mozilla version 1 as a starting point. For a really successful open-source browser, one needs to look at Firefox.

Originally called Firebird, a synonym for Phoenix that led to quite a few comments about rising from the ashes of Netscape, Firefox is sort of doing to Internet Explorer what Internet Explorer did to Netscape. I say "sort of" because the nibbles seem larger. Maybe this is due to foxes having relatively larger mouths for their size. The actual reason is that it seems that when the goal of dominating the market was achieved, Microsoft lost interest in enhancing Internet Explorer.

As I stated earlier, Firefox is my favorite browser, which doesn't mean that there isn't something that I find troubling with it. Consider the size of the download compared to other web browsers; it is a fraction of the size of most of the others, yet every feature is in there. I'm not troubled enough to give up using Firefox or to lose any sleep—well, maybe just a little sleep. Which is probably how my twisted mind came up with a logical method of how they did it.

Because the majority of web browsers are produced by corporations, they are limited in the number of potential developers to employees and consultants of the corporation. Firefox, on the other hand, is open source. This means that although there is still a limited potential pool of developers, the pool is much larger—say, about the population of the planet, minus two (Bill Gates and Steve Baulmer).

This line of reasoning makes the most sense, far more than my other possible explanation. Open source has better-trained Bit-Gnomes, little people that live in the computer and move the data around. But this theory really makes sense only after the better part of a bottle of Scotch, so I'll stop here.

1.3.3   Linux Browsers (Konqueror, Ephiphany, Galeon, Opera, and Firefox)

Forgive me, Father, for I have sinned: I really don't use Linux very much. The reason for this omission can be explained in a brief conversation that occurred between my then boss and me. It started when out of the blue he said, "It must really piss you off."

My reply was both logical and to the point. "What?"

"The idea that you can't know everything."

After a moment of thought, I replied in the only way I could. I said "Yes, it does!"

For me, Linux is like that. I read about it, but before I get a chance to use what I've read, something comes up and the promise of knowledge fades like a dream in the first light of day. What I do know, however, is that Firefox is probably comparable to the Windows versions, and all of the rest are all open source. This means that if I say that browser A doesn't support B today, by next Thursday, it will, so I'm keeping my mouth shut. If you want to know whether a browser supports a particular feature, the only way to learn is to try it.

However, I'd like to point out one thing: Look at the previous subheading—I'll wait. Alright, notice anything? Yeah, Firefox is listed there. Being open source, Firefox really gets around, which is really comforting. It is a bit like visiting a city far away, feeling lonely, and finding an old friend there.

1.3.4   The Others (Opera, Safari)

These are the browsers that fight for a percentage of what's left over from the big players: Microsoft Internet Explorer and Firefox. Although taken together they don't command a large percentage of the browsers out there, they shouldn't be ignored. It is very possible that the next Internet Explorer or Firefox will come from this group.

Opera, considered a minor player by some, has taken up two spots in the current top ten. And, no, they're not being piggy; it's Opera version 8 and Opera version 7. The interesting thing is that Opera appears to be the sole stand-alone web browser that until very recently charged, although a free version was available for those willing to tolerate advertisements. In this day of "free" web browsers, any browser that charged and survived definitely deserves a closer look.

A relative newcomer, Apple Computer's Safari is, at least, according to the specs and everything I've heard from Mac worshippers, a solid feature-packed browser. Although Apple is currently only a minor player in the computing world, excluding the iPod, its ease-of-use is bound to keep it going for the foreseeable future. So Safari shouldn't lightly be ignored.

In addition to the aforementioned web browsers, there are a slew of others with much smaller user bases. These relative unknowns include browsers for the visually impaired, text-only browsers, and browsers that run on mobile devices. Unfortunately, having used Microsoft's Pocket Internet Explorer 2002 (PIE), I really wouldn't expect much in the way of Ajax support in the near future.

1.4   A Brief Introduction to Cross-Browser Development

Knowledge of different browsers, their capabilities, or merely their existence is often an aid in a discipline called cross-browser development. Cross-browser development can be one of the most exciting programming disciplines; unfortunately, in programming, "exciting" isn't usually a good thing. The problem is that, in most instances, cross-browser development is essentially writing the same routines two or more times, slightly different each time. Personally, I get a feeling of satisfaction whenever I get a routine to work, but when coding a cross-browser, getting it to work in one browser is only half the job.

The issue with cross-browser development is that some "features" that are available on one browser either aren't available on another or have slightly different syntax. Imagine the feeling of satisfaction of solving a particularly thorny problem in Firefox only to have the same page crash and burn in Internet Explorer. Take, for example, the serialization of XML in Firefox; it works great, but try the same code in Internet Explorer, and here be monsters!

To avoid the monsters, it is necessary to understand where they usually hang around waiting for the unsuspecting developer. But first let's establish where the monsters don't reside; for example, the standard data types such as Boolean, numeric, and string are pretty safe. The same can be said for the statements, such as flow-control statements and assignment statements.

It is just too bad the same cannot be said for objects and event handlers. At least for me, this is where most of the problems arise. Everything will be going along fine, with the page working perfectly right up to point that either there is a spectacular failure, or worse, the page just simply stops working. Fortunately, with a little knowledge and a little planning, it is possible to avoid these web development monsters that live where the standards don't quite mesh with reality.

1.4.1   Casualties of the Browser Wars

Cross-browser compatibility was probably the first casualty of the Browser Wars that began about 20 minutes after the second web browser was developed. In those days, browser developers had a tendency to play fast and loose with things in an effort to pack features into their browser before the competition. In the rush to be the first with a new feature, or to play catch-up, no thought was given to the web developers who would actually have to program for these browsers.

Because of this, it wasn't unusual to see two browsers with essentially the same functionality, but having entirely different approaches. Look at how the XMLHttpRequest object is implemented in Microsoft Internet Explorer and in Gecko-based browsers such as Firefox. Internet Explorer, which was the first to implement this object, made it part of ActiveX. This means that to create an instance of this object in Internet Explorer, the following syntax is used:

```
var objXMLHTTP = new ActiveXObject('Microsoft.XMLHTTP');
```

With Firefox and any other browser that implements the XMLHttpRequest object, the syntax is as follows:

```
var objXMLHTTP = new XMLHttpRequest();
```

The reason for this is that ActiveX is a Microsoft-only technology, which means that short of trying to license it from Microsoft, which I can't imagine would come cheap, it was necessary to find another way. And, when found, this other way became the standard for all non-Microsoft web browsers.

1.4.2   Market Share Does *Not* Equal Right

While I'm on the subject of proprietary technologies, I'd like to point out that market share does not equate to being right. History is full of cases in which the leader, the one with the largest market share, was blindsided by something that he or she didn't realize was a threat until too late. Does anybody remember Digital Research's CP/M? If you haven't, CP/M was the premier operating systems in the days when 64K was considered a lot of memory. In a fractured landscape of operating systems, it had more than half of the operating system market.

Then there was the release of the IBM PC, which offered a choice of three operating systems: CP/M-86, PC DOS, and UCSD D-PASCAL. At the time, everybody thought that Digital Research had the new landscape of the Intel 8086 as theirs for the foreseeable future. Unfortunately, because Microsoft's DOS was $50 less, market share yielded to economic pressure. Microsoft went on to become the leader in computer operating systems, while Digital Research faded into history.

1.4.3   The World Wide Web Consortium, Peacekeepers

During the height of the Browser Wars, there was the definite feeling that web browser technology was advancing at a breakneck pace, so much so that the World Wide Web Consortium seemed to be playing catch-up. It was a case of putting the cart before the horse, with the web browsers getting features and then the recommendations being published, which explains the weirdness with the XMLHttpRequest object.

Now the war is, if not over, at least at intermission, giving us time to get some popcorn and a soda. In addition, whether by accident or by design, this break has given the World Wide Web Consortium time to move once more into the lead. Unfortunately, the damage is done and we're all forced to code around the little differences in the various browsers.

1.5   THE SERVER SIDE OF THINGS

The purpose of this book is to explain how Ajax works, paying particularly close attention to the web browser; however, a web browser is only part of the equation. Even for the biggest client-side fan in the world, it is impossible to totally ignore the web server. A web browser without a web server is totally cut off, limited to little client-side tasks such as Fahrenheit-to-Celsius conversions or some equivalent. But add a web server to the mix, and all of a sudden there is an entire universe at your fingertips.

As with the choice of a web browser, the choice of a web server is a deeply personal experience. Requiring much thought as to the capabilities and features of each and every server available, it is also important to take into consideration knowledge and training before coming to a decision.

For these reasons and others, in large corporations, decisions like this are usually made by upper management. After exhausting research consisting of a round of golf and a 17-martini lunch, managers decide to use whatever their golfing buddy Bob is using and issue a decree. The fact that Bob thinks that a megabyte is what sharks do to swimmers never really comes up.

But maybe your manager doesn't know Bob, so the decision is up to you. The question comes down to, what is the middle tier going to be? The answer to this question is totally up to you. Open source or proprietary? Whether to use PHP, ASP, JSP, ASPX, or Ruby? The answer isn't as clear as you'd think. Feel like using PHP and Internet Information Server? Not a problem, just download and install PHP. If ASP .Net and Apache is your thing, try Mono. I'm not here to make the decision for you; regardless of the server side, Ajax will work on the client side.

1.5.1   Apache

First and foremost, Apache is not a web server developed by Native Americans; the name is, in fact, a pun. In the early days of the Apache Project, the server was patched nearly daily, leading someone to declare that it was "a patchy" server. Needless to say, the name stuck.

Things have changed quite a bit since those early days; Apache has been the most popular server since the latter half of the 1990s. At the time that I'm writing this, more than two-thirds of web servers use Apache, which says a lot about stability.

1.5.2   Internet Information Server

IIS, as it is known to those of us who use it, is Microsoft's answer to Apache. In fact, most of the examples in this book use IIS on the server side. Don't get excited—it isn't because it is better; it is only because it comes bundled with Windows XP Pro. It comes down to the whole Internet Explorer thing; I'm lazy, and I use it at my day job.

1.5.3   The Remaining Players

Yes, there are other web servers beyond the big two. For example, there is the CERN Server, brought to you by the same people who created the World Wide Web. Another choice is NCSA HTTPd, from the National Center for Supercomputing Applications at the University of Illinois in Urbana, Illinois. Unfortunately it is no longer under development, which is too bad; I, for one, would like a web server from HAL's hometown.

I'd like to mention another "minor" server: WEBrick. Technically considered an "HTTP server library" for creating web servers, it is included with downloads of the Ruby programming language. Note that the quotes are mine because it just isn't natural to be able to create a web server with only a few lines of code. WEBrick falls into the "tools to make tools" category, which I cover later.

1.6   WE LEARN BY DOING

The problem with working in the computing field is that technology insists on advancing. Learn something new today, and 2 years down the road, it is obsolete. Because of this, it's necessary to continue learning the latest new technology, which means lots of reading and lots of training. While at Bell Labs, I formulated two rules of training that I'd like to share with you:

1. Training will be given far enough in advance of the project that there is sufficient time to forget everything learned.
2. If sufficient time does not exist for the first rule, the training will take place a minimum of 6 months after the project has been completed.

These rules have proved true every place that I have ever worked throughout my career. Banks, insurance, manufacturing, whatever—it doesn't matter. These rules have always held true.

There is, however, a way to skirt these rules. Simply try the examples, play with them, alter the code, make it better, break it, and fix it. There is no substitute for immersing yourself in any subject to learn that subject. It might be difficult at first, and sometimes it might even be painful, but the easiest way to learn is by doing.

1.6.1   Coding by Hand

Currently, coding web applications by hand has fallen out of favor, and rightly so, replaced by packaged components that can be dragged and dropped. Unfortunately, although the practice of using components means that individual pages are developed quicker, it also means that it isn't always easy to determine what the components are actually doing behind the scenes. This is especially true when the underlying code isn't fully understood because the developers skipped ahead to the parts that will keep them employed.

However, when learning something new, or trying to explain it to someone else, I have a strong tendency to code an application by hand. In part, the reason for this is that it gives me a better feel for the new subject. Of course, the other part is that I coded classic ASP for quite some time and spend a great deal of time writing client-side workarounds for managers who insisted on the use of design-time controls. Although it improved developers' JavaScript skills considerably, it had the same effect upon those developers that mercury had upon hat makers in the nineteenth century. Don't believe me? Go ask Alice.

Seriously, though, the idea of coding at least the first couple of applications by hand is to attempt to get a feel for the technology. Feel free to ignore my advice on this subject. What does matter, however, is making it easier for us in the end, which is why tools are important.

1.6.2   Tools to Make Tools

If the idea of coding by hand is repugnant to you, consider this: On some level, somebody coded something by hand. It is a pretty sure bet that there are no software tool trees, although I have used several that weren't quite ripe yet.

Many developers have issues with the very concept of creating their own common tools for web development. The first issue probably relates to the idea of job security; after all, if a company has a "developer in a box," why would it pay for the real thing? The answer to this is relatively simple: What if they want changes to what's in the box? Let me put it another way: Have you ever written some code and played the "I bet you can't guess what this does" game? I have, and not only is it good for feeding the old ego, but it is a blast, too! Of course, there is the tendency to strut around like Foghorn Leghorn afterward, but as long as you avoid the young chicken hawk developer and the old dog developer, everything will be fine. Also remember that, by himself, the weasel isn't a real threat.

Another issue is the "I can tell you, but then I'll have to kill you" mindset. A while back, I had a manager with this mindset; she seemed to withhold required information just for fun from every assignment. For example, she once gave me the assignment to produce a report from a payroll file and then told me that I didn't have high enough security to see either the file or the file layout. Somebody once said that information is power, and some people take it to heart. The danger with this philosophy is that information can literally be taken to the grave, or it is so out-of-date that it no longer applies.

Finally, there's what I believe to be the biggest issue, which I call "The Wonder Tool"; it dices, it slices, and it even makes julienne fries. Similar to the "feature creep" that we're all familiar with, but with a difference, it starts out unrealistic. "The Wonder Tool" is a mouse designed to government specifications, more commonly called an elephant. For the interest of sanity (yeah, right, me talking about sanity), it makes far more sense to break up the tool into more manageable pieces. For example, let's say that we need common tools to do X and Y, both of which need a routine to do Z. Rather than code Z twice as part of X and Y, it makes more sense to code a separate tool to do Z and have X and Y use this tool. And who knows? Sometime in the future, you might need a few Zs, and you'll already have them.

1.7 SUMMARY

The intention behind this chapter is that it serve as something of an explanation of the humble beginnings of the World Wide Web, starting with a single server and growing into the globe-spanning network that it is today.

First there was a brief explanation of both static and dynamic web pages, including the components that go into building each type of page. Components such as HTML, CSS, and JavaScript were briefly covered. Several examples of "DHTML out of control" were also mentioned; I, for one, can't wait for the video.

There was also a brief description, or, in some cases, an honorable mention, of several different web browsers. These browsers included some of the more popular web browsers for Linux, Windows, and Mac OS X. In addition, mention was made of some of the more annoying problems with cross-browser development.

The server side of things was briefly covered, to illustrate that there are always alternatives to whatever is being used currently. Also, I mentioned how it might be possible to mix and match technology, such as ASP.NET on Linux.

Finally, I covered the biggest problem with technical training today: how to apply it and how to circumvent it. Regardless of who we are, we learn by doing, and that information is like cookies; it's meant to be shared.

Introducing Ajax

A little more than a year ago, an article by Jesse James Garrett was published describing an advanced web development technique that, even though individual components of it have existed for years, few web developers had ever stumbled across. I can guess the reason for this lack of knowledge; basically, in the last few years, the need to produce measurable results has gotten in the way of the need to practice our craft. Or, as a former manager of mine would say, it's "that mad scientist stuff," except, as I recall, he used another word in place of *stuff*. Unfortunately, nine times out of ten, the need to produce measurable results gets in the way of "that mad scientist stuff."

However, it's the tenth time that's important. The article didn't stop at just describing the technique; it went on to say that Google used the very same technique. Invoking that single name, Google, was enough to change a point of view. Quicker than you could say, "Igor, the kites!" the phrase "that mad scientist stuff" morphed into "Why aren't we doing it this way?" The reason for this change of perception is that the name Google made this a technique that could produce measurable results. All it took was that single name, Google, to make using the XMLHttpRequest object so that the browser could communicate with the server without the page ever unloading and reloading into an acceptable practice.

This chapter introduces you to that practice, the practice of updating web pages with information from the server. Beyond the XMLHttpRequest object, which has been around for several years as a solution looking for a problem, there is nothing weird needed. Basically, it is how the individual pieces are put together. When they're put together in one way, it is nothing more than a pile of parts; however, when put together in another way, the monster essentially rises from its slab.

2.1   NOT A MOCKUP

A few years ago, I demonstrated an application that did what I just described. The demo ran for more than 2 hours with the same questions repeated over and over.

"It's a mockup, right?"

"No, it is the actual application."

"It can't be. The screen doesn't blink."

"That's because XML, HTTP, and SOAP are used to get the data directly from the server. JavaScript then updates only the parts of the page that have changed."

"It's a mockup, right?"

And so on. It took the client more than 2 hours to realize that the database was actually being updated without the page "blinking," as he referred to it.

2.2   A TECHNIQUE WITHOUT A NAME

Now, if I had been smart, I would have given the technology a name then and there, and thus ensured my place in Web history, shutting up the client as well. After all, a name is a thing of power, and the client, not wanting to sound stupid for not knowing what the acronym meant, would have saved more than 2 hours of my life that were spent re-enacting the scene of peasants with pitch forks from the 1931 version of *Frankenstein,* minus the tongs. Unfortunately, I drew an absolute blank and just called it as it was.

With apologies to the people who make the cleanser and the detergent, legend has it that the original Ajax was the second most powerful of the Greek warriors at Troy. Even though he had some issues (who in the *Illiad* didn't?), his strength and skill in battle were second to none (well, okay, second only to Achilles). In naming the technology Ajax, Jesse James Garrett gave the technology both Ajax's strengths and issues.

2.2.1   Names

An old idea dates back to the dawn of human civilization that to know someone's or something's true name is to have power over that person or thing. It is one of the basic concepts of what is commonly referred to as magic, and although magic isn't real, the idea that names can hold power isn't very far from the truth. Consider, if you will, a resumé. If ever a document held names of power, a resumé is it. Not very long ago, resumés invoking words such as *JavaScript, DHTML,* and *XML* were looked upon with envy, perhaps even awe. After all, for a little while, it seemed as though web developers were rock stars that, thankfully, were never asked to sing. Unfortunately, those names are now considered passé or even a little old-fashioned.

In his essay describing this web development technique, Mr. Garrett did one final thing; he gave it a name, Ajax, and thus gave us power over it. The acronym refers to Asynchronous JavaScript And XML, and whether you love or hate the name, the technology now has a name. At the very least, this naming means that we can describe what we've been doing at work. Ajax is a lot easier to say than, "I've been using client-side JavaScript, SOAP, and XML to obtain data directly from the server using XMLHTTP instead of the standard unload/reload cycle."

2.3   WHAT IS AJAX?

As stated previously, Ajax stands for Asynchronous JavaScript And XML, but what exactly does that mean? Is the developer limited to only those technologies named? Thankfully, no, the acronym merely serves as a guideline and not a rule. In some ways, Ajax is something of an art, as with cooking. Consider, for a moment, the dish called shrimp scampi; I've had it in restaurants up and down the East Coast of the United States, and it was different in every restaurant. Of course, there were some common elements, such as shrimp, butter, and garlic, but the plethora of little extras added made each dish unique.

The same can be said of Ajax. Starting with a few simple ingredients, such as HTML and JavaScript, it is possible to cook up a web application with the feel of a Windows or, if you prefer, a Linux application. You might have noticed earlier that my ingredients list omitted XML; the reason for that omission is that XML is one of those optional ingredients. This might sound strange because the x in *Ajax* stands for XML, but it is also useful in those instances when a particular client does not support XML or doesn't support some of the more "mad scientist" methods of communicating with the server.

2.3.1   The Ajax Philosophy

How the client—in this case, a web browser—communicates with the server is one of the cornerstones of Ajax. Designed with the philosophy of not using bandwidth just because it's there, a web page coded using these techniques won't go through the unload/reload cycle, or "blink," as some refer to it, unless absolutely necessary. Why send 100,000 bytes back and forth to the server when 300 bytes will suffice?

Of course, this means that, to the casual observer, the browser is behaving strangely because sometimes only selected parts of a web page are updated.

This means that the page won't "blink," as the peasant—er, client—so elegantly put it. Instead, in a wink of an eye, parts of the page will update quicker than they believed possible. The speed difference can be compared to the difference between accessing a file on a floppy disk and accessing a file on the hard disk. Personally, my reaction was along the lines of "I am never going back!" But individual results can vary, so consult your doctor.

Another concept that Ajax uses is, why not make the client work for a living? Have the client's web browser handle parts of the processing rather than just parrot preprocessed information on the screen. The initial page load would consist of data and JavaScript, instructions on what to do with the data. To expand upon the earlier mad scientist analogy, imagine a do-it-yourself "mad scientist" kit consisting of a pile of parts and a minion that answers to Igor, and you'll get the idea.

With an Ajax application, the browser is expected to actually process the data supplied by the server. This means not only the little things that DHTML did, such as rollovers and hierarchical drop-down navigation menus, but real things, such as posting to the server and handling the response, whether it is handling it either synchronously or asynchronously. In addition, Ajax applications need to be able to not only find objects on the HTML page but also, if necessary, update them.

This leads to the question of how, short of the whole kites and Igor methodology, does one accomplish this unholy task? The answer is that it depends on just how and how far one wants to pursue this course. There are three ways to bring life to an Ajax application, and each has its own advantages and disadvantages. It all depends on just which parts of the Ajax toolset the developers are comfortable with. It also depends on how comfortable you are with excluding certain members of the planet from the application. Yes, I'm talking about those people who are still running Internet Explorer version 2.0. Fortunately, it isn't my job to issue decrees concerning browser compatibility; however, it is my job to cover how to implement an Ajax application.

2.3.2   Meddling with Unnatural Forces

Earlier I explained how I, and probably quite a few others, stumbled upon the then nameless technique that was to become Ajax. However, that was not my first brush with what my supervisor called "mad scientist stuff." Several years earlier, as a consultant for the group insurance division of a large insurance company, I had the good fortune to get the assignment to automate a paper-based request system.

Armed with a file layout, salespeople would try to sell group insurance to companies and, theoretically, would explain that enrollee information needed to conform to the file layout. However, possibly in an effort to make the sale and thereby get the commission, they would accept it in any conceivable electronic format. XML, Excel, or flat files—it was all the same to them because they would fill out a multipage form and the minions in systems would take care of it. Needless to say, quite a few of these pieces of paper got lost, got coffee spilled on them, or simply got filed under "it's real work and I don't want to do it" by the folks in systems.

Arriving onsite, I quickly got to work researching the various forms and how they were handled, which led to documenting how the process should work. Because I was the sole designer and developer for this new system, there was, shall I say, some freedom as to the technologies at my disposal. The back end was classic ASP and SQL Server, both of which are beyond the scope of this book. The front end, however, was a combination of HTML, JavaScript, and DOM, with a little CSS thrown in for good measure.

Here's how it worked: The user would enter multiple pages of information concerning the request. This information would be cached on the client side until the user reached the end of the chain of pages and clicked the final submit button. The caching was accomplished through the use of HTML frames; the first frame, as the user input frame, filled the entire browser's window. However, the second frame, the data frame, was the interesting one because it wasn't visible even though it was always there.

This trick, for lack of a better word, with hidden frames was that they had the advantage of speeding up the application. The speeding up was due to reduced interaction with both the web server and the database server. Another benefit was that, in addition to the performance improvements, the application seemed to flow better because the input was broken into convenient chunks instead of the usual approach of entering between 80 and 200 items at one time.

2.4 AN AJAX ENCOUNTER OF THE FIRST KIND

Now that I've gushed about the *why* of this technique, let me offer a little insight on the *how* of this technique. Let's start with the three HTML documents shown in Listing 2-1, Listing 2-2, and Listing 2-3. Some readers might not consider this a true example of Ajax, but it does share many of the same qualities of Ajax, in much the same way that a *Star Trek* fan and a *Star Wars* fan share many of the same qualities.

Listing 2-1   HTMLfs.htm

```
<html>
  <head>
    <title>HTMLfs</title>
  </head>
  <frameset rows="100%,*">
    <frame name="visible_frame" src="visible.htm">
    <frame name="hidden_frame" src="hidden.htm">
    <noframes>Frames are required to use this Web site.</noframes>
  </frameset>
</html>
```

Listing 2-2   visible.htm

```
<html>
  <head>
    <title>visible</title>
    <script language="javascript">
/*
    Perform page initialization.
*/
function initialize() { }

/*
    Handle form visible form onchange events.  Values from the visible
    form are copied to the hidden form.
*/
function changeEvent(obj)
{
  parent.frames[1].document.getElementById(obj.id).value = obj.value;
}

/*
    Submits the form in the hidden frame then reloads the hidden frame.
*/
function submitForm() {
  parent.frames[1].document.getElementById('hidden_form').submit();
  parent.frames[1].document.location = "hidden.htm";
}
    </script>
  </head>
    <body onload="initialize()">
      <form name="visible_form" id="visible_form"></form>
    </body>
</html>
```

Listing 2-3   hidden.htm

```
<html>
  <head>
    <title>hidden</title>
    <script language="javascript">
var reBrowser = new RegExp('internet explorer','gi');

/*
    Perform page initialization, waits for the visible frame to load and
clones the hidden form to the visible form.
*/
function initialize()
{
  var hiddenForm = document.getElementById('hidden_form');

  if(reBrowser.test(navigator.appName))
  {
    while(parent.document.frames.item(0).document.readyState !=
'complete') { }

    parent.frames[0].document.getElementById('visible_form').innerHTML =
hiddenForm.innerHTML;
  }
  else
  {
    var complete = false;

    while(!complete)
    {
      try
      {

parent.frames[0].document.getElementById('visible_form').appendChild
(hiddenForm.cloneNode(true));

        complete = true;
      }
      catch(e) { }
    }
  }

}
    </script>
  </head>
  <body onload="initialize()">
    <form name="hidden_form" id="hidden_form" action="post.aspx">
      <h1>Address Information</h1>
      <table border="0" width="100%">
        <tr>
          <th width="30%" align="right">Name: </th>
          <td align="left">
```

continues

Listing 2-3   continued

```
            <input type="text" name="name" id="name" value=""
onchange="changeEvent(this)">
          </td>
        </tr>
        <tr>
          <th align="right">Address Line 1: </th>
          <td align="left">
            <input type="text" name="address1" id="address1" value=""
onchange="changeEvent(this)">
          </td>
        </tr>
        <tr>
          <th align="right">Address Line 2: </th>
          <td align="left">
            <input type="text" name="address2" id="address2" value=""
onchange="changeEvent(this)">
          </td>
        </tr>
        <tr>
          <th align="right">City: </th>
          <td align="left">
            <input type="text" name="city" id="city" value=""
onchange="changeEvent(this)">
          </td>
        </tr>
        <tr>
          <th align="right">State: </th>
          <td align="left">
            <input type="text" name="state" id="state" value=""
onchange="changeEvent(this)">
          </td>
        </tr>
        <tr>
          <th align="right">Zip Code: </th>
          <td align="left">
            <input type="text" name="zip" id="zip" value=""
onchange="changeEvent(this)">
          </td>
        </tr>
      </table>
      <br>
      <input type="button" value="Submit" onclick="submitForm()">
    </form>
  </body>
</html>
```

2.4.1   A World Unseen

Any developer familiar with the use of frames and framesets will find Listing 2-1 pretty normal looking. However, one item isn't plain vanilla: the `rows="100%,*"` attribute on the frameset element, which states that the first frame gets 100 percent of available rows. The asterisk (`*`) states that anything left over goes to the second frame. In this example, there is nothing left over, so it is the equivalent of coding zero. This results in the first frame being visible and the second frame being hidden. In essence, this is a sneaky way to hide what's going on from prying eyes—namely, the user. The next two listings are the visible frame, Listing 2-2, and the hidden frame, Listing 2-3. Listing 2-3 is where the real mad science happens.

2.4.2   Enter JavaScript

Listing 2-2 is short and sweet, basically two short JavaScript functions that don't appear to do anything. The first of these functions, `changeEvent`, is just what it says it is, a handler for an `on change` event. When fired, it copies the value associated with the current object on the current frame to one with the same ID on the hidden frame. The second function, `submitForm`, submits a form; however, like the previous function, it works with the hidden frame by locating and submitting the form there.

This leaves just one question: Where does the HTML for the visible form come from? The answer lies in Listing 2-3, the one for the hidden frame. Like the visible frame, it has JavaScript functions and a form. There is, however, a major difference in the form. Unlike its visible counterpart, it has all of the HTML necessary to make a nice little form. The trick is getting it from the hidden frame to the visible frame.

This magic is accomplished in the pages' `on load` event handler, `initialize`. This function waits for the other frame to load and then copies this form's inner HTML to the other frame. When this is done, the result is the normal-looking web page shown in Figure 2-1. The way it behaves, however, is almost application-like, with parts of the visible page being updated each time the hidden frame does an unload/reload cycle.

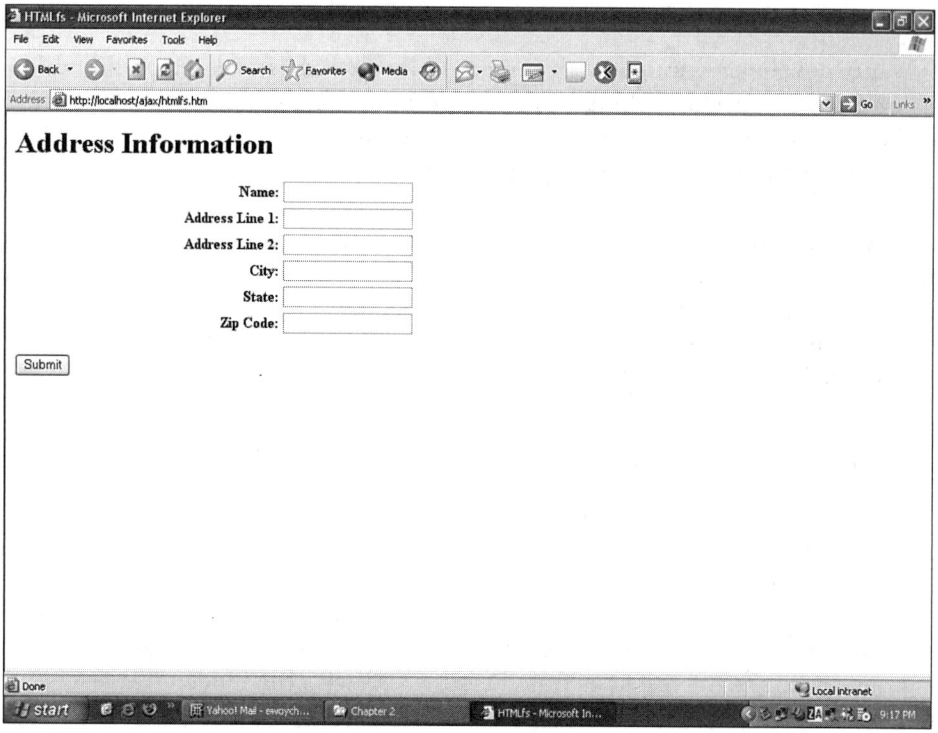

Figure 2-1   A normal-looking web page that functions almost like a desktop application

2.5   AN AJAX ENCOUNTER OF THE SECOND KIND

As flexible and cross-browser capable as the "hidden frames" method of implementing Ajax is, all that has been accomplished is the "AJ" part of Ajax. Which is sort of like the sound of one hand clapping, and that usually means that Igor has been slacking off again. Thankfully, there's another part—eh, make that technology—available: XML. The problem with XML is that it has developed a reputation of being difficult; however, it doesn't have to be. Just keep in mind that, in those situations, code has a tendency to follow you around, like Igor.

2.5.1   XML

In its simplest form, XML is nothing more than a text file containing a single well-formed XML document. Come to think of it, the same is pretty much true in its most complex form as well. Looking past all of the hype surrounding XML, it is easy to see that XML is merely the text representation of self-describing data in a tree data structure. When this is understood, all that is left are the nitty-gritty little details, like "What's a tree data structure?" and "How exactly does data describe itself?"

A tree data structure is built of nodes, with each node having only one node connected above it, called a *parent* node. The sole exception to this rule is the *root* node, which has no parent node. Nodes can also have other nodes connected below, and these are called *child* nodes. In addition, nodes on the same level that have the same parent node are called children. Figure 2-2 is a graphical representation of a tree data structure.

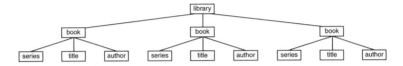

Figure 2-2 Tree data structure

Figure 2-2 can also be represented as the XML document shown in Listing 2-4.

Listing 2-4 XML Representation of the Same Information as in Figure 2-2

```xml
<?xml version="1.0" encoding="UTF-8" standalone="yes"?>
<library>
  <book>
    <series>The Wonderland Gambit</series>
    <title>The Cybernetic Walrus</title>
    <author>Jack L. Chalker</author>
  </book>
  <book>
    <series>The Wonderland Gambit</series>
    <title>The March Hare Network</title>
    <author>Jack L. Chalker</author>
  </book>
  <book>
    <series>The Wonderland Gambit</series>
    <title>The Hot-Wired Dodo</title>
    <author>Jack L. Chalker</author>
  </book>
</library>
```

The nodes shown in Listing 2-4 are called *elements,* which closely resemble HTML tags. And like HTML tags, start tags begin with < while end tags begin with </. However, unlike HTML tags, all XML tags either must have a closing tag or be self-closing or must be empty elements. Self-closing tags are recognizable by the ending />; if the forward slash was omitted, the document would not be a *well-formed* XML document. In addition, to all elements being either closed or self-closing, the tags must always match up in order. This means that the XML document in Listing 2-5 is well formed but the XML document in Listing 2-6 is not well formed. In a nutshell, "well formed" means that there is a right place for everything. Feet are a good example of this: Imagine if Igor used two left feet; the monster wouldn't be well formed and wouldn't be able to dance, either.

Listing 2-5   A Well-Formed XML Document

```
<?xml version="1.0" encoding="UTF-8" standalone="yes"?>
<one>
  <two>
    <three>
      <four/>
    </three>
  </two>
</one>
```

Listing 2-6   An XML Document That Is Not Well Formed

```
<?xml version="1.0" encoding="UTF-8" standalone="yes"?>
<one>
  <two>
    <three>
      <four/>
  </two>
    </three>
</one>
```

As neat and nifty as the hidden frames method of communicating with the server is, the addition of an XML document provides another option, XMLHTTP, or, as some refer to it the XMLHttpRequest object. Note all those capital letters, which are meant to indicate that it is important. The XMLHttpRequest object sends information to and retrieves information from the server. Although it doesn't have to be, this information is usually in the form of XML and, therefore, has the advantage of being more compact than the usual HTML that the server sends. Just in case you're interested, this was the means of communication for that page that I had handwritten and was using during the "it doesn't blink" fiasco.

2.5.2 The XMLHttpRequest Object

Unlike the hidden frames approach, in which the unload/reload cycle is still there but is tucked out of the way, using the XMLHttpRequest object means finally saying good-bye to the unload/reload cycle that we've all come to know and loathe. This means that, in theory, if not in practice, a single page could conceivably be an entire website. Basically, it's a load-and-go arrangement.

In theory, the original page loads and a user enters information into a form and clicks submit. A JavaScript event handler sends the user's information to the server via XMLHTTP and either waits penitently for a response (synchronous) or sets an event handler for the response (asynchronous). When the response is received, the JavaScript takes whatever action that it is programmed to, including updating parts of the page, hence the lack of an unload/reload cycle or "blink." This is great theory, but a theory is pretty useless if it cannot be put into practice; let's take a look in Listings 2-7 and 2-8 at how this can be implemented from a client-side perspective.

Listing 2-7   Example Ajax Web Page

```
<html>
  <head>
    <title>AJAX Internet Explorer Flavor</title>
    <script language="javascript">
var dom = new ActiveXObject('MSXML2.FreeThreadedDOMDocument.3.0');
var objXMLHTTP = new ActiveXObject('Microsoft.XMLHTTP');

/*
    Obtain the XML document from the web server.
*/
function initialize()
{
  var strURL = 'msas.asmx/getTime';

  objXMLHTTP.open('POST',strURL,true);
  objXMLHTTP.onreadystatechange = stateChangeHandler;

  try
  {
    objXMLHTTP.send();
  }
  catch(e)
  {
  alert(e.description);
  }
}

/*
    Handle server response to XMLHTTP requests.
*/
function stateChangeHandler()
```

continues

Listing 2-7   continued

```
{
  if(objXMLHTTP.readyState == 4)
    try
    {
      dom.loadXML(objXMLHTTP.responseText);
      document.getElementById('time').innerText =
dom.selectSingleNode('time').text;
    }
  catch(e) { }
}
    </script>
  </head>
  <body onload="initialize()">
    <div id="time"></div>
  </body>
</html>
```

Listing 2-8   XML Document

```
<?xml version="1.0" encoding="utf-8" ?>
<time>3:30 PM</time>
```

If this were *CSI, Columbo* or *The Thin Man,* now is the time when the hero explains how the deed was done. It goes something like this: The HTML page loads, which causes the onload event handler, initialize, to fire. In this function, the XMLHttpRequest object's open method is invoked, which only sets the method (POST), gives the relative URL of a web service, and states that the request will be asynchronous (true). Next, the onreadystatechage event handler is set; this is the function that handles what to do when the web service responds. Finally, the send method of the XMLHttpRequest object is invoked, sending our request on its merry way.

When a response is received from the web service, the stateChangeHandler is fired. You've probably noticed the test of the readyState property. The reason for this is that there are more than one possible readyState values, and we're interested in only four, complete. When the response is complete, the result is loaded into an XML document, the appropriate node is selected, and the HTML is updated.

Listings 2-7 and 2-8 could be considered by some a pure example of Ajax. Unfortunately, the way it is currently coded, browsers other than Microsoft Internet Explorer would have real issues with it. What sort of issues? The code simply won't work because of differences in how XML and the XMLHttpRequest object work in various browsers. This doesn't mean that this form of Ajax is an

IE-only technology; it simply means that careful planning is required to ensure cross-browser compatibility.

On the subject of compatibility, I don't want to scare you off, but let me point out that the more advanced the client-side coding is, the more likely it is that there will be issues. The majority of these issues are merely little annoyances, similar to flies buzzing around. These "flies" aren't fatal, but it is a good idea to keep these things in mind.

2.6   AN AJAX ENCOUNTER OF THE THIRD KIND

The fifth part of Ajax, an optional part, isn't for the faint of heart. It transcends the "mad scientist stuff" into the realm of the magical, and it is called eXtensible Stylesheet Language for Transformations, or XSLT. In other words, if Ajax really was mad science and it was taught in school, this would be a 400-level course. Why? The reason is that the technology is both relatively new and very, very browser dependent. However, when it works, this method provides an incredible experience for the user.

2.6.1   XSLT

XSLT is an XML-based language that is used to transform XML into other forms. XSLT applies a style sheet (XSLT) as input for an XML document and produces output—in most cases, XHTML or some other form of XML. This XHTML is then displayed on the browser, literally in the "wink of an eye."

One of the interesting things about XSLT is that, other than the XML being well formed, it really doesn't make any difference where the XML came from. This leads to some interesting possible sources of XML. For example, as you are probably aware, a database query can return XML. But did you know that an Excel spreadsheet can be saved as XML? XSLT can be used to transform any XML-derived language, regardless of the source.

Listing 2-9 shows a simple Internet Explorer–only web page along the same lines as the earlier examples. By using XSLT and the `XMLHttpRequest` object to retrieve both the XML and XSLT shown in Listing 2-10, it is extremely flexible. This is because after the initial page is loaded, any conceivable page can be generated simply by changing the XML and/or the XSLT. Sounds pretty powerful, doesn't it?

Listing 2-9   A Simple IE-Only Web Page

```
<html>
  <head>
    <title>AJAX Internet Explorer Flavor</title>
```

continues

Listing 2-9   continued

```
    <script language="javascript">
var dom = new ActiveXObject('MSXML2.FreeThreadedDOMDocument.3.0');
var xslt = new ActiveXObject('MSXML2.FreeThreadedDOMDocument.3.0');
var objXMLHTTP;

/*
    Obtain the initial XML document from the web server.
*/
function initialize()
{
  doPOST(true);
}

/*
    Use the XMLHttpRequest to communicate with a web service.
*/
function doPOST(blnState) {
  var strURL = 'http://localhost/AJAX/msas.asmx';

  objXMLHTTP = new ActiveXObject('Microsoft.XMLHTTP');

  objXMLHTTP.open('POST',strURL,true);

  if(blnState)
    objXMLHTTP.setRequestHeader('SOAPAction','http://
tempuri.org/getState');
  else

  objXMLHTTP.setRequestHeader('SOAPAction','http://tempuri.org/getXML');

  objXMLHTTP.setRequestHeader('Content-Type','text/xml');

  objXMLHTTP.onreadystatechange = stateChangeHandler;

  try
  {
    objXMLHTTP.send(buildSOAP(blnState));
  }
  catch(e)
  {
  alert(e.description);
  }
}

/*
    Construct a SOAP envelope.
*/
function buildSOAP(blnState) {
  var strSOAP = '<?xml version="1.0" encoding="UTF-8"?>';
```

```
    strSOAP += '<soap:Envelope
xmlns:xsi="http://www.w3.org/2001/XMLSchema-instance"
xmlns:xsd="http://www.w3.org/2001/XMLSchema"
xmlns:soap="http://schemas.xmlsoap.org/soap/envelope/">';
    strSOAP += '<soap:Body>';

    if(blnState)
    {
      strSOAP += '<getState xmlns="http://tempuri.org/">';
      strSOAP += '<state_abbreviation/>';
      strSOAP += '</getState>';
    }
    else
    {
      strSOAP += '<getXML xmlns="http://tempuri.org/">';
      strSOAP += '<name>xsl/state.xsl</name>';
      strSOAP += '</getXML>';
    }

    strSOAP += '</soap:Body>';
    strSOAP += '</soap:Envelope>';

    return(strSOAP);
}

/*
    Handle server response to XMLHTTP requests.
*/
function stateChangeHandler()
{
  if(objXMLHTTP.readyState == 4)
    try
    {
      var work = new ActiveXObject('MSXML2.FreeThreadedDOMDocument.3.0');

      work.loadXML(objXMLHTTP.responseText);

      switch(true) {
        case(work.selectNodes('//getStateResponse').length != 0):
          dom.loadXML(objXMLHTTP.responseText);
          doPOST(false);

          break;
        case(work.selectNodes('//getXMLResponse').length != 0):
          var objXSLTemplate = new
ActiveXObject('MSXML2.XSLTemplate.3.0');


xslt.loadXML(work.selectSingleNode('//getXMLResult').firstChild.xml);

          objXSLTemplate.stylesheet = xslt;

          var objXSLTProcessor = objXSLTemplate.createProcessor;

          objXSLTProcessor.input = dom;
```

continues

Listing 2-9 continued

```
        objXSLTProcessor.transform();

        document.getElementById('select').innerHTML =
objXSLTProcessor.output;

        break;
      default:
        alert('error');

        break;
    }
  }
  catch(e) { }
}
    </script>
  </head>
  <body onload="initialize()">
  <div id="select"></div>
</html>
```

Listing 2-10 The XML and XSLT Part

```
<?xml version="1.0" encoding="UTF-8"?>
<xsl:stylesheet version="1.0"
xmlns:xsl="http://www.w3.org/1999/XSL/Transform">
  <xsl:output method="html" version="1.0" encoding="UTF-8" indent="yes"/>

  <xsl:template match="/">
    <xsl:element name="select">
      <xsl:attribute name="id">state</xsl:attribute>
      <xsl:attribute name="name">selState</xsl:attribute>
      <xsl:apply-templates select="//Table[country_id = 1]"/>
    </xsl:element>
  </xsl:template>

  <xsl:template match="Table">
    <xsl:element name="option">
      <xsl:attribute name="value"><xsl:value-of
select="state_abbreviation"/></xsl:attribute>
      <xsl:value-of select="state_name"/>
    </xsl:element>
  </xsl:template>
</xsl:stylesheet>
```

2.6.2   Variations on a Theme

At first glance, the JavaScript in the previous example appears to be very similar to that shown in Listing 2-7; however, nothing could be further from the truth. The first of these differences is due to two calls being made to a web service and the use of XSLT to generate the HTML to be displayed in the browser. Let's look at this in a little more detail.

First, the only thing that the `initialize` function does is call another function, `doPOST`, passing a `true`. Examining `doPOST` reveals that the purpose of the `true` is to indicate what the `SOAPAction` in the request header is, `http://tempuri.org/getState` to get information pertaining to states and provinces from the web service, or `http://tempuri.org/getXML` to get XML/XSLT from the web service. The first time through, however, we're getting the XML.

The second difference, also in `doPOST`, is the addition of a call to `buildSOAP` right smack in the middle of the `XMLHttpRequest` object's `send`. This is how arguments are passed to a web service, in the form of text—a SOAP request, in this instance. Checking out `buildSOAP`, you'll notice that `Boolean` from `doPOST` is passed to indicate what the body of the SOAP request should be. Basically, this is what information is needed from the web service, states or XSLT.

You'll remember the `stateChangeHandler` from the earlier set of examples, and although it is similar, there are a few differences. The first thing that jumps out is the addition of a "work" XML document that is loaded and then used to test for specific nodes; `getStateResponse` and `getXMLResponse`. The first indicates that the SOAP response is from a request made to the web service's `getState` method, and the second indicates a response from the `getXML` method. Also notice the `doPOST` with an argument of `false` in the part of the function that handles `getState` responses; its purpose is to get the XSLT for the XSL transformation.

Speaking of a transformation, that is the purpose of the code that you might not recognize in the `getXML` portion of the `stateChangeHandler` function. Allow me to point out the `selectSingleNode` method used, the purpose of which is to remove the SOAP from the XSLT. The reason for this is that the XSLT simply won't work when wrapped in a SOAP response. The final lines of JavaScript perform the transformation and insert the result into the page's HTML.

The use of XSLT to generate the HTML "on the fly" offers some interesting possibilities that the other two methods of implementing Ajax do not. For instance, where in the earlier example the look of the page was dictated by the hard-coded HTML, this doesn't have to be the case when using XSLT. Consider for a moment the possibility of a page using multiple style sheets to change the look and feel of a page. Also, with the speed of XSLT, this change would occur at Windows application speeds instead of the usual crawl that web applications proceed at.

2.7   THE SHAPE OF THINGS TO COME

The sole purpose of this chapter is to offer a glimpse of the shape of things to come, both in this book and in the industry. All joking aside, this glimpse wasn't the result of mad science or any other dark art. It is the result of several years of beating various web browsers into submission, consistently pushing a little further to create rich application interfaces with consistent behavior.

The wide range of technologies that comprise Ajax can be a double-edged sword. On one hand, there is extreme flexibility in the tools available to the developer. On the other hand, currently Ajax applications are often sewn together in much the same way that DHTML pages were in the late 1990s. Unfortunately, although the hand-crafted approach works for furniture and monsters, it relies heavily on the skill level of Igor—eh, the developer.

In future chapters, it is my intention to elaborate on the various techniques that were briefly touched upon in this chapter. Also, even though Ajax is currently considered a technique that takes longer to develop than the "traditional" methods of web development, I'll show some ideas on how to reduce this time. After all, what self-respecting mad scientist cobbles together each and every monster by hand? It's all about tools to make tools—eh, I mean monsters.

2.8   SUMMARY

This chapter started with a brief introduction to Ajax that included some of the origins and problems associated with using "mad scientist stuff," such as the accusations of attempting to pass off a mock-up as an actual application and the inability to describe just how something works. Of course, some people still will think Corinthian helmets and hoplites at the very mention of Ajax, but you can't please everyone.

Next there was a brief outline of the philosophy behind Ajax, which centers on the idea of not bothering the server any more than is necessary. The goal is that of reducing, if not eliminating, the unload/reload cycle—or "blink," as some call it. The Ajax philosophy also includes the idea of making the client's computer work for a living. After all, personal computers have been around in some form for close to 30 years; they should do some work—take out the trash, mow the lawn, or something.

Finally, I presented the three simple examples of how Ajax can be implemented. The first example, although not quite Ajax, does much to show something of the first attempts to implement a web application with the feel of a Windows application. Although it's primitive by today's standard, it is still better than 99 percent of the web pages out there today.

Using the XMLHttpRequest object, the second example is dead on as to what is expected from an Ajax application. Broken are the bonds that limit updates to the unload/reload cycle that has been confronting us on the Web since Day 1. In addition, XML plays well with the concept of reducing traffic.

The third and final example pushes Ajax to the current limits with the addition of XSLT to the mix. XSLT allows XML to be twisted and stretched into any conceivable shape that we can imagine. No longer are our creations limited to the parts that we can dig up here and there; we can make our own parts on demand.

CHAPTER 3

HTML/XHTML

If you've made it this far, you're now in the "road warrior" section of the book, where all the reference materials and bizarre ideas dwell. The origin of this section goes all the way back to the trunk of my car—unless you're British, in which case, the origin of this section goes all the way back to the boot of my automobile. Until relatively recently, as I previously stated, I was a consultant, a hired gun, a one-man medicine show, or a resident visitor. No matter which term you prefer, a permanent office with bookshelves was not an option. So I was forced to carry books in and out with me each day.

This was a real educational experience. I've learned things from computer books that you wouldn't believe. First, regardless of the subject and the type, hardcover or paperback, computer books are heavy. Also, there is a little-known law of computer books—let's call it Ed's Law of Computer Books. It goes something like this: "Regardless of the subject, whatever you need to know is in another book."

It is true; I've lost count of the number of times that the information needed was in a book that was still in my car. So if the car was parked somewhere nearby, I'd trek downstairs and out to my car, grab the book, and then go back upstairs, only to find that I needed yet another book. This is the purpose of this section: so that I can plant my tush and not have to travel out to my car.

If, unlike myself, you're not too lazy to carry more than one book, consider this chapter something of a refresher on a few of the basic building blocks of Ajax. Well, maybe it's technically not a refresher because XHTML is still considered by some to be a little mysterious. That is probably due to the *X*.

This chapter covers some of the background material that is necessary to develop an Ajax application, specifically HTML and XHTML. Odds are, you're familiar with much, if not all, of the material covered here. But because I'm in Pennsylvania writing this and you're wherever you are reading this, it is kind of hard to tailor this specifically to your needs.

3.1 THE DIFFERENCE BETWEEN HTML AND XHTML

From its very beginning, Hypertext Markup Language is what has made the World Wide Web possible. It both conveys the thoughts of the person who created the page and defines nearly every aspect of what we see on each and every web page visited. Like English, French, Spanish, Japanese, Russian, or any other language in use today, it is a living language, evolving and growing.

Early on, this growth was fast and sudden, with "features" often doing an end-run around the World Wide Web Consortium. Add to that the fact that many of the designers of web pages play fast and loose in an effort to have more content than the next guy. So what if some corners were cut? It was all about content, and content was king.

Enter XHTML, considered by some as an effort to reign in the Wild West approach to web development by making HTML a dialect of XML. XHTML came in three flavors: transitional, strict, and frameset, with each flavor offering either different capabilities or different degrees of conformance to the XML standard.

3.1.1 Not Well Formed

Probably the biggest single difference between HTML and XHTML is that XHTML must be well formed. "Not a big deal," you say. Well, it could be. The part of the document that isn't well formed doesn't have to be glaring, like a foot being attached to the forehead. Because an XHTML document is essentially XML, simply following the HTML practices that we've followed for years is enough to get us into trouble. Consider the following two HTML input statements:

```
<input type="text" name="bad" id="bad" value="Not well-formed">

<input type="text" name="alsobad" id="alsobad"
value="Not well-formed" disabled>
```

Both statements are perfectly acceptable HTML, but as XHTML, they don't make the grade because neither is well formed. The problem with the first statement is that the tag isn't closed—perfectly acceptable in HTML, but verboten in XHTML. Fortunately, correcting it is a simple matter; just close the tag in the manner of self-closing tags or treat it as a container tag. The problem with the second statement might be a little harder to spot. I'll give you a hint: attributes. Yes, in XML, attributes must always have values, so give it one. `disabled="disabled"` might look goofy, but it works.

3.1.2   Well Formed

At first glance, it might appear that all that is required to convert HTML into XHTML is to slap a DTD before the HTML tag, close some tags, and clean up some attributes. Voilà, instant XHTML! Well, maybe, sometimes, occasionally, except on Tuesdays or at night during a full moon. You see, unfortunately, there is still a potential source of problems.

I stumbled on this problem approximately 5 minutes after creating my first XHTML page, and I immediately felt betrayed. The source of the problem was compares in my JavaScript functions. With the assorted compares using ampersand (&), greater than (>), and less than (<), the document wasn't well formed. In my despair, I knew how Victor Frankenstein felt, brought down by creatures of my own creation. Oh, the irony!

3.1.3   A Well-Formed Example

Thankfully, my despair didn't last very long. It wasn't like there was a death in the family, or *Stargate SG-1* had been cancelled, or anything important like that. It was merely a technical speed bump (or white tail deer, to those of you in Pennsylvania) on the road of life. I wasn't worried because I knew a trick that would make anything well formed.

XHTML is really nothing more than a dialect of XML, in the same way that both XSL and SVG are. This means that although it falls under the rules of XML, it also falls under the exceptions to those rules. For example, there are two ways to ensure that a greater than is well formed, but because JavaScript can't handle > entities aren't an option. This leaves only CDATA as the way to hide the JavaScript from the browser.

If you're unfamiliar with CDATA, it is the XML equivalent of saying "Pay no attention to that man behind the curtain." Basically, anything that is within the CDATA won't be parsed as XML, which is quite convenient for this case. There is, however, one problem with using CDATA; certain web browsers have issues with it, so it is necessary to hide it from the browser in the manner shown in Listing 3-1.

Listing 3-1   Hiding CDATA

```
<!-- <![CDATA[
function xyzzy(a,b) {
  if(a > b)
    alert('a is bigger');
  else
    if(a = b)
```

continues

Listing 3-1   continued

```
    alert('a & b are equal');
  else
    alert('b is bigger')
}
// ]]> -->
```

The purpose of the HTML/XML comments is to hide the CDATA section from HTML. The JavaScript comment prevents select browsers from having issues from a JavaScript perspective. Although it might not be pretty to look at, it does work well.

3.2   ELEMENTS AND ATTRIBUTES

I'm not sure why, but there seems to be a law stating that the sections of books intended for reference must be both dry and boring. Please bear with me as I try to conform to this law while describing the relationship between elements and attributes. Unfortunately, the American educational system falls short when attempting to teach students how to write in a monotone, but I'll do my best.

3.2.1   A Very Brief Overview of XHTML Elements and Their Attributes

In the interest of being boring, I put together Table 3-1 which covers attributes along with the elements associated with them. Because this is a high-level overview—say, around 30,000 feet—there isn't much beyond the "this element goes with that attribute" kind of thing. However, it is important to remember two things when referring to this table.

The first is that although this table was created from the request for HTML 4.01, it is by no means gospel. There will always be web browsers that either don't support select attributes and/or elements, and browsers that add some of their own. Also, if you recall our escapade with binding XML and HTML, web browsers don't get the least bit cranky if developers make up their own attributes and elements, or even use `onchange` when it should have been `onclick`.

Table 3-1 XHTML Elements and Associated Attributes

Element	Description	Deprecated	Attributes
a	Anchor		accesskey, charset, class, coords, dir, href, hreflang, id, lang, name, onblur, onclick, ondblclick, onfocus, onkeydown, onkeypress, onkeyup, onmousedown, onmousemove, onmouseout, onmouseover, onmouseup, rel, rev, shape, style, tabindex, target, title, type
abbr	Abbreviated		class, dir, id, lang, onclick, ondblclick, onkeydown, onkeypress, onkeyup, onmousedown, onmousemove, onmouseout, onmouseover, onmouseup, style, title
acronym			class, dir, id, lang, onclick, ondblclick, onkeydown, onkeypress, onkeyup, onmousedown, onmousemove, onmouseout, onmouseover, onmouseup, style, title
address	Author information		class, dir, id, lang, onclick, ondblclick, onkeydown, onkeypress, onkeyup, onmousedown, onmousemove, onmouseout, onmouseover, onmouseup, style, title
applet	Java applet	Yes	align, alt, archive, class, code, codebase, height, hspace, id, name, object, style, title, vspace, width
area	Client-side image map area		accesskey, alt, class, coords, dir, href, id, lang, nohref, onblur, onclick, ondblclick, onfocus, onkeydown, onkeypress, onkeyup, onmousedown, onmousemove, onmouseout, onmouseover, onmouseup, shape, style, tabindex, target, title
b	Bold		class, dir, id, lang, lang, onclick, ondblclick, onkeydown, onkeypress, onkeyup, onmousedown, onmousemove, onmouseout, onmouseover, onmouseup, style, title

continues

Table 3-1　continued

Element	Description	Deprecated	Attributes
base	Base URI of document		href, lang, target
basefont	Document base font size	Yes	color, face, id, size
bdo	BiDi override		class, id, lang, style, title
big	Large text		class, dir, id, lang, onclick, ondblclick, onkeydown, onkeypress, onkeyup, onmousedown, onmousemove, onmouseout, onmouseover, onmouseup, style, title
blockqoute	Block quotation		cite
body	Document body		alink, background, bgcolor, class, dir, id, lang, link, onclick, ondblclick, onkeydown, onkeypress, onkeyup, onload, onmousedown, onmousemove, onmouseout, onmouseover, onmouseup, onunload, style, text, title, vlink
br	Line break		class, clear, id, style, title
button	Button object		accesskey, class, dir, disabled, id, lang, name, onblur, onclick, ondblclick, onfocus, onkeydown, onkeypress, onkeyup, onmousedown, onmousemove, onmouseout, onmouseover, onmouseup, style, tabindex, title, type, value
caption	Table caption		align, class, dir, id, lang, onclick, ondblclick, onkeydown, onkeypress, onkeyup, onmousedown, onmousemove, onmouseout, onmouseover, onmouseup, style and title
center	Center contents	Yes	class, dir, id, lang, onclick, ondblclick, onkeydown, onkeypress, onkeyup, onmousedown, onmousemove, onmouseout, onmouseover, onmouseup, style, title

Element	Description	Deprecated	Attributes
code	Code fragment		class, dir, id, lang, onclick, ondblclick, onkeydown, onkeypress, onkeyup, onmousedown, onmousemove, onmouseout, onmouseover, onmouseup, style, title
col	Table column		align, char, charoff, class, dir, id, lang, onclick, ondblclick, onkeydown, onkeypress, onkeyup, onmousedown, onmousemove, onmouseout, onmouseover, onmouseup, style, title, valign, width
colgroup	Table column group		align, char, charoff, class, dir, id, lang, onclick, ondblclick, onkeydown, onkeypress, onkeyup, onmousedown, onmousemove, onmouseout, onmouseover, onmouseup, span, style, title, valign, width
dd	Definition description		class, dir, id, lang, onclick, ondblclick, onkeydown, onkeypress, onkeyup, onmousedown, onmousemove, onmouseout, onmouseover, onmouseup, style, title
del	Deleted text		cite, class, datetime, dir, id, lang, onclick, ondblclick, onkeydown, onkeypress, onkeyup, onmousedown, onmousemove, onmouseout, onmouseover, onmouseup, style, title
dfn	Instance definition		class, dir, id, lang, onclick, ondblclick, onkeydown, onkeypress, onkeyup, onmousedown, onmousemove, onmouseout, onmouseover, onmouseup, style, title
dir	Directory list	Yes	class, compact, dir, id, lang, onclick, ondblclick, onkeydown, onkeypress, onkeyup, onmousedown, onmousemove, onmouseout, onmouseover, onmouseup, style, title

continues

Table 3-1   continued

Element	Description	Deprecated	Attributes
div	Style container		align, class, dir, id, lang, onclick, ondblclick, onkeydown, onkeypress, onkeyup, onmousedown, onmousemove, onmouseout, onmouseover, onmouseup, style, title
dl	Definition list		class, compact, dir, id, lang, onclick, ondblclick, onkeydown, onkeypress, onkeyup, onmousedown, onmousemove, onmouseout, onmouseover, onmouseup, style, title
dt	Definition term		class, dir, id, lang, onclick, ondblclick, onkeydown, onkeypress, onkeyup, onmousedown, onmousemove, onmouseout, onmouseover, onmouseup, style, title
em	Emphasis		class, dir, id, lang, onclick, ondblclick, onkeydown, onkeypress, onkeyup, onmousedown, onmousemove, onmouseout, onmouseover, onmouseup, style, title
fieldset	Form control group		class, dir, id, lang, style, title
font	Font change	Yes	class, color, dir, face, id, lang, onclick, ondblclick, onkeydown, onkeypress, onkeyup, onmousedown, onmousemove, onmouseout, onmouseover, onmouseup, size, style, title
form	Input form		accept-charset, accept, action, class, dir, enctype, id, lang, method, name, onclick, ondblclick, onkeydown, onkeypress, onkeyup, onmousedown, onmousemove, onmouseout, onmouseover, onmouseup, onreset, onsubmit, style, target, title
frame	Frameset window		class, frameborder, id, longdesc, marginheight, marginwidth, name, noresize, scrolling, src, style, title, width

Element	Description	Deprecated	Attributes
frameset	Collection of window subdivisions		class, cols, id, onload, onunload, style, title
h1	Heading		align, class, dir, id, lang, onclick, ondblclick, onkeydown, onkeypress, onkeyup, onmousedown, onmousemove, onmouseout, onmouseover, onmouseup, style, title
h2	Heading		align, class, dir, id, lang, onclick, ondblclick, onkeydown, onkeypress, onkeyup, onmousedown, onmousemove, onmouseout, onmouseover, onmouseup, style, title
h3	Heading		align, class, dir, id, lang, onclick, ondblclick, onkeydown, onkeypress, onkeyup, onmousedown, onmousemove, onmouseout, onmouseover, onmouseup, style, title
h4	Heading		align, class, dir, id, lang, onclick, ondblclick, onkeydown, onkeypress, onkeyup, onmousedown, onmousemove, onmouseout, onmouseover, onmouseup, style, title
h5	Heading		align, class, dir, id, lang, onclick, ondblclick, onkeydown, onkeypress, onkeyup, onmousedown, onmousemove, onmouseout, onmouseover, onmouseup, style, title
h6	Heading		align, class, dir, id, lang, onclick, ondblclick, onkeydown, onkeypress, onkeyup, onmousedown, onmousemove, onmouseout, onmouseover, onmouseup, style, title
head	HTML document head		dir, lang, profile

continues

Table 3-1   continued

Element	Description	Deprecated	Attributes
hr	Horizontal rule		align, class, dir, id, lang, noshade, onclick, ondblclick, onkeydown, onkeypress, onkeyup, onmousedown, onmousemove, onmouseout, onmouseover, onmouseup, size, style, title, width
html	HTML document root		dir, lang, version
i	Italic		class, dir, id, lang, marginwidth, onclick, ondblclick, onkeydown, onkeypress, onkeyup, onmousedown, onmousemove, onmouseout, onmouseover, onmouseup, style, title
iframe	Inline frame		align, class, frameborder, height, id, longdesc, marginheight, name, scrolling, src, style, title
img	Embedded image		align, alt, border, class, dir, height, hspace, id, ismap, lang, longdesc, name, onclick, ondblclick, onkeydown, onkeypress, onkeyup, onmousedown, onmousemove, onmouseout, onmouseover, onmouseup, src, style, title, usemap, vspace, width
input	Form input control		accept, accesskey, align, alt, checked, class, dir, disabled, id, ismap, lang, maxlength, name, onblur, onchange, onclick, ondblclick, onfocus, onkeydown, onkeypress, onkeyup, onmousedown, onmousemove, onmouseout, onmouseover, onmouseup, onselect, readonly, size, src, style, tabindex, title, type, usemap, value

Element	Description	Deprecated	Attributes
ins	Inserted text		cite, class, datetime, dir, id, lang, onclick, ondblclick, onkeydown, onkeypress, onkeyup, onmousedown, onmousemove, onmouseout, onmouseover, onmouseup, style, title
isindex	Single-line input prompt	Yes	class, dir, id, lang, prompt, style, title
kbd	Keyboard text entry		class, dir, id, lang, onclick, ondblclick, onkeydown, onkeypress, onkeyup, onmousedown, onmousemove, onmouseout, onmouseover, onmouseup, style, title
label	Form text field		accesskey, for, onblur, onfocus
legend	Fieldset legend		accesskey, align, class, dir, id, lang, onclick, ondblclick, onkeydown, onkeypress, onkeyup, onmousedown, onmousemove, onmouseout, onmouseover, onmouseup, style, title
li	List item		class, dir, id, lang, onclick, ondblclick, onkeydown, onkeypress, onkeyup, onmousedown, onmousemove, onmouseout, onmouseover, onmouseup, style, style, title, title, type, value
link	Media-independent link		charset, class, dir, href, hreflang, id, lang, media, onclick, ondblclick, onkeydown, onkeypress, onkeyup, onmousedown, onmousemove, onmouseout, onmouseover, onmouseup, rel, rev, style, target, title
map	Client-side image map		class, dir, id, lang, name, onclick, ondblclick, onkeydown, onkeypress, onkeyup, onmousedown, onmousemove, onmouseout, onmouseover, onmouseup, style, title

continues

Table 3-1   continued

Element	Description	Deprecated	Attributes
menu	Menu list	Yes	class, compact, dir, id, lang, onclick, ondblclick, onkeydown, onkeypress, onkeyup, onmousedown, onmousemove, onmouseout, onmouseover, onmouseup, style, title
meta	Document meta-information		content, dir, http-equiv, lang, name, scheme
noframes	Alternate text when frames are not supported		class, dir, id, lang, onclick, ondblclick, onkeydown, onkeypress, onkeyup, onmousedown, onmousemove, onmouseout, onmouseover, onmouseup, style, title
noscript	Alternate text when JavaScript is not supported		class, dir, id, lang, onclick, ondblclick, onkeydown, onkeypress, onkeyup, onmousedown, onmousemove, onmouseout, onmouseover, onmouseup, style, title
object	Embedded object		align, archive, border, class, classid, codebase, codetype, data, declare, dir, height, hspace, id, lang, name, onclick, ondblclick, onkeydown, onkeypress, onkeyup, onmousedown, onmousemove, onmouseout, onmouseover, onmouseup, standby, style, tabindex, title, usemap, vspace, width
ol	Ordered list		class, compact, dir, id, lang, onclick, ondblclick, onkeydown, onkeypress, onkeyup, onmousedown, onmousemove, onmouseout, onmouseover, onmouseup, start, style, style, title, title, type
optgroup	Option group		class, dir, disabled, id, label, lang, onclick, ondblclick, onkeydown, onkeypress, onkeyup, onmousedown, onmousemove, onmouseout, onmouseover, onmouseup, style, title

Element	Description	Deprecated	Attributes
option	Select option		class, dir, disabled, id, label, lang, onclick, ondblclick, onkeydown, onkeypress, onkeyup, onmousedown, onmousemove, onmouseout, onmouseover, onmouseup, selected, style, title, value
p	Paragraph		align, class, dir, id, lang, onclick, ondblclick, onkeydown, onkeypress, onkeyup, onmousedown, onmousemove, onmouseout, onmouseover, onmouseup, style, title
param	Applet/ object parameter		id, name, type, value, valuetype
pre	Preformatted text		class, dir, id, id,·lang, onclick, ondblclick, onkeydown, onkeypress, onkeyup, onmousedown, onmousemove, onmouseout, onmouseover, onmouseup, style, title, width
q	Inline quotation		cite, class, dir, id, lang, onclick, ondblclick, onkeydown, onkeypress, onkeyup, onmousedown, onmousemove, onmouseout, onmouseover, onmouseup, style, title
s	Strike- through	Yes	class, dir, id, lang, onclick, ondblclick, onkeydown, onkeypress, onkeyup, onmousedown, onmousemove, onmouseout, onmouseover, onmouseup, style, title
samp	Sample		class, dir, id, lang, onclick, ondblclick, onkeydown, onkeypress, onkeyup, onmousedown, onmousemove, onmouseout, onmouseover, onmouseup, style, title
script	Container for scripts		charset, defer, language, src, type

continues

Table 3-1   continued

Element	Description	Deprecated	Attributes
select	Option select		class, dir, disabled, id, lang, multiple, onblur, onchange, onclick, ondblclick, onfocus, onkeydown, onkeypress, onkeyup, onmousedown, onmousemove, onmouseout, onmouseover, onmouseup, size, style, tabindex, title
small	Small text		class, dir, id, lang, onclick, ondblclick, onkeydown, onkeypress, onkeyup, onmousedown, onmousemove, onmouseout, onmouseover, onmouseup, style, title
span	Style container		class, dir, id, lang, onclick, ondblclick, onkeydown, onkeypress, onkeyup, onmousedown, onmousemove, onmouseout, onmouseover, onmouseup, style, title
strike	Strike-through	Yes	class, dir, id, lang, onclick, ondblclick, onkeydown, onkeypress, onkeyup, onmousedown, onmousemove, onmouseout, onmouseover, onmouseup, style, title
strong	Strong emphasis		class, dir, id, lang, onclick, ondblclick, onkeydown, onkeypress, onkeyup, onmousedown, onmousemove, onmouseout, onmouseover, onmouseup, style, title
style	CSS		class, dir, lang, media, type
sub	Subscript		class, dir, id, lang, onclick, ondblclick, onkeydown, onkeypress, onkeyup, onmousedown, onmousemove, onmouseout, onmouseover, onmouseup, style, title
sup	Superscript		class, dir, id, lang, onclick, ondblclick, onkeydown, onkeypress, onkeyup, onmousedown, onmousemove, onmouseout, onmouseover, onmouseup, style, title

Element	Description	Deprecated	Attributes
table	HTML table		align, bgcolor, border, cellpadding, cellspacing, class, dir, frame, id, lang, onclick, ondblclick, onkeydown, onkeypress, onkeyup, onmousedown, onmousemove, onmouseout, onmouseover, onmouseup, rules, style, summary, title, width
tbody	Table body		align, char, charoff, class, dir, id, lang, onclick, ondblclick, onkeydown, onkeypress, onkeyup, onmousedown, onmousemove, onmouseout, onmouseover, onmouseup, style, title, valign
td	Table data cell		abbr, align, axis, bgcolor, char, charoff, class, colspan, dir, headers, height, id, id, lang, nowrap, onclick, ondblclick, onkeydown, onkeypress, onkeyup, onmousedown, onmousemove, onmouseout, onmouseover, onmouseup, rowspan, scope, style, title, valign, width
textarea	Multiline text-input area		accesskey, class, cols, dir, disabled, id, lang, name, onblur, onchange, onclick, ondblclick, onfocus, onkeydown, onkeypress, onkeyup, onmousedown, onmousemove, onmouseout, onmouseover, onmouseup, onselect, readonly, rows, style, tabindex, title
tfoot	Table footer		align, char, charoff, class, dir, id, lang, onclick, ondblclick, onkeydown, onkeypress, onkeyup, onmousedown, onmousemove, onmouseout, onmouseover, onmouseup, style, title, valign

continues

Table 3-1   continued

Element	Description	Deprecated	Attributes
th	Table header cell		abbr, align, axis, bgcolor, char, charoff, class, colspan, dir, headers, height, id, lang, nowrap, onclick, ondblclick, onkeydown, onkeypress, onkeyup, onmousedown, onmousemove, onmouseout, onmouseover, onmouseup, rowspan, scope, style, title, valign
thead	Table header		align, char, charoff, class, dir, id, lang, onclick, ondblclick, onkeydown, onkeypress, onkeyup, onmousedown, onmousemove, onmouseout, onmouseover, onmouseup, style, title, valign, width
title	Document title		cite, class, dir, id, lang, onclick, ondblclick, onkeydown, onkeypress, onkeyup, onmousedown, onmousemove, onmouseout, onmouseover, onmouseup, style, title
tr	Table row		align, bgcolor, char, charoff, class, dir, id, lang, onclick, ondblclick, onkeydown, onkeypress, onkeyup, onmousedown, onmousemove, onmouseout, onmouseover, onmouseup, style, title, valign
tt	Teletype text style		class, dir, id, lang, onclick, ondblclick, onkeydown, onkeypress, onkeyup, onmousedown, onmousemove, onmouseout, onmouseover, onmouseup, style, title
u	Underlined	Yes	class, dir, id, lang, onclick, ondblclick, onkeydown, onkeypress, onkeyup, onmousedown, onmousemove, onmouseout, onmouseover, onmouseup, style, title

Element	Description	Deprecated	Attributes
ul	Unordered list		class, compact, dir, id, lang, onclick, ondblclick, onkeydown, onkeypress, onkeyup, onmousedown, onmousemove, onmouseout, onmouseover, onmouseup, style, title, type
var	Variable		class, dir, id, lang, onclick, ondblclick, onkeydown, onkey-press, onkeyup, onmousedown, onmousemove, onmouseout, onmouseover, onmouseup, style, title

3.2.2 Frames Both Hidden and Visible

The question is, exactly what purpose can HTML frames serve in the brave new world of Ajax applications?

To be perfectly honest, I don't exactly know, but I can offer some possible suggestions.

The first suggestion that I can offer is to use an IFRAME with CSS positioning instead of either a JavaScript alert or a JavaScript prompt to convey information to and from the visitor. Not only would it allow for additional opportunities regarding the physical layout, but it wouldn't have the stigma associated with pop-ups. In fact, it might even provide a way around some pop-up-blocking software.

Here's how it would work: A zero-sized IFRAME would be created along with the original page. When needed, it could be moved about the page using CSS positioning and could be resized to display the required information. The source of the information could be from the page's JavaScript, another page on the web server, or a web service.

My second suggestion is to use the frames, especially hidden ones, as somewhere to cache information. I'm not only referring to the garden variety forms of information, such as XML or XSL stylesheets, but also to in-line Cascading Style Sheets. Imagine the reaction of visitors discovering that they can customize their browsing experience on a website that already feels like an application. Think along the likes of using the CSS from the fifth IFRAME for Bob, and you'll get the idea.

The same technique can also be used to cache large XML documents, of the kind that eat up bandwidth. Caching whole or nearly whole pages that

don't often load is also a possibility, as with the Items page from earlier examples. Instead of retrieving the XML every time the visitor wanders to the page,
just build the page once and cache. This would also have the advantage of further increasing application speed.

3.2.3   Roll Your Own Elements and Attributes

We use Microsoft Internet Explorer's XML element in both IE and Firefox. The
interesting thing is that, unlike Internet Explorer, Firefox doesn't support the
XML element, so how exactly did it work? According to several recommendations published by the World Wide Web Consortium, when an unrecognized
document element is encountered, it needs to be handled gracefully. Most
likely, this is a "plan for future expansion" thing.

Think about it; this makes a great deal of sense because if you go without
it, boom, the web browser would just roll over and die whenever somebody
with sausage fingers mistyped a tag. The World Wide Web wouldn't be a pretty
sight without this feature. Interestingly, the same feature is also available for
attributes, which explains how the home-grown data binding works.

A number of times in the past, I took advantage of this in regard to
attributes. I took advantage of this little trick in several different ways, but I
have a couple of favorites. The first was stashing the original values of HTML
input objects for the purposes of resets. Click a button, and a client-side
JavaScript event handler would update the value attribute from the `oldvalue`
attribute.

Another one of my favorite uses was to use it as a "value has changed"
indicator. This indicator would be checked when the form was submitted.
Based upon the result of a test, any number of actions could be taken, including producing a client-side error message.

However, my most favorite was to stash other options for selects. You
see, the system that I worked on had pages with several HTML `select` objects
with the contents of each `select` based upon the selection made in the previous
`select`. Originally, whenever a visitor came to the website and made a selection, that visitor was forced to wait through an unload/reload for each
selection.

The "mad scientist" solution was to create a series of attributes consisting
of the various attributes. Each select had an `onchange` event handler that would
update the options of the next logical `select` object. Although this wasn't an
Ajax application, the change that I made gave it one of the same characteristics; it didn't bother the server any more than absolutely necessary.

3.2.4 A Little CSS

Before the introduction of Cascading Style Sheets, when a developer wanted to change the font name or color, there was only one option, the HTML FONT element. If you've never seen a page written using the FONT element, consider yourself lucky. They were bloated, like a balloon in the Macy's Thanksgiving Day parade.

They also seemed to attract managers who felt the need to change the font from 11 point to 12 point or use color for bold text. "You know, it would look better in Magenta or Peach Puff." So there I was looking up the RGB values for Magenta (#FF00FF) and Peach Puff (#FFDAB9), which was much easier than hunting throughout the document looking for all the FONT elements. Needless to say, the day I found out that the FONT element was deprecated was one of my happiest days.

Now instead of being forced to use the HTML FONT element, I'm presented with a choice. Basically, it comes down to setting the font for the document as a whole, individual element types, or individual elements. This presents a quandary, unless, of course, you're like me: a bad typist in a career that requires typing. In that case, I recommend applying Cascading Style Sheets in the following manner:

1. Set the overall style of the document by setting the style for the BODY, TABLE, DIV, and SPAN elements. This is one area where trickle down economics actually works.

2. Next concentrate on the other elements that you plan to use, such as the INPUT element. This is also the time and the place for handling any homegrown elements, such as the XML element in Firefox.

3. Third, take care of the classes, those elements that go a long way toward giving a website a particular look and feel. The rowHeader and rowData classes from the earlier examples reflect this philosophy.

4. Finally, deal with the style of the individual elements themselves: positional CSS and the scrollable DIV.

Finally, because the main purpose of this chapter is to serve as a reference, there is Table 3-2, whose purpose is to describe some of the more common CSS 1 elements.

Table 3-2   Some of the More Common CSS 1 Elements

Property	CSS	Description
font-family	1	Sets the font name or font family name
font-style	1	Either normal, italics, or oblique
font-variant	1	Either normal or small-caps
font-weight	1	Either normal, bold, bolder, lighter, 100, 200, 300, 400, 500, 600, 700, 800, or 900.
font-size	1	Size of the font as an absolute, relative, length, or percentage
font	1	Sets all font properties at once
color	1	Sets the color for the element specified
background-color	1	Sets the background color for an element
background-image	1	Sets the background image for an element
background-repeat	1	Sets the repeat for the background image
background-attachment	1	Sets the scroll for the background image
background-position	1	Sets the position of the background image
background	1	Sets all background properties at once
word-spacing	1	Sets the spacing between words
letter-spacing	1	Sets the spacing between letters
text-decoration	1	Sets the text decoration: blink, line-through, none, overline, or underline
vertical-align	1	Sets the vertical positioning: baseline, bottom, middle, percentage, sub, super, text-bottom, text-top, or top
text-transform	1	Sets the text transformation: capitalize, lowercase, none, or uppercase
text-align	1	Sets the text alignment: left, right, center, or justify
text-indent	1	Sets the indent property for container elements
line-height	1	Sets the spacing between lines
margin-top	1	Sets the property as a percentage, length, or auto
margin-right	1	Sets the property as a percentage, length, or auto
margin-bottom	1	Sets the property as a percentage, length, or auto
margin-left	1	Sets the property as a percentage, length, or auto
margin	1	Sets all margin properties at once
padding-top	1	Sets the property as either a percentage or a length

Property	CSS	Description
padding-left	1	Sets the property as either a percentage or a length
padding-right	1	Sets the property as either a percentage or a length
padding-bottom	1	Sets the property as either a percentage or a length
padding	1	Sets all the padding properties at once
border-top-width	1	Sets the property to thin, medium, thick, or length
border-bottom-width	1	Sets the property to thin, medium, thick, or length
border-right-width	1	Sets the property to thin, medium, thick, or length
border-left-width	1	Sets the property to thin, medium, thick, or length
border-width	1	Sets all of the border properties at once
border-color	1	Sets the color of the border
border-style	1	Sets the border style to one of the following: none, dotted, dashed, solid, double, groove, ridge, inset, or outset
border-top	1	Sets the border width, style, and color
border-bottom	1	Sets the border width, style, and color
border-right	1	Sets the border width, style, and color
border-left	1	Sets the border width, style, and color
border	1	Sets the border width, style, and color for all the borders at once
width	1	Sets the width for an element
height	1	Sets the height for an element
float	1	Indicates that text can wrap around an element
clear	1	Specifies whether floating elements can float to the side
display	1	Sets how and whether an element will display: lock, inline, list-item, or none
white-space	1	Sets how whitespace is treated: normal, pre, or nowrap.
list-style-type	1	Specifies the type of a list item marker: disc, circle, square, decimal, lower-roman, upper-roman, lower-alpha, upper-alpha, or none
list-style-image	1	Sets the image
list-style-position	1	Sets the position
list-style	1	Sets all the list-style properties at once

Although Cascading Style Sheets is about as different as you can get from HTML/XHTML, they work together—actually, they work together extremely well. Before the adoption of CSS, the task of giving web pages a common look and feel was handled using the font tag, which, thankfully, has been deprecated (or, as I like to think of it, taken out and shot!). Sorry, I have never liked the font tag since the time a little cosmetic change to a web page took 2 days, mostly because there were about 700 instances scattered throughout a page. Think of the combination of technologies as a kind of synergy, like deuterium and a fission bomb or peanut butter and chocolate.

3.3   SUMMARY

In this, hopefully, refresher/reference chapter, some of the differences between the older HTML and the new and improved XHTML were covered. Special attention was paid to the fact that XHTML, unlike its cousin HTML, must be well formed and what exactly that means. Additionally, this chapter showed how to hide JavaScript, which is about as well formed as a platypus, within XHTML.

Next, some of the basics of the HTML/XHTML elements were covered: specifically which attributes go along with which elements, and which elements are deprecated. Next frames, the visible kind and otherwise, were discussed, followed by the advantages of being able to add custom elements and attributes. I wrapped things up with a high-level overview of Cascading Style Sheets.

JavaScript

I would like to point out that JavaScript has nothing to do with the Java programming language itself. Many people unfamiliar with JavaScript have a real problem with this, thinking that the word *Java* in *JavaScript* denotes some kind of relationship. Well, the relationship is similar to the relationship between "pine" trees and pineapples, or apples and pineapples. Yes, they are all distantly related, but that is the end of it.

My first encounter with coding JavaScript was in a web development class that was taught at Penn State as part of a web design certificate program. Impatiently I took the precursors, waiting for the class in which my programming skills would help. About 5 minutes into the class, it quickly became apparent that certain experiences would be more useful JavaScript precursors than others. For example, other than providing somewhere for the JavaScript to go, the HTML class wouldn't be of much use. Knowledge of C or any similar language, such as C++, Java, Pascal, or even PL/I, on the other hand, would go a long way toward helping to learn JavaScript.

In this chapter, I cover the following aspects of JavaScript:

+ Data types
+ Variables
+ Operators
+ Flow-control statements
+ Functions
+ Recursion
+ Constructors
+ Event handling

4.1 DATA TYPES

As with its ancestor, the C programming language of Kernighan and Ritchie, JavaScript supports a number of data types. Although the number isn't nearly as large as C, representatives of the basic data types are all present, and methods of describing your own data types exist. In fact, with only a little delving into the "dark arts," it is quite possible that many problems can be solved on the client side using JavaScript.

4.1.1   Numeric

In JavaScript, all numbers are 64-bit double-precision floating-point numbers, whether they are floating point or integer. This means that 18,437,736,874, 454,810,624 values divided evenly between positive and negative can be represented in JavaScript. In addition, there are three "special" values, increasing the total to 18,437,736,874,454,810,627. And you thought that you were being robbed.

The first of the three "special" values is NaN, which means Not a Number or "oops," as I like to think of it. From my point of view, it means that I made some kind of boneheaded mistake and am doomed to suffer for it. The second and third values are positive and negative infinity, which are, well, infinite.

4.1.2   String

JavaScript strings are UTF-16 strings or 16-bit Unicode Transformation Formats: character encoding. What it comes down to is that each character in a string is represented in 2 bytes, which means that the potential for display of non-English characters exists. This might not seem like a big deal, but it very well could be when the boss walks into your office and asks about internationalization. Ooh, scary.

Seriously, though, quite a number of things can be done in JavaScript along the lines of string manipulation. For example, it is quite easy to make an entire line either upper case or lower case, a really nice feature when testing for a particular string value. In addition, other functions allow for the searching, extracting, and replacing of substrings. Table 4-1 outlines these features.

Table 4-1   JavaScript String Functions

Name	Type	Description
escape(string)	Method	Converts the characters that would be illegal in a URL into legal escape sequences.
string.charAt(n)	Method	Returns the character at the position n, where n is a positive integer.
string.charCodeAt(n)	Method	Returns the encoded character at the position n, where n is a positive integer.
string.concat(stringB)	Method	Returns a string consisting of both strings concatenated.

Name	Type	Description
`String.fromCharCode` `(u1,...,uN)`	Static Method	Returns a string constructed from a series of Unicode characters.
`string.indexOf(stringB,n)`	Method	Starting at position n or 0, if n is omitted, returns the start position of the second string in the first string. A -1 is returned when the second string isn't found within the first.
`string.lastIndexOf` `(stringB,n)`	Method	Starting at position n or the end of the string, if n is omitted, returns the start position of the second string in the first string starting at the end of the string. A -1 is returned when the second string isn't found within the first.
`string.length`	Property	The length of the string in characters.
`string.match(regexp)`	Method	Returns an array consisting of matches to the pattern in the regular expression regexp.
`string.replace` `(regexp,text)`	Method	Replaces of one or more instances that match the pattern with text.
`string.search(regexp)`	Method	Returns a Boolean indicating whether a match to the pattern is found in the string.
`string.slice(n,m)`	Method	Returns the portion of the string starting at n and continuing to m, where both n and m are integers. In addition, if either value is negative, it indicates the position from the end of the string.
`string.split(regexp)`	Method	Returns an array consisting of the strings that were separated by instances of the pattern in the regular expression regexp.
`string.substr(n,m)`	Method	Returns a substring starting at position n for a length of m characters. In instances where m is omitted or exceeds the length of the string, the final character is the final character of the string.

continues

Table 4-1   continued

Name	Type	Description
string.substring(*n*,*m*)	Method	Returns a substring starting at position *n* for a length of *m* characters. In instances where *m* is omitted or exceeds the length of the string, the final character is the final character of the string.
string.toLowerCase()	Method	Converts the string to lower case.
string.toString()	Method	Returns the string value.
string.toUpperCase()	Method	Converts the string to upper case.
string.valueOf()	Method	Returns the value of the string.
unescape(string)	Method	The inverse of escape; the escape sequences are converted back into the original characters.

In my opinion, one of the coolest ways to manipulate strings has got to be regular expressions, although, come to think of it, it is also probably one of the most obscure ways to manipulate strings as well. If you're unfamiliar with regular expressions, they are an object that stores a pattern for use in the searching of strings. This pattern is then applied to a string using either a regular expression method or a string method.

The theory behind regular expressions is relatively easy to grasp, but the actual practice is not. The reason for this comes down to the pattern; it needs to be specific enough to find only what you are actually looking for, yet it also needs to be general enough to be able to find sequences that aren't always easy to find. Maybe you'll be able to understand how this works a little better after looking at Table 4-2, which describes the special characters that go into constructing a pattern.

Table 4-2   Characters Used to Create Regular Expressions

Pattern	Description
\	Designates the next character as either a literal or a special character.
^	Designates the beginning of a string.
$	Designates the end of a string.
*	Specifies a match to the preceding character zero or more times.
+	Specifies a match to the preceding character one or more times.
?	Specifies a match to the preceding character zero or one time.
.	Matches any single character, excluding newline.
( )	Matches the contents of the parenthesis. Note that this is a pattern match and is remembered.

Pattern	Description
a¦b	Specifies a match to either a or b.
{n}	Specifies a match to the preceding pattern exactly *n* times, where *n* is a nonzero positive integer.
{n,}	Specifies a match to the preceding pattern at least *n* times, where *n* is a nonzero positive integer.
{n,m}	Specifies a match to the preceding pattern at least *n* times and at most *m*, where *n* and *m* are nonzero positive integers.
[xyz]	Matches any single character enclosed by the brackets.
[^xyz]	Matches any single character not enclosed by the brackets.
[0-9]	Matches the range of characters enclosed by the brackets.
[^0-9]	Matches the characters not included in the range of characters enclosed by the brackets.
\b	Matches a word boundary.
\B	Matches a nonword boundary.
\d	Matches a numeric character, synonym for [0-9].
\D	Matches a non-numeric character, synonym for [^0-9].
\f	Matches a form feed.
\n	Matches a newline.
\r	Matches a carriage return.
\s	Matches any single whitespace character.
\S	Matches any single nonwhitespace character.
\t	Matches a tab.
\v	Matches a vertical tab.
\w	Matches any single word character or underscore.
\W	Matches any character that is not a word character or an underscore.
\n	When preceded by a pattern (), matches *n* times, where *n* is a positive integer. When not preceded by a pattern, matches an octal escape value.
\x*n*	Matches a hexadecimal escape value where *n* is a positive integer.

Alright, now for a quickie example. Let's say, for instance, that we want to replace all instances of either the word red or the word blue in a string with the word purple. Although this could be done programmatically, as shown in Listing 4-1, it isn't the easiest thing in the world. However, with a regular expression, also shown in Listing 4-1, it really isn't too bad.

Listing 4-1   Programmatic and Regular Expression Approaches to String Substitution

```
function initialize() {
  var colors = 'redorangebluegreenblueyellow';

  /*
    Call the substitute function twice, once for blue and once for
    red.
```

continues

Listing 4-1   continued

```
   */
   alert(substitute(substitute(colors,'blue','purple'),'red','purple'));

   /*
      Define the regular expression to search for red or blue, in
      addition set the options for global and ignore case.
      The available options are:
         g  = global (all occurrences in a string)
         i  = ignore case
         gi = global and ignore case
   */
   var re = new RegExp('red¦blue','gi');

   /*
      Perform the replacement.
   */
   alert(colors.replace(re,'purple'));
}

function substitute(text,word,replacement) {
   var temp = text;

   /*
      perform string replacement using substring.
   */
   while(temp.indexOf(word) >= 0) {
      temp = temp.substr(0,temp.indexOf(word)) + replacement +
temp.substr(temp.indexOf(word)+word.length);
   }

   return(temp);
}
```

I would like to point out that, at the time of this writing, Microsoft Internet Explorer appears to have a bug with regular expressions. It occurs when performing regular expressions in a loop. Occasionally, even though a pattern match exists, it isn't recognized. Fortunately, there is a workaround. Within the body of the loop, use the compile method to "reset" the pattern. When this is done, pattern matches are always recognized. Yes, it is something of a kludge, but regular expressions are too useful to ignore, and we should also be kind to those less fortunate than ourselves by accommodating their broken web browsers.

4.1.3   Boolean

JavaScript Boolean data types are the standard true/false data types that we've all been exposed to umpteen times, end of story.

4.1.4   Miscellaneous

These are the two data types that don't cleanly fit into any category: null and undefined. The null data type represents nothing, and the undefined data type represents something that is not defined.

4.1.5   Arrays

Although it's not an object type, I've chosen to include arrays here because they are a useful mechanism for grouping related information. A relatively simple data structure, arrays permit the access of information based upon an integer index. In JavaScript arrays, this index begins at zero and increases by one for each element of the array.

An item of interest about arrays in JavaScript is that it isn't necessary for the individual elements of an array to all be of the same type, although it might be a good idea to ignore this capability because it presents a world of opportunities to really screw up. However, some really nice goodies built into JavaScript more than make up for the potential issues that might arise from weak typing.

First things first. Let's take a look at the three ways to define a JavaScript array: defining an empty array, defining an array with a set number of elements, and defining an array with a set number of elements with values. Each of these three ways uses the `Array()` constructor, as shown in the following snippets:

```
var one = new Array();
var two = new Array(3);
var three = new Array('red', 'green', 'blue');
```

Earlier I stated that there are some really nice goodies built into JavaScript arrays, but they're rather numerous, so I've chosen to list them in Table 4-3.

Table 4-3   Features of JavaScript Arrays

Method	Description
`array.concat(arrayb)`	Concatenates two arrays into a single array
`arraylength()`	Returns the length of an array, as in the number of elements
`array.reverse()`	Returns the array with the elements in reverse order
`array.slice(start,end)`	Returns a portion of an array
`array.sort()`	Sorts the array into ascending order

continues

Table 4-3 continued

Method	Description
`array.join()`	Converts all elements to strings and concatenates them, separated by commas
`array.push(item)`	Adds an element to the end of an array
`array.pop()`	Removes and returns an element from the end of the array
`array.splice(r,a…a)`	Removes the element specified by the first parameter and adds subsequent elements
`array.unshift(item)`	Adds an element to the beginning of an array
`array.shift()`	Removes and returns an element from the beginning of an array

4.1.6 Object

In JavaScript, the Object type is an unordered collection of name and value pairs. Although this doesn't sound like much, it is a type of data structure that is commonly referred to as an associative array. I have a tendency to use an associative array.

4.2 VARIABLES

Unlike many other programming languages, in JavaScript, variables are not strongly typed, which means that what once contained a number could now be a string. This can sometimes cause some issues when developing on the client side; think about the idea of running across a string when a number is expected. A situation like that could prove somewhat embarrassing, especially because applications are like dogs; they can smell fear. This explains why applications always fail during a demo to upper management.

The names of variables in JavaScript consist of alpha characters followed by a number. The underscore character is also permitted; I usually use it to remind myself that a particular variable is not to be touched. Along the line of the wires that hold up Buck Rogers' spaceship, if you mess with it, bad things could happen.

As with many programming languages, variables in JavaScript have a scope. Before you have an attack of paranoia ("They're watching me!"), please allow me to explain what scope is in reference to variables. Variable scope refers to where the variable is defined. In JavaScript, variables can have either local scope or global scope.

In local scope, the variable is defined within a particular function. The simplest way to explain it is by examining the two functions in Listing 4-2. The first function, `Jeckle`, defines a variable named `monster`. The second function, `Frankenstein`, also defines a variable named `monster`. Because both variables are local, `Jeckle`'s `monster` is a different `monster` than `Frankenstein`'s.

Listing 4-2 Two Local Variables

```
function Jeckle() {
  var monster = 'Mister Hyde';
}

function Frankenstein() {
  var monster = 'Bob';
}
```

Global scope refers to variables that are defined throughout the entire page. They are defined in one of two ways, either using a var and declaring the variable outside a function, or omitting the var and declaring it within a function. I don't have a problem with the first method of declaring a global variable, but I have some definite issues with the second. All that it takes is one case of "sausage fingers"; a mistyped variable name, and I'm debugging for hours.

4.3 OPERATORS

JavaScript has a number of operators that you might or might not be familiar with. These include the ever-present == (equals) and != (not equals), to which you have undoubtedly been exposed; there are a number of others. Although some of these operators are familiar, some others might not be as familiar, so Table 4-4 briefly touches upon these.

Table 4-4 JavaScript Operators

Operator	Type	Description
a + b	Arithmetic	Addition
$a - b$	Arithmetic	Subtraction
$a * b$	Arithmetic	Multiplication
a / b	Arithmetic	Division
$a \% b$	Arithmetic	Modulus, the remainder to division
++a	Arithmetic	Increment by one
--a	Arithmetic	Decrement by one

continues

Table 4-4   continued

Operator	Type	Description
$a = b$	Assignment	Set equal to
$a \mathrel{+}= b$	Assignment	Increment by the value on the right
$a \mathrel{-}= b$	Assignment	Decrement by the value on the right
$a \mathrel{*}= b$	Assignment	Multiply by the value on the right
$a \mathrel{/}= b$	Assignment	Divide by the value on the left
$a \mathrel{\%}= b$	Assignment	Modulus by the value on the right
$a == b$	Comparison	Equal to, value
$a === b$	Comparison	Equal to, value and type
$a \mathrel{!}= b$	Comparison	Not equal to
$a > b$	Comparison	Greater than
$a < b$	Comparison	Less than
$a >= b$	Comparison	Greater than/equal to
$a <= b$	Comparison	Less than/equal to
a && b	Logical	And
a ¦¦ b	Logical	Or
$!a$	Logical	Not
$a + b$	String	String concatenation
$a=(condition)?b:c$	Comparison	Comparison operator
typeof(a)	Special	Returns a string consisting of the operand type
void a	Special	Suppresses the return of a variable

I'll bet you didn't know that typeof was an operator.

4.4   FLOW-CONTROL STATEMENTS

My first job straight out of college was working on an order-entry system that was developed by the elves at Bell Labs. Needless to say, I found myself in the Promised Land; although the salary was only alright, the tools and some of the code were brilliant. Notice that I said "some of the code." There was also some code that really, really stunk.

One particular "utility" comes to mind. Its purpose was to simulate an order being sent to manufacturing and billing. It had absolutely no conditions or loops—just the brute-force changing of the order status, totally disregarding whether the order was ready for transmittal. I'm not 100 percent sure why, but this inelegant code bothers me to this day.

One possible reason could be that I visualize code as a river with currents and eddies. As with a river, the flow of the program slows down and speeds up, depending upon the existing conditions. In my mind, I can almost see the flow following a particular channel, branching left or right and occasionally looping back upon itself. Maybe this is a strange way to look at it, but I consider flow-control statements to be elegant.

4.4.1   Conditionals

The granddaddy of all conditional statements has to be the if statement. In some form, the if statement is present in every programming language that I've ever used, seen, read about, or just plain stumbled across. Because of JavaScript's C roots, the if statement syntax is like a function with the condition being enclosed in parenthesis and the following statement being executed only when the condition is true. Sometimes there is an else followed by the statement to execute when the condition is false, and sometimes there isn't. When multiple statements need to be executed, they are enclosed in curly braces. Listing 4-3 shows the basics.

Listing 4-3   The Basics of the JavaScript if Statement

```
if(a == 1)
  alert('a is one');
else {
  alert('a is not one');

  if(b == 1) {
    if(c == 1)
      alert('Both b and c are one');
  } else
    alert('b is not one');
}
```

Almost as if it were cloned right from the pages of Kernighan and Ritchie's *The C Programming Language* (Prentice Hall, 1988), the conditional operator is a ternary operator, essentially an entire if statement/else statement shrunken into a convenient package for those of us who suffer from the sausage fingers affliction. The only problem is that many developers consider it too confusing and, therefore, avoid it. But it isn't really that hard; just remember that it breaks down in the following manner:

```
room != 'y2' ? 'xyzzy' : 'plugh'
```

Most often you'll see the result assigned to a variable like this:

```
magicWord =  room != 'y2' ? 'xyzzy' : 'plugh'
```

To those of you with mad scientist tendencies, the answer is, yes, conditional operators can be nested. The answer to the next question is also, yes, I have nested conditional operators.

The next four flow-control statements go together; in fact, you'll never see three of them by themselves. I am referring to the conditional structure that is known in various programming languages by a number of names, including *case, select, choose,* or *switch,* as it is called in JavaScript.

The `switch` statement evaluates a series of conditions until a condition is met. When this happens, execution begins at the `case` statement with the `true` condition. If none of the conditions is true, the execution begins at the default statement or after the `switch`, if there is no default statement. Listing 4-4 shows the basic structure of the `switch` statement.

Listing 4-4   Basic Structure of the `switch` Statement

```
switch(number) {
  case(0):
    alert('zero');

    break;
  case(1):
  case(3):
    alert('odd < 5');

    break;
  case(2):
  case(4):
    alert('even < 6');

    break;
  default:
    alert('many');

    break;
}
```

In addition to the "standard" version of the `switch` statement shown in Listing 4-4, there is a little known variant. Instead of using a variable as the expression, `true` or `false` can be used. This allows for the possibility of using a `switch` statement instead of a series of nested `if` statements, as Listing 4-5 illustrates.

Listing 4-5   A `switch` Statement Acting Like a Series of Nested `if` Statements

```
switch(true) {
  case(number == 0):
    alert('zero');
```

```
      break;
  case(color == 'red'):
    alert('#FF0000');

      break;
  case(color == 'green'):
    alert('#00FF00');

      break;
  case(color == 'blue'):
    alert('#0000FF');

      break;
  case((color % 2) == 0):
    alert('even');

      break;
  default:
    alert('whatever');

      break;
}
```

4.4.2   Looping

The purpose of looping in programs is to execute a series of statements repeatedly, thus cutting down on the required lines to code. This reduction in the number of lines has the advantage of improving the overall readability. In addition, loops allow for a variable number of executions. Personally, loops mean that I don't have to type any more than I have to, but, hey, I'm a hunt-and-peck typist.

It has been a while since CSC 100, "Introduction to Computer Science," but if I remember correctly, the `for` loop was the first type of looping structure taught. Most likely the reason for this is that it is really hard to mess it up, even for virgin programmers. A block of code is executed a specific number of times, incrementing a variable for each iteration.

The `for/in` loop is a close relative of the `for` loop. However, unlike the `for` loop, which specifies the number of iterations using a numeric value, an object is used. The really unfortunate thing about the `for/in` loop is that most people forget it exists, myself included. Listing 4-6 has several examples of both `for` and `for/in` loops.

Listing 4-6   Examples of `for` and `for/in` Loops

```
var factorial = 1;
var numbers = new Array(1,2,3,4,5);
var index;

for(var i=1;i < 6;i++)
  factorial *= i;

factorial = 1;

for(var i=5;i > 0;i—)
  factorial *= i;

factorial = 1;

for(index in numbers)
  factorial *= numbers[index];

alert(factorial);
```

Because they are so similar in function, the `while` loop and the `do/while` loop offer a quandary concerning which to use. They both execute a block of instructions while a condition is `true`. So why are there two different loops, you ask? Go on, ask; I'll wait.

The reason there are two different loops is that one tests *before* executing the block of code, and the other tests *after* executing the block of code. The `while` loop performs the test and then executes the code block only if the condition is `true`. Iteration continues until the condition is no longer `true`, at which time execution continues with the code immediately following the loop.

On the other hand, the `do/while` loop executes the code block before performing the test. Because the test is performed after the execution of the code block, it guarantees that the code block will be executed at least once. This is quite useful when it is necessary to execute the code block once, regardless of whether the condition is `true`.

The majority of times that I code a loop, it is because I'm looking for something. Where I'm looking isn't important, although it is usually either in an array or in the DOM. However, what is important is that I need to find it. So I'll write a little routine that loops through whatever, looking for something. Let's say that there are 600 whatevers and I find what I'm looking for at number 20. Wouldn't it be nice to be able to stop looking?

It is possible; remember the `break` statement from the `switch`? It also terminates a loop-dropping execution to the statement immediately following the loop. Heck, it is even elegant.

But what if you don't want to exit the loop, but rather continue with the next iteration? Then you use the `continue` statement, which causes the current iteration to stop and the next iteration to begin. It is sort of like going back for a second helping of the entreé when you haven't finished your vegetables, but hey, unlike your mother, JavaScript doesn't complain.

One more issue arises with exiting loops; JavaScript allows labels to be placed on statements, like looping statements. This provides a way to refer to the statement from elsewhere in the script. This means that a `break` or `continue` can refer to a specific loop so that it is possible to break or continue an outer loop from an inner loop. Listing 4-7 gives an example of how this works—a useless example, but an example nonetheless.

Listing 4-7   A Useless Example of Using `break` and `continue` to Refer to a Specific Loop

```
var result = 1;

Iloop: for(var i=0;i < 5;i++)
Jloop:    for(var j=0;j < 5;j++)
            if(j == 2)
              break Jloop;
            else
Kloop:        for(var k=0;k < 5;k++)
                if(k == 3)
                  continue Iloop;
                else
                  result += k;

alert(result);
```

4.5   FUNCTIONS

Fromsome points of view, JavaScript functions are a little bit on the strange side when compared to other programming languages. This is because even though they are functions, they don't necessarily return a value. JavaScript functions are really groupings of code designed to perform a specific task. Quick, imagine yourself writing a JavaScript function that concatenates two strings. Visualize it fully in your mind before looking at the example in Listing 4-8.

Listing 4-8   A Function That Concatenates Two Strings

```
function concatenate(a,b) {
  return a.toString() + b.toString();
}
```

Don't be surprised if the function that you visualized looks remarkably similar to the one in Listing 4-8. There is a perfectly logical reason for this similarity; my mind-reading machine has been perfected. Either that or I'm aware that the majority of developers know only a couple ways to define a JavaScript function. Which is the truth? I'll give you a hint: It is currently the fall of 2005, and I'm writing this on the SEPTA R5 line on my way to Doylestown, Pennsylvania. If I actually could read minds across space and time, I would have won Powerball last week and I'd be writing this on the beach in Tahiti.

This means that, as web developers, we're all in a rut, doing the same thing the same way day after day and year after year. Yeah, I know the drill: "It works, so why change it?" and "I always do it that way" are usually the statements used. To these statements, I have one response, "You learn more from your mistakes than you do from your successes!"

When you actually get down to it, there are several separate and distinct ways to define a function in JavaScript. Why so many ways to define a function? I can't rightfully say, but I can take a guess. It has always seemed to me that the more ways there are to perform a single task, the more flexible the language is and the more problems can be solved.

Getting back to our function that concatenates two strings, we've already seen one possible method of implementing the solution, so let's take a look at another way. JavaScript has the Function() constructor for, interestingly enough, constructing functions. The Function constructor, an example of which is shown here, is used to create a function and assign it to a variable or an event handler.

```
var concatenate = new Function('a','b','return a.toString()
+ b.toString()');
```

In addition to the Function constructor, the function operator can be used to assign a function to a variable. One of the more interesting "features" of the Function constructor is that it shows that JavaScript is really an interpreted language because the function is stored as a string. This is an example of our string concatenation example defined using the function operator:

```
var concatenate = function(a,b) {return a.toString() + b.toString()}
```

4.6   RECURSION

Feel free to skip over this section if you're one of those developers with a fear of recursion; not only is this considered an advanced topic, but it can also literally cause headaches. If you should decide to read on, good for you! The only real way to get over the headaches is to use recursion as much as possible and work your way through them. After all, what's a couple of weeks of pain compared to being able to write some really tight code?

Are you still there? Rats! I guess I'll have to write this part of the chapter. So much for kicking back and watching *My Name Is Nobody* on DVD.

In its simplest form, recursion occurs when a function calls itself repeatedly to achieve some kind of result. Some examples of functions that readily lend themselves to recursion are mathematical, such as the Euclidean algorithm, the Ackerman Function and the functions to compute factorials, Fibonacci numbers, and Catalan numbers.

When setting out to create a recursive function, one thing to keep in mind is that anything that can be done recursively can also be done iteratively. In fact, sometimes it is actually more efficient to code an iterative function. This is because there are limits on how deep the recursion can go, usually around 32K. Attempts to exceed this built-in limitation will result in a nicely worded error message that essentially means "stack overflow." Keep this in mind when implementing recursive functions.

With the disclaimer about the perils of recursion out of the way, let's examine one of the older examples of recursive algorithms, the Euclidean algorithm. Dating from approximately 200 B.C., the Euclidean algorithm is a method for computing the Greatest Common Divisor of two integers. Listing 4-9 shows a recursive implementation of the Euclidean algorithm.

Listing 4-9   A Recursive Implementation of the Euclidean Algorithm

```
function gcd(m, n) {
  if ((m % n) == 0)
    return n;
  else
    return gcd(n, m % n);
}
```

To show how this function works, let's call the gcd function with the values 24 and 18. Because 24 % 18 is 6, the function is called again with the values 18 and 6. Because 18 % 6 is 0, we're done, and the value 6 is returned as the Greatest Common Divisor.

Just in case you were wondering what an iterative version of the gcd function would look like, it is shown in Listing 4-10.

Listing 4-10   An Iterative Implementation of the Euclidean Algorithm

```
function gcd(m, n) {
  var t;

  while(n != 0) {
    t = n;
    n = m % n;
    m = t;
  }

  return(m);
}
```

4.7   CONSTRUCTORS

The capability to create custom objects is what separates modern program-ming languages from the programming languages of yore. Unfortunately, in JavaScript, this capability is one of those language features that is often either ignored or overlooked. Believe it or not, there is actually a good reason for this; it is all a matter of perception. You see, JavaScript is often viewed as a lightweight language or a kid's programming language, good only for tasks such as creating pop-ups or handling mouseover events.

Although I believe that everybody is entitled to their opinion, I also believe that this opinion has kept web applications mired in their original unload/reload glory. For this reason, as well as the fact that I'm not terribly fond of writing hundreds or thousands of lines of custom code, I began to play around with JavaScript constructors. Yes, with some planning and design work in the beginning, it is very possible to free up some time for the occa-sional mad scientist project later.

The first question is, how do we start writing a constructor? Do we just jump in and create a constructor and use it? Or should we work out the details of how something works and then use that to write a constructor? Which approach is better?

Tough questions, and, unfortunately, I can't say what will work for you. I can, however, tell you what works for me. Whenever I'm developing a construc-tor, the first thing that I do is write a sample application that does what I want it to do, but not using a constructor. After the sample application is developed the next step is to rewrite it using a constructor. This might seem like more work than it's worth, but it works for me. Also, I have a tendency to see a better way to accomplish tasks with each subsequent rewrite.

   With that explained, let's take a look at some of the coding details of creating JavaScript constructors. I've always been fond of palindromes (words,
numbers, or sentences that are spelled the same forward and backward), so
let's create a constructor something along those lines. Without further ado,
here is an introduction to the two ways of coding class constructors in
JavaScript.

   Yes, there are two different ways to code class constructors in JavaScript.
The first, which is probably the easier of the two, involves creating a function
and then creating an instance of that function using the new operator. Listing
4-11 shows an annotated example of using this method to create a constructor.

Listing 4-11   An Annotated Example of Creating a Class Constructor

```
function Monster(text) {
  /*
     The purpose of the following code is to increment a global
     variable for each instance of this class.  In the event of the
     global variable being undefined it will be initialized with a
     value of one.
  */
  try {
    ++_monster;
  }
  catch(e) {
    _monster = 1;
  }


  /*
     This code, which is executed whenever a new instance is
     created, initializes new occurrences of this object.  Private
     and public properties are defined and initialized.  In
     addition, methods are exposed making them public.
  */
  var occurrence = _monster;              // Private property
  this.string = text;                     // Public property
  this.palendrome = _palendrome;          // Public method
  this.number = _number;                  // Public method

  /*
     The following function is a method which has been made public
     by the above: this.palendrome = _palendrome; statement.
  */
  function _palendrome() {
    var re = new RegExp('[ ,.!;:\']{1,}','g');
    var text = this.string.toLowerCase().replace(re,'');

    return(text == _reverse(text))
  }
```

                                                                    continues

Listing 4-11   continued

```
/*
   The following function is a public read only method that gets
   the value of the private property occurrence.  Through
   techniques like this it is possible to maintain control over
   the inner workings of objects.
*/
function _number() {
  return(occurrence);
}

/*
   The _reverse function is a private method.  Methods are private
   when they are not exposed using the this.[external name] =
   [internal name] statement as _palendrome and _number were.
*/
function _reverse(string) {
  var work = '';

  for(var i=string.length;i >= 0;−i)
    work += string.charAt(i);

  return(work);
}
}
```

To instantiate (a fancy way to say "create an instance") this class, all that is necessary is to use the new operator in the following manner:

```
var myMonster = new Monster();
```

Using the newly instantiated class is just a matter of using the various public properties and methods that were defined by the constructor. For example, to set and get the string property for the myMonster instance of the Monster class, the code would look like this:

```
myMonster.string = 'Able was I ere I saw Elba!';
alert(myMonster.string);
```

To use the properties methods, statements would look like the following:

```
alert(myMonster.palendrome());
alert(myMonster.number());
```

However, there is another way to create a class constructor in JavaScript: use the prototype property. This is shown in Listing 4-12.

Listing 4-12   Using the `prototype` Property to Create an `sclass` Constructor

```
Creature.prototype = new Creature;
Creature.prototype.constructor = Creature;

function Creature() {
  /*
     The purpose of the following code is to increment a global
     variable for each instance of this class.  In the event of the
     global variable being undefined it will be initialized with a
     value of zero.
  */
  try {
    ++_creature;

    /*
       This is a public property which really shouldn't be accessed
       externally.
    */
    this._instance = _creature;
  }
  catch(e) {
    /*
       Zero is used here due to the fact that this constructor is
    executed at class definition time.
    */
    _creature = 0;
  }
}

Creature.prototype.string;                         // Public property

   /*
      The following function is a method which has been made public
      by the Creature.prototype.palendrome = _Creature_palendrome;
      statement below.
   */
function _Creature_palendrome() {
  var re = new RegExp('[ ,.!;:\'']{1,}','g');
  var text = this.string.toLowerCase().replace(re,'');

  return(text == _reverse(text))

   /*
      The _reverse function is a private method available only within
      the enclosing method.
   */
   function _reverse(string) {
     var work = '';

     for(var i=string.length;i >= 0;—i)
       work += string.charAt(i);
```

continues

Listing 4-12   continued

```
    return(work);
  }
}
Creature.prototype.palendrome = _Creature_palendrome;

  /*
    The following function is a method which has been made public
    by the Creature.prototype.number = _Creature_Number; statement
    below.
  */
function _Creature_Number() {
    return(this._instance);
}
Creature.prototype.number = _Creature_Number;
```

4.8   EVENT HANDLING

Bring up the subject of client-side events among a group of web developers, and the first (sometimes the only) one mentioned is the `onclick` event handler. Occasionally, someone will acknowledge the `onmouseover` and the `onmouseout` events, but that is usually a rare occurrence, such as leap year or a pay raise after Y2K. Come to think of it, you're more likely to hear a story about someone holding a door open for Walter Koenig than to hear the smallest utterance about another event.

The problem is that developers get into a rut, a comfort zone, and use the same events day in and day out. After a few months of this, we have a tendency to forget that the event handlers are even there. One of the reasons for this is that developing web applications is like riding a bike; when you don't remember how to do it right, there isn't even time to scream before the splat. For this reason, I have compiled Table 4-5, which covers the event handlers common to most browsers. Yes, Bill, that means that the `beforeunload` event is omitted.

Table 4-5   Event Handlers Common to Most Browsers

Operator	Syntax	Description
blur	*object*.onblur = *function*	Fires when an object loses focus, such as when Tab is pressed or another object is clicked.
focus	*object*.onfocus = *function*	Fires when the object gets focus, either programmatically or through user interaction.

Operator	Syntax	Description
load	*window.*onload = *function*	Fires when the page is loaded. This event can be simulated by periodically checking the document's readystate property.
resize	*window.*onresize = *function*	Fires when the window is resized.
scroll	*window.*onscroll = *function*	Fires when the page's scroll bars are used.
unload	*window.*onunload = *function*	Fires just before the page is onloaded. Although it is commonly used by pop-ups to spawn more pop-ups, it does have some legitimate uses.
onclick	*object.*onclick = *function*	Fires when an object is clicked.
dblclick	*object.*ondblclick = *function*	Fires when an object is double-clicked.
mousedown	*object.*onmousedown = *function*	Fires when the mouse button is pressed.
mouseup	*object.*onmouseup = *function*	Fires when the mouse button is released.
mousemove	*object.*onmousemove = *function*	Fires when the mouse is moved.
mouseover	*object.*onmouseover = *function*	Fires when the mouse pointer moves over the specified object.
mouseout	*object.*onmouseout = *function*	Fires when the mouse pointer moves off the specified object.
change	*object.*onchange = *function*	Fires when the object's value changes.
reset	*object.*onreset = *function*	Fires when the object (form) is reset.
select	*object.*onselect = *function*	Fires when a different option is selected on the object (select).
submit	*object.*onsubmit = *function*	Fires when the object (form) is submitted.
keydown	*object.*onkeydown = *function*	Fires when a keyboard key is pressed when the specified object has focus.
keyup	*object.*onkeyup = *function*	Fires when a keyboard key is released when the specified object has focus.
keypress	*object.*onkeypress = *function*	A combination of both the keydown and keyup events.

Unfortunately, knowing the events is only half the battle. For this knowledge to be of any use, it is necessary to know how to assign a JavaScript event to the handler. And as with many endeavors in JavaScript, there are two ways to accomplish this task. No, I'm not referring to a right way and a wrong way; I'm referring to assigning via HTML and via JavaScript. Listing 4-13 shows both ways to assign an event handler.

Listing 4-13   The Two Ways to Assign an Event Handler in JavaScript

```
document.getElementById('myButton').onclick = new
Function('alert(\'Ouch! You clicked me!\')');

<input type="button" id="myButton" value="Don't click">

<input type="button" id="myButton" value="Click" onclick="alert('Oooh! Do
it again!')">
```

Before wrapping up this chapter, there are some important items that could fall under the umbrella of event handling. Although they aren't really events, they do raise events. The items that I am referring to are the `window.setTimeout()` and `window.setInterval()` methods. Don't be surprised if you've never heard of them; they're a little "out there."

The purpose of these methods is to delay the execution of a JavaScript function for a specific number of milliseconds. Why? Well, let's say, for example, that you'd like to check later to see if an event has taken place and leave it at that. The real question is really, why are there two methods instead of one? The reason for two methods is that `setTimeout` executes a function once, whereas `setInterval` executes a function repeatedly until told otherwise. Think of `setInterval` as being afflicted with lycanthropy, and you get the concept. The syntax, shown here, for both of these methods is identical:

```
var oTime = window.setTimeout('myFunction()',1000);

var oInterval = window.setInterval('myYour()',100);
```

All that is left is what to do when it is necessary to clear a timeout or an interval. It is simple; just do the following, and they're cleared:

```
window.clearTimeout(oTime);

window.clearInterval(oInterval);
```

Remember one important thing when coding in JavaScript: Bending the rules is allowed. Experiment, and delve into matters that man, or woman, was not meant to delve into. After all, it is the mad scientist way.

4.9   SUMMARY

In this chapter, we started with the basics of JavaScript data types and variables; with a side trip to operators, we covered the basics and a little more.

Our trek continued through the flow-control statements, the conditional ones such as `if-then-else` and the `switch` statement. In addition, the looping statements were covered, from the common `for` loop to the more obscure `for-in` loop.

Next, JavaScript functions were covered along with the somewhat feared topic of recursive functions. In the same vein as functions, constructors we covered, starting with the "function" method of creating constructors. The `prototype` method also was covered. Finally, event handling was discussed—specifically, how to set handlers and how to deal with the event when it fires.

CHAPTER 5

Ajax Using HTML and JavaScript

Human beings, as well as other life forms, are made up of chemicals such as iron, nitrogen, and water. However, simply mixing everything together in a cauldron and giving it a quick stir won't result in someone climbing out of the cauldron. The reason for this is that it isn't the type of ingredients put together; it is how the ingredients are put together. After all, if girls really were made of sugar and spice and everything nice, there would be a lot more geeky guys with dates at the prom. If you've ever read Lester Del Rey's short story *Helen O'Loy,* you might be accustomed to the concept of building a date from things lying about.

The same is true for web applications. Consider for a moment what is commonly referred to as Dynamic HTML, or DHTML, for short. Still commonly used in web applications, it is distinguished from plain HTML only by the fact that things happened based upon events. This is where the *dynamic* part comes in. I would like to point out that at no time did I mention the word *JavaScript*. The reason for this is that not only is it possible to have DHTML without JavaScript, but it is also possible to have JavaScript without DHTML.

Just in case you're curious, the way to have DHTML without JavaScript is to use Cascading Style Sheets in event handlers instead of JavaScript. Although it wouldn't be quite as flexible as JavaScript, and it could be used only for things such as mouseovers and mouseouts, it does fulfill the dynamic requirement. After all, it really is how the various parts are put together, not the parts themselves. Let's dig a little into the pile of client-side parts available when starting an Ajax application and see what can be of use in building our monster.

In this chapter, however, I intend to take advantage of the tools available to us. Most of these tools are used in the traditional manner. However, some are not; what fun would it be if everything was done according to the manual? Consider frames, for example. Whether or not you're aware of it, you can abuse frames in quite a number of ways. Other tools that I use are the cross-browser

Document Object Model and HTML tables for displaying information. Hey, torture the information enough, and eventually it will confess.

In addition to these tools, I cover the ultimate database "tool," stored procedures, but with a quirky difference. The difference is that I'm using MySQL, not Oracle or Microsoft SQL Server. Just in case you're wondering why, I have three very good reasons. The first is that MySQL is an open source database. The second is that stored procedures are rather new in MySQL, so there isn't very much written about them. The final reason, and, in my opinion the most important, is that my wife keeps me on a budget; alas, no Tesla coils for me.

5.1   HIDDEN FRAMES AND IFRAMES

Frames and iframes (in-line frames), for some reason, are one of those things that strike fear into the heart of web developers everywhere. It is one of those deep-seated fears, like tanning products are to a vampire or advertisements for having your pet spayed or neutered are to a werewolf. Several reasons for this primal fear of frames exist; fortunately, there is a countermeasure for each of these reasons.

The first of these reasons is the mistaken belief that frames are nonstandard and, therefore, are supported by only a handful of "unholy" web browsers. Fortunately, this belief is a total and complete myth because frames and iframes have the blessing of the World Wide Web Consortium. In fact, the only unholy—eh, make that unusual—part is that the frames are hidden, but, then, that's the entire point of this endeavor.

Now let's get into the actual specifics of making frames behave like Claude Rains, who, if I may digress for a moment, brilliantly played a mad scientist even if he didn't start that way. First starting with the older frame instead of the more recent iframe, the hiding entirely takes place in the frameset, as Listing 5-1 shows.

Listing 5-1   The Older Frame

```
<frameset rows="100%,*">
      <frame name="visible_frame" src="visible.htm">
      <frame name="hidden_frame" src="hidden.htm">
      <noframes>
            Frames are required to use this web site.
      </noframes>
</frameset>
```

As mentioned in the previous chapter, the `rows="100%,*"` performs the magic, but it isn't the only method available to us. In fact, looking at only the opening frameset tag, the following eight examples all produce the desired results:

```
<frameset rows="100%,*">

<frameset rows="100%,0">

<frameset rows="*,0%">

<frameset rows="*,0">

<frameset cols="100%,*">

<frameset cols="100%,0">

<frameset cols="*,0%">

<frameset cols="*,0">
```

The reason for this plethora of choices is that this is one of those times when we really don't care how the hiding is accomplished—all that matters is that the hiding *is* accomplished. Oh, this is a good time for me to point out that when developing a new application using hidden frames, it isn't a violation of the mad scientist rules to make the hidden frame visible for testing. It is, however, a violation to let others see the frame with the hidden frame visible, both because it gives the impression that something is wrong with our fiendish plans and because it looks ugly.

Unlike framesets, in which the hiding is accomplished through the use of either rows or columns, iframes have the much-easier-to-remember `height` and `width` attributes, as the following tag shows:

```
<iframe height="0" width="0" src="hidden.htm">
```

That's it—just the one measly little tag, and we've got something that kind of looks a lot like Ajax. Right about now you're either taking my name in vain or wondering why I didn't start with iframes. In fact, there are probably some out there who are doing both. Well, the answer is both personal and simple. Whenever I learn something new, I try to immerse myself totally in it, avoiding all shortcuts until whatever I learned becomes second nature. To be totally honest, after learning to swim, I was wrinkled for a week.

5.2 CROSS-BROWSER DOM

Now that we have either classic frames or iframes, we have reached one of the most widespread reasons for their avoidance: the matter of access. Short of a crystal ball and tea leaves, or maybe two soup cans and a piece of string, just how do the various frames communicate? I've worked with some web developers who believed that it was easier to talk with the ghost of Elvis than to have individual frames communicate with one another. However, to be honest, most of those web developers talked of black helicopters and wore aluminum foil hats to ward off mind control.

As much as it seems otherwise, interframe communications is relatively simple and can be dealt with using one word: *DOM*. Alright, you caught me in a fib; DOM is an acronym, so it's really three words, Document Object Model. Coming in both HTML and XML flavors, in this instance, the DOM is a hierarchical representation of a web page that allows JavaScript to access and modify a page. Actually, careless coding when using the DOM is a most excellent way for a page to self-destruct, a la "Good morning, Mister Phelps."

As formidable as the DOM sounds, it is nothing more than a hierarchical representation of a document, which, in this case, is an HTML document. Think trees—the data structure trees, not the green woody things. And, no, not binary trees; we want the ones that can have more than two children.

Just in case you need a little refresher in the structure of trees, it goes like this:

+ Each of the tags in an HTML document can be referred to as a node or element.
+ There is only one topmost node, which is called the root node.
+ All nodes are descendants of the root node, either directly or indirectly.
+ With the exception of the root node, all nodes have a single parent node.
+ Nodes that occur on the same tree level that share a parent are called siblings.
+ The immediate descendants of a particular node are referred to as that node's children.

However, you must remember one thing when accessing the Document Object Model: Here be monsters. This is one of those places where it is really necessary to test things on several different browsers. The reason for this is the usual; it is basically a question of interpretation of the World Wide Web Consortium's DOM specifications. This might sound a little like the schisms that occur between different sects of the same religion, but depending on the application, it can cause some major headaches. Listing 5-2 shows an example of this potential problem.

Listing 5-2   Example of a Problem Created by Differing Interpretations of the W3C's DOM Specs

```
<html>
      <head>
            <title>DOM Test</title>
```

```
            <script language="JavaScript">
/*
     Recursively transverse the HTML DOM using the passed
                    node as a starting point.
*/
function transverse(obj) {
     var strNode = ancestor(obj) + obj.nodeName.toString() + '\n';

     for(var i=0;i < obj.childNodes.length;i++)
          strNode += transverse(obj.childNodes.item(i));

     return(strNode);

     function ancestor(obj) {
          if(obj.parentNode != null)
               return('>' + ancestor(obj.parentNode));
          else
               return('');
     }
}
          </script>
     </head>
     <body onload="document.getElementById('textarea1').value =
transverse(document)">
          <table width="300" border="1" cellspacing="1" cellpadding="1">
          <tr>
             <td>
                    <input type="text" id="input1" name="input1" />
             </td>
          </tr>
             <tr>
                <td>
                       <textarea id="textarea1" name="textarea1"
cols="80" rows="20"></textarea>
                </td>
             </tr>
          </table>
        </body>
</html>
```

Consisting of an HTML document with an embedded JavaScript function whose sole purpose is to transverse the document, the page just shown yields some interesting results, depending on the web browser. Listings 5-1, 5-2, and 5-3 show the result of loading the document in Microsoft Internet Explorer, Firefox, and Opera, respectively.

Listing 5-3   Microsoft Internet Explorer

```
#document
>HTML
>>HEAD
```

continues

Listing 5-3   continued

```
>>>TITLE
>>>SCRIPT
>>BODY
>>>TABLE
>>>>TBODY
>>>>>TR
>>>>>>TD
>>>>>>>INPUT
>>>>>>>#text
>>>>>TR
>>>>>>TD
>>>>>>>TEXTAREA
>>>>>>>>#text
>>>>>>>#text
```

Listing 5-4   Firefox

```
#document
>HTML
>>HEAD
>>>TITLE
>>>>#text
>>>#text
>>>SCRIPT
>>>>#text
>>#text
>>BODY
>>>#text
>>>TABLE
>>>>#text
>>>>TBODY
>>>>>TR
>>>>>>#text
>>>>>>TD
>>>>>>>#text
>>>>>>>INPUT
>>>>>>>#text
>>>>>>#text
>>>>>#text
>>>>>TR
>>>>>>#text
>>>>>>TD
>>>>>>>#text
>>>>>>>TEXTAREA
>>>>>>>#text
>>>>>>#text
>>>>>#text
>>>#text
```

Listing 5-5 Opera

```
#document
>HTML
>>HEAD
>>>TITLE
>>>>#text
>>>SCRIPT
>>BODY
>>>#text
>>>TABLE
>>>>TBODY
>>>>>TR
>>>>>>TD
>>>>>>>#text
>>>>>>>INPUT
>>>>>>>#text
>>>>>TR
>>>>>>TD
>>>>>>>#text
>>>>>>>TEXTAREA
>>>>>>>>#text
>>>>>>>#text
>>>#text
>>>#text
>>>#text
```

Interesting, isn't it? You can't even play the *Sesame Street* "One of these things ain't like the other" song because none of them is like the others. However, more similarities exist than differences, such as the basic structure and the existence of specific nodes. What is important to remember is that, depending on the web browser, #TEXT elements can be sprinkled here and there.

Now that this is out of the way, let's take a closer look at the HTML document in Listing 5-6, with the goal of locating specific elements, such as the BODY element. As a matter of fact, grab a number 2 pencil; it's time for a pop quiz. Which of the following JavaScript statements can be used to locate the BODY element in the HTML document shown in Listing 5-6?

1. `window.document.body;`

2. `document.body;`

3. `self.document.body;`

4. `document.getElementsByTagName("body").item(0);`

Listing 5-6   Sample HTML Document

```html
<html>
  <head>
    <title>Sample</title>
  </head>
  <body>
    <p>Hello, World!</p>
  </body>
</html>
```

Pencils down. The correct answer is: all of them. Yes, it is a trick question, but it points out that there are many ways to reach the same destination. Think of it as an "All roads lead to Rome" thing, and no one will get hurt. Of course, it might be important to remember that some of the routes to a destination could be quicker than others.

I'd like to cover one additional, often overlooked, DOM topic. When dealing with frames, there will always be more than one #document. Not only does the frameset have a #document, but each frame will have a #document of its own.

5.2.1   JavaScript, ECMAScript, and JScript

Regardless of the name they call it by, people either love or hate JavaScript, which is probably why opinions range from it being either the greatest thing since sliced bread or the tool of the devil. Personally, I believe that cheeseburgers are the greatest thing since sliced bread and that the tool of the devil is cellphones. Nothing worse than enjoying a good cheeseburger, with onion rings on the side, and the damn phone starts playing "The Monster Mash." But I digress.

JavaScript is a tool, neither good nor bad, like any other tool; it's all in how the tool is used. Give ten people a box of tools and a job to do, and nine of them will get the job done in various degrees, while the tenth will require a call to 911. With human nature being what it is, you'll never hear about the first nine; you'll only hear about poor old Bob who did himself serious bodily harm with a router. For this reason, people will decide that routers are evil.

JavaScript essentially falls into the same category, a lightweight, interpreted object-based language, and it is extremely flexible and tightly coupled with the browser. For instance, you're now aware that by using JavaScript and DOM it is possible to modify the contents of the page as previously demonstrated without bothering the server, but are you also aware that by using JavaScript it is also possible to create objects?

Let's say, for instance, that you've got a website that uses a handful of standard-sized pop-ups. Well, rather than code them each by hand and possibly have typos on a few pages, why not create an object to open a number of standard-sized windows? Three different-sized pop-ups should suffice; add to that the capability to override the various properties, and we end up with the "function," which is really a class shown in Listing 5-7.

Listing 5-7 JavaScript `childWindow` Class

```
function childWindow(strURL, strName, strChildType) {
     /*    The purpose of this function is to act as a
       class constructor for the childWindow object.

            The properties for this object are the following:
                          url           = uniform resource locator
                          name          = child window name
                          child         = child window object
                          attributes    = child window attributes

            The methods for this object are the following:
            open()                     = Opens and sets focus to the
                                         childWindow
            close()                    = Closes the childWindow
            focus()                    = Sets focus to the childWindow
            closed()      = Returns a boolean indicating if the

                                         childWindow is open.
     */
     var reName = new RegExp('[^a-z]','gi'); // Regular expression
     var e;
// Dummy for error code

// Properties
     this.url = strURL; // Uniform resource locator
     this.name = strName.toString().replace(reName,'');
     this.childType = strChildType; // Child window type
     this.child = null; // Child window object
     this.alwaysRaised = 'no'; // Window always raised
     this.copyhistory = 'yes'; // Copy browser history
     this.height = ''; // Window's height
     this.left = 0; // Window's left start position
     this.location = 'no'; // Window's location box
     this.menubar = 'no'; // Window's menu bar
     this.resizable = 'yes'; // Window's resizable
     this.scrollbars = 'yes'; // Window's scroll bars
     this.status = 'yes'; // Window's status bar
     this.toolbar = 'yes'; // Window's tool bar
     this.width = ''; // Window's width
     this.top = 0; // Window's top start position

// Methods
     this.open = childWindowOpen; // Open method
     this.close = childWindowClose; // Close method
     this.focus = childWindowFocus; // Focus method
```

continues

Listing 5-7   continued

```
// Determine attributes based on type
     try {
           if(typeof this.childType != 'undefined')
                switch(this.childType.toLowerCase()) {
                     case 'info':
                          this.height = Math.round(screen.availHeight
* 0.4);
                          this.width = Math.round(screen.availWidth *
0.4);
                          this.left = (screen.availWidth -
Math.round(screen.availWidth * 0.4) - 8) / 2;
                          this.top = (screen.availHeight -
Math.round(screen.availHeight * 0.3) - 48) / 4;
                          this.toolbar = 'no';

                          break;
                     case 'help':
                          this.height = Math.round(screen.availHeight
* 0.7);
                          this.width = Math.round(screen.availWidth *
0.8);
                          this.left = screen.availWidth -
Math.round(screen.availWidth * 0.8) - 8;
                          this.top = (screen.availHeight -
Math.round(screen.availHeight * 0.7) - 48) / 4;

                          break;
                     case 'full':
                          this.height = screen.availHeight - 48;
                          this.width = screen.availWidth - 8;
                          this.toolbar = 'no';

                          break;
                     default:
                          throw(null);

                          break;
                }
           else
                throw(null);
     }
     catch(e) {
           this.height = screen.availHeight - 147;
           this.width = screen.availWidth - 8;
           this.menubar = 'yes';
           this.resizable = 'yes';
           this.scrollbars = 'yes';
           this.status = 'yes';
           this.toolbar = 'yes';
           this.location = 'yes';
     }
```

```
        function childWindowOpen() {
                /*      The purpose of this function is to act as the open
        for the childWindow object by
opening a window with attributes based upon
                    the window type specified.
                */

                var strAttributes; // Window attributes
                var e;
           // Dummy error

                // Build window attribute string
                strAttributes = 'alwaysRaised=' + this.alwaysRaised;
                strAttributes += ',copyhistory=' + this.copyhistory;

                if(typeof this.height == 'number')
                        if(this.height > 0)
                                strAttributes += ',height=' + this.height;

                strAttributes += ',left=' + this.left;
                strAttributes += ',location=' + this.location;
                strAttributes += ',menubar=' + this.menubar;
                strAttributes += ',resizable=' + this.resizable;
                strAttributes += ',scrollbars=' + this.scrollbars;
                strAttributes += ',status=' + this.status;
                strAttributes += ',toolbar=' + this.toolbar;
                strAttributes += ',top=' + this.top;

                if(typeof this.width == 'number')
                        if(this.width > 0)
                                strAttributes += ',width=' + this.width;

           // Try to open a child window
                try {
                        this.child = window.open(this.url, this.name,
        strAttributes);

                        if(window.opener.name == this.name)
                                this.child = window.opener;
                        else
                                if(window.opener.opener.name == this.name)
                                        this.child = window.opener.opener;
                                else
                                        if(window.opener.opener.opener.name ==
        this.name)
                                                this.child =
        window.opener.opener.opener;
                                        else
                                                if(window.opener.opener.opener.name ==
        this.name)
                                                        this.child =
        window.opener.opener.opener;
```

continues

Listing 5-7   continued

```
                this.focus();
        }
        catch (e) {
                this.focus();
        }
    }

    function childWindowClose() {
        /*    The purpose of this function is to act as the
close method for the childWindow
            object and close the child window.
        */
        var e;
    // Dummy for error code

        try {
                this.child.close();
        }
        catch (e) { }
    }

    function childWindowFocus() {
        /*    The purpose of this function is to act as the
focus method for the childWindow
            object.  In other words, set focus to the
                child window.
        */
        this.child.focus();
    }
}
```

As with the more traditional languages, to use our window object, it is necessary to instantiate the class—in other words, create an instance of the class. Listing 5-8 shows how instantiation is accomplished, and Figure 5-1 displays the result.

Listing 5-8   Example of Using the `childWindow` Class

```
var child = new childWindow('child.html','child','info');
child.open();
```

Another often overlooked feature of JavaScript is its recursive capabilities, although, come to think of it, this might be an intentional omission. For some reason, the majority of developers avoid recursion like it's an Osmonds' or a Carpenters' album. I'm of the opinion that the reason for this is that, as with the albums from either of the two mentioned groups, recursion can cause headaches. Of course, it might be more because, unless trained, our minds don't readily lend themselves to thinking recursively.

Figure 5-1 childWindow class in action

Nevertheless, sometimes recursion is the easiest way to handle a particular coding issue. And not computing Fibonacci numbers or the factorial of a number, which are those "make work tasks" designed to keep computer science professors off the street. Group those two problems with singly- and doubly-linked lists, and they're good for a whole semester.

Instead, let's examine the transverse() function from Listing 5-2, which, for convenience, has been copied here to Listing 5-9. With the exception of the enclosed ancestor() function, the transverse() function is pretty much a classic example of recursion coded in JavaScript. The same can be said of the ancestor() function, whose sole purpose is to return a greater-than sign for every ancestor of the current node.

Listing 5-9   Listing 5-2 Repeated

```
/*
      Recursively transverse the HTML DOM using the passed
                        node as a starting point.
*/
function transverse(obj) {
      var strNode = ancestor(obj) + obj.nodeName.toString() + '\n';

      for(var i=0;i < obj.childNodes.length;i++)
            strNode += transverse(obj.childNodes.item(i));

      return(strNode);

      function ancestor(obj) {
            if(obj.parentNode != null)
                  return('>' + ancestor(obj.parentNode));
            else
                  return('');
      }
}
```

5.2.2   A Problem to Be Solved

With all due respect to one of my previous managers who believed that there were no such thing as problems, only opportunities, there is one problem that I've been meaning to solve for a while now. It's one of those things that the average person, one without mad scientist tendencies, doesn't realize exists. Where do mad scientists shop online? Oh, sure, there's Amazon.com and Walmart.com, but have you ever tried to purchase a cask of Amontillado, or stones and mortar from either website? These essential tools of the trade just aren't readily available online.

The big websites just don't appreciate the needs of the lonely mad scientist. In fact, it might be a good idea to include some of the other often-underrepresented groups as well. I imagine that alchemists and sorcerers have some issues shopping for the tools of their trades as well. I, for one, have never seen either site offer retorts or grimoires or anything along those lines. Not that I know what a retort is; I imagine that it is some kind of backup Linzer torte or something along those lines. There is definitely an untapped market here, so much so that, had I conceived of this idea about six years ago, it would be necessary to beat off potential investors with a stick.

I envision this website as a pretty normal series of web pages, starting with a splash page that takes the visitor to a page displaying items for the various guilds: mad scientist, alchemist, and sorcerer. The visitor would then have the option of browsing all the items available or filtering by guild.

Shoppers could view the details of the individual items and, if desired, add them to their shopping cart, which can be displayed at any time. When they were sure that they had everything they want, they could proceed to checkout, enter their shipping and billing information, and be off.

So with that idea in mind, the various web pages fall into a few simple categories:

+ Those that display tabular information that cannot be altered, such as the items for sale

+ Pages that display tabular information that can be updated, such as the quantities of items in the shopping cart

+ Static form-type pages, such as those that verify your shipping address page

+ Updateable forms, such as the page where the visitor enters the shipping billing information

Oh, and the other thing I forgot to mention: This site needs to work with a selection of different web browsers. I have a couple of totally logical reasons to require this cross-browser capability. The first reason is to appeal to as wide a customer base as possible because the more customers, the more sales. The second is, it might not be a good idea to tick off someone who is potentially creating a Moon-Mounted Death Ray. Hmm, note to self: Use a P.O. Box as a corporate address.

Before proceeding any further, now is a good time to delve a little into the server-side environment. Let's start with the operating system and web server; I'm using Windows XP Professional and Internet Information Server. The reason for this is the usual: It came on the machine, and I'm too lazy to change it. Besides, I'm pretty sure that "Age of Mythology" doesn't run on Linux. Note to self: Make sure that you don't get caught by Mary Ann playing when you should be writing.

So far, my environmental choices have been pretty boring, and the open source people are thinking that Firefox alone doesn't cut it for a book. Alright, how about MySQL version 5? In fact how, about MySQL version 5 with stored procedures? Interested? Well, then, read on.

In version 5, MySQL introduced a feature that had been in the proprietary databases for quite some time: stored procedures. Just in case you were abducted by aliens in 1974 and only recently got back to Earth, let me explain what stored procedures are. Stored procedures are preparsed SQL that accepts parameters and can return results.

Let's say, for example, that we have a table consisting of the states and territories of the United States and the provinces of Canada. Let's also say that we'd like the option of passing the procedure a two-character abbreviation to receive the name of the state or province, or passing a null value to obtain the names and abbreviations of all. We would create a stored procedure that looks a lot like the one shown in Listing 5-10.

Listing 5-10   A MySQL Stored Procedure

```
DELIMITER $$

DROP PROCEDURE IF EXISTS 'ajax'.'stateSelect'$$
CREATE PROCEDURE 'ajax'.'stateSelect'(
  stateAbbreviation VARCHAR(2)
)
BEGIN
  SELECT   state_abbreviation,
           state_name
  FROM     state
  WHERE    (stateAbbreviation IS NULL OR stateAbbreviation =
state_abbreviation);
END$$

DELIMITER ;
```

Now that we have a stored procedure, the big question is, what do we do with it? Fortunately, that's an easy question; we call it as shown in the first example here. However, I'd like to point out that because of the way the stored procedure is called, when a parameter is null, a null must, in fact, be passed as shown in the second example.

```
CALL stateSelect('NJ');

CALL stateSelect(NULL);
```

Now that the database issue is out of the way, it is time to figure out what to code the server side in. My first thought was to pick a language that has a proven track record and was widely accepted, but I could not find a reliable source of punch cards, so COBOL wasn't a viable option. The really scary part is that I've seen it attempted at companies because they thought that they could port their mainframe CICS code to the Web, but that is another story.

I finally decided on PHP 5. My reasons for this are several. The first is that I've seen it and know that, not only does it work, but it works well. Another reason is that it appears to be a combination of C and UNIX Shell, both of which I've worked with in the past. The third reason is that it plays well with MySQL and stored procedures—at least, once configured correctly and if I remember to use the mysqli library instead of the older mysql library.

The final reason is that it is open source, and, therefore, several slick IDEs such as PHP Designer 2005 from MPSOFTWARE are available to those of us on limited budgets.

5.3   TABULAR INFORMATION

As stated previously, the first two types of web pages required both deal in some way with tabular information, either for display or for updates.

When I was in high school, I took quite a few drafting classes, thinking that perhaps a career in architecture lay in my future. But I discovered computers, and, eh, a career in a different kind of architecture lay in my future. And that is exactly what we need now: an architecture upon which to build our creature—eh, er, e-commerce—site. So let's send Igor to get a cold beverage and queue the storm sound effects before we start.

Back already?

Because programming is one of those fields, like politics, in which trotting out an old idea is a virtue, we'll drag the frameset from Chapter 2, "Introducing Ajax," into this chapter and use it again. If Congress can recycle the same bills year after year, surely we can do the equivalent with some code. Just in case you've forgotten what it looks like, Listing 5-11 shows it in its entirety, without commercial interruption.

Listing 5-11   Frameset

```
<!DOCTYPE HTML PUBLIC "-//W3C//DTD HTML 4.0 Transitional//EN">
<html>
      <head>
             <title>MSAWSS</title>
      </head>
      <frameset rows="100%,*">
             <frame name="visible_frame" src="visible.html">
             <frame name="hidden_frame"
src="customer.php?email=ewoychowsky@yahoo.com">
             <noframes>
                 Frames are required to use this web site.
          </noframes>
         </frameset>
</html>
```

Unfortunately, because of scope creep, the visible page from Chapter 2 doesn't make the grade for this chapter. It is almost there, but it needs a little more functionality—basically, additional logic to make it bulletproof. By *bulletproof*, I mean able to withstand attack by Machinegun Kelly or any other "guest" who can click a mouse button upward of 200 times a minute.

But before adding the necessary logic, let's see what JavaScript functions we already have that can be cloned for our nefarious purpose. The first JavaScript function to be cloned is `changeEvent`, which itself does a little cloning. The sole purpose of this little cross-browser-capable function is to handle an `onchange` event for HTML `input`, `textarea`, and `select` tags. The second function that can be cloned is `submitForm`, which, surprisingly, is also cross-browser-capable.

At this point in designing the architecture, I have run out of code to clone and now must write code from scratch. But before I do, allow me to explain what I'd like to do. After all, explaining plots is a common weakness that we mad scientists all have, and if I can't explain it to you, I'll have to explain it to Igor, and the blank, glassy stare that he gets is so unnerving.

First I'd like a routine that ensures that the peasants—eh, guests—don't muck around with the Back button. This is because the Back button is like fire to Victor's monster—it causes unpredictable results. With any kind of HTML frames, hitting the Back button is just as likely to cause the hidden page to go back as the visible page. In short, it is not a good thing. Fortunately, in this instance, a little JavaScript goes a long way, as the following line of code shows:

```
window.history.forward(1);
```

Doesn't look like much, does it? Well, it isn't the size of the boat, but the, um, never mind. Let's just say that it is all that is necessary to ensure that the current page is always the top page in the history, which is exactly what this does. Of course, it needs to be included on every page, both visible and hidden. It is also important to remember to provide some means of navigation; otherwise, shoppers will be lost in a "twisty little maze of passages, all alike," which isn't real good for repeat business.

The next function isn't really a function at all; it is actually a Boolean global variable that merely indicates whether the web browser is Microsoft Internet Explorer or another browser. The reason this is an Internet Explorer indicator isn't because I'm in love with IE; it is because the larger the software company is, the more likely that it has wandered off the path when it comes to following standards. So with this in mind, the following code was written:

```
var _IE = (new RegExp('internet explorer','gi')).test(navigator.appName);
```

The third function that is necessary to this project is one that "clones" a form on the hidden frame to the visible. Although this sounds pretty simple, it is anything but simple. In fact, most developers never ask one major question unless they try this kind of thing for themselves:

When loading the frameset for the first time, which page loads first?

Fortunately, there is a simple answer to this question; unfortunately, the answer is that I don't know, which is a rather big stumbling block to overcome to complete the website. This means that not only will the function need to clone the hidden form to the visible form, but it might have to sit around waiting for the visible form to finish loading. The good thing is that the process of checking for frame completeness is very similar to what was done in Chapter 2, as shown in Listing 5-12.

Listing 5-12   initialize Function

```
/*
        Update the visible frame with information from this page.
*/
function initialize()
{
  var hiddenForm = document.getElementById('hidden_form');

  if(_IE)
  {
    if(parent.document.frames.item('visible_frame').document.readyState
!= 'complete')
      window.setTimeout('initialize()',100);
    else

parent.frames['visible_frame'].document.getElementById('visible_form').
innerHTML = hiddenForm.innerHTML;
  }
  else
  {
    try
    {
      var node =
parent.frames['visible_frame'].document.getElementById('visible_form').
firstChild;

      try
      {

parent.frames['visible_frame'].document.getElementById('visible_form').
removeChild(node);
      }
      catch(e) { }

parent.frames['visible_frame'].document.getElementById('visible_form').
appendChild(hiddenForm.cloneNode(true));
    }
    catch(e)
```

continues

Listing 5-12   continued

```
  {
    window.setTimeout('initialize()',100);
  }
 }
}
```

The `initialize()` function is invoked by the hidden frame's `onload` event handler, and the first thing that it does is use the `_IE` Boolean that I created earlier. The reason for this is that occasionally I do give in to temptation and use a nonstandard browser feature. In this instance, the feature is the document object's `readyState` property. Just test it against "complete," and we're good to go (that is, if the browser is Microsoft Internet Explorer; otherwise, it is necessary to give it the old college `try` and `catch`).

If the visible frame isn't ready, it is necessary to use the `window.setTimeout()` method to invoke the `initialize()` function again after waiting the specified number of milliseconds. Don't confuse this method with the `window.setInterval()` method because `setTimeout` invokes the specified function only once. With `setInterval()`, the function repeats like salami does until it is stopped, which is bad, unless you are fond of debugging really weird client-side happenings.

The next function that I want to add is one to restrict keyboard input to numeric values. Although the appropriate elements can be tested at submission time, we're dealing with guests who could potentially unleash a plague of giant hedgehogs on Spotswood, New Jersey, when ticked off. So why not avoid any problems before they occur? Listing 5-13 shows this function in all its glory.

Listing 5-13   `restrict` Function

```
/*
      Restrict keyboard input for the provided object using the
        passed regular
                    expression and option.
*/
function restrict(obj,rex,opt) {
      var re = new RegExp(rex,opt);
      var chr = obj.value.substr(obj.value.length - 1);

      if(!re.test(chr)) {
            var reChr = new RegExp(chr,opt);

            obj.value = obj.value.replace(reChr,'');
      }
}
```

The final two functions are the changeEvent() and the submitForm() functions, which have been copied directly from Chapter 2. Listing 5-14 shows both of these functions.

Listing 5-14   changeEvent and submitForm Functions

```
/*
    Handle form visible form onchange events.  Values from the
        visible form are copied to the hidden form.
*/
function changeEvent(obj)
{
    parent.frames[1].document.getElementById(obj.id).value = obj.value;
}


/*
    Submits the form in the hidden frame.
*/
function submitForm() {
    parent.frames[1].document.getElementById('hidden_form').submit();
}
        </script>
    </head>
    <body onload="initialize()">
        <form name="visible_form" id="visible_form"></form>
    </body>
</html>
```

5.3.1 Read Only

As strange as it sounds, when I'm creating a website from scratch, I often find it simpler to begin coding nearer to the end than the beginning. This is probably some sort of unique mental defect, but it works, so I'm not about to mess with it. So let's start with the page that shows the garbage that the sucker ordered—eh, the items that the customer selected for purchase. In fact, let's play nice and try to refer to customers as "guests" instead of "users" or "suckers"—at least, to their faces (remember the Moon-Mounted Death Ray).

So with my new and enlightened attitude, let's determine what information the guests require. Well, the order number would be nice, if only for our own protection. The same can be said for item numbers, item names, quantity, and both unit price and total item price. Showing the total along with any shipping charges and tax (at least, until our own Death Ray is operational) is an absolute must.

So let's see, we have the following:

+ One order number
+ A variable number of item lines consisting of item numbers, item names, quantity ordered, unit price, and total item price
+ One shipping total
+ One tax total, at least for the near future
+ One grand total

Now that we've got something that remotely resembles a plan, it is time to implement it. First there are the database tables that describe the guild (Mad Scientist, Alchemist, or Sorcerer), orders, items, and lines. From this SQL it is pretty easy to infer what some of the other tables are, but we ignore them for now because they're not needed at this point. Listing 5-15 shows the SQL necessary to define these tables.

Listing 5-15   SQL to Create MySQL Database Tables

```
CREATE TABLE guild (
      guild_id int(6) auto_increment NOT NULL,
      guild_name varchar(255)  NOT NULL,
      PRIMARY KEY (guild_id),
      UNIQUE id (guild_id)
);

CREATE TABLE orders (
      orders_id int(6) auto_increment NOT NULL,
      customer_id int(6) NULL,
      ship_address_id int(6) NULL,
      orders_date datetime NOT NULL,
      PRIMARY KEY (orders_id),
      UNIQUE id (orders_id),
      KEY customer_key (customer_id),
      KEY ship_address_key (ship_address_id)
);

CREATE TABLE item (
      item_id int(6) auto_increment NOT NULL,
      item_name varchar(255) NOT NULL,
      item_description varchar(255) NULL,
      item_price decimal(10,2) NOT NULL,
      PRIMARY KEY (item_id),
      UNIQUE id (item_id)
);

CREATE TABLE line (
      line_id int(6) auto_increment NOT NULL,
      orders_id int(6) NOT NULL,
```

```
            item_id int(6) NOT NULL,
            line_quantity int NOT NULL,
            line_item_price decimal(10,2) NOT NULL,
            PRIMARY KEY (line_id),
            UNIQUE id (line_id),
            KEY orders_key (orders_id),
            KEY item_key (item_id)
);
```

If you recall, earlier I stated that MySQL version 5 and higher support stored procedures; in fact, I even gave you an example. We've just covered the tables we're using for this example, so now is a good time to cover the stored procedure. The stored procedure `lineSelect` (see Listing 5-16) is relatively simple, just a `select` statement with a bunch of inner joins. Although it isn't heavy duty—no cursors, transactions, or anything like that—it is an example of a stored procedure in MySQL, currently a thing only slightly more common than unicorns.

However, there are a number of reasons for the inclusion of stored procedures, especially in MySQL. The first of these is to avoid the use of Microsoft Access, which is technically a database; however, it really isn't very robust. Some might argue that Access is a replacement for SQL Server, which I agree to, but I'm on a budget here and a stripped-down developers' edition isn't what I want. Besides, both Access and SQL Server are Windows-only databases. Oracle, on the other hand, runs a number of platforms and is robust, but it isn't open source. As for my final reason for stored procedures, speed thrills.

Listing 5-16 `lineSelect` stored procedure

```
DELIMITER $$

DROP PROCEDURE IF EXISTS `ajax`.`lineSelect`$$
CREATE PROCEDURE `ajax`.`lineSelect`(
  ordersId INTEGER(6)
)
BEGIN
  SELECT    line_id,
            item_id,
            line_quantity,
            line_item_price
  FROM      line
  WHERE     (ordersId IS NULL OR ordersId = orders_id)
  ORDER BY  line_id ASC;
END$$

DELIMITER ;
```

Earlier I said that the examples would be in PHP, and because stored procedures are being used, it is necessary to use the mysqli library instead of the mysql library. This might not sound like a big deal, but it would be a good idea to provide some basic information on the parts of mysqli that are used in this example. Table 5-1 outlines these "parts."

Table 5-1   mysqli

Method/Property	Type	Description
mysqli	Constructor	Returns a connection
connect_errno()	Property	Returns the result of the connection attempt
query	Method	Executes the provided SQL statement
error	Property	Returns the result of the command
fetch_array	Method	Returns the result of a query as an array
close()	Method	Closes the connection

The odd thing is that after all the little details are covered, such as the client-side JavaScript, database tables, and stored procedures, there is actually very little code to write. Mostly it comes down to putting the pieces together and using the Cascading Style Sheets (CSS) shown in Listing 5-17 to give the website a consistent look and feel.

Listing 5-17   CSS

```
A:active
{
  color: 0000FF
}
A:visited
{
  color: 0000FF
}
A:hover
{
  color: 800080;
  text-decoration: none
}
BODY
{
  background-color: F0F8FF;
  font-family: tahoma;
  font-size: 12px
}
BUTTON
{
  cursor: hand;
  font-family: tahoma;
```

```
    font-size: 12px
}
INPUT
{
  cursor: hand;
  font-family: tahoma;
  font-size: 12px
}
H1
{
  font-family: tahoma;
  font-size: 18px
}
TABLE
{
  border: collapse
}
TH
{
  font-family: tahoma;
  font-size: 12px
}
TD
{
  font-family: tahoma;
  font-size: 12px
}
.cellAlert
{
  color: FF0000;
  font-weight: bold
}
.pageHeader
{
  background-color: 000080
}
.pageCell
{
  color: FFFFFF;
  font-family: tahoma;
  font-size: 16px;
  font-weight: bold
}
.rowHeader
{
  background-color: 6495ED;
  color: FFFFFF;
  font-weight: bold
}
.rowData
{
  background-color: D3D3D3
```

continues

Listing 5-17   continued

```
}
.numeric
{
  font-family: tahoma;
  text-align: right
}
```

The end result of this endeavor is the page shown in Figure 5-2, whose code is shown in Listing 5-18 along with some common PHP variables and routines shown in Listing 5-19. While we're on the subject of common routines, I should state now that there are several different approaches to handling inclusion of common code. The first, which I'm using here, is to include everything that could possibly be of any use from a single file. Later, however, I switch to an approach that breaks up variables and routines by function. For example, database-related items are here and rendering-related items are there, and anything else is handled on a case-by-case basis. This might seem like overkill now, but it falls under the category of defensive programming.

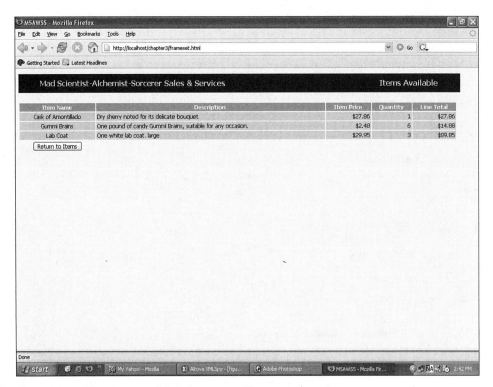

Figure 5-2   The page resulting from our efforts

Listing 5-18   Code for the Page in Figure 5-2

```
<!DOCTYPE HTML PUBLIC "-//W3C//DTD HTML 4.0 Transitional//EN">
<html>
<?php
include('common.php');

$title="Order Detail";
$order = substr(@$_SERVER['QUERY_STRING'],6);
$order = 1;
$query = "CALL lineSelect(" . $order . ")";
$mysqli = new mysqli($server,$user,$password,$database);

if(mysqli_connect_errno())
{
  printf("Connect failed: %s\n", mysqli_connect_error());

  exit();
}

if(!$result = $mysqli->query($query))
{
  printf("Error: %s\n", $mysqli->error);

  exit();
}
?>
    <head>
        <link rel="stylesheet" type="text/css" href="common.css"/>
        <title><?php echo $title; ?></title>
        <script language="javascript" src="library.js"></script>
    </head>
    <body onload="initialize()">
        <form name="hidden_form" id="hidden_form" action="post.aspx">
<?php
pageHeader($system,$title);
?>
            <table border="0" width="980px" ID="Table1" border="1"
cellpadding="2" cellspacing="2">
                <tr class="rowHeader">
                    <th>Item Name</th>
                    <th>Description</th>
                    <th>Quanity</th>
                    <th>Unit Price</th>
                    <th>Price</th>
                </tr>
<?php
$total = 0;

while($row = $result->fetch_array(MYSQLI_ASSOC))
{
  printf("<tr class='rowData'><td
align='center'>%s</a></td>",$row["item_name"]);
  printf("<td align='left'>%s</a></td>",$row["item_description"]);
```

continues

Listing 5-18   continued

```php
  printf("<td class='numeric'>%s</td>",$row["line_quantity"]);
  printf("<td class='numeric'>$%s</td>",$row["line_item_price"]);
  printf("<td class='numeric'>$%s</td></tr>",($row["line_item_price"] *
$row["line_quantity"]));

  $total += ($row["line_item_price"] * $row["line_quantity"]);
}
?>
                <tr class="rowData">
                    <td> </td>
                    <td> </td>
                    <td> </td>
                    <th class='numeric'>Total</th>
<?
  printf("<td class='numeric'>$%s</td>",$total);
?>
                </tr>
              </table>
          </form>
      </body>
<?php
$result->close();
?>
</html>
```

Listing 5-19   PHP Variables and Routines

```php
<?php
$server="localhost";           //  MySQL database server
$user="root";                  //  MySQL user id
$password="wyvern";            //  MySQL password
$database="ajax";              //  MySQL database

$system="Mad Scientist-Alchemist-Sorcerer Sales & Services";

/*
     Write the header for a web page.
*/
function pageHeader($systemName,$pageName)
{
?>
<table border="0" height="60px" width="975px" ID="<?php $pageName ?>"
border="0" cellpadding="0" cellspacing="0">
    <tr class="pageHeader" height="40px">
        <td width="5%"> </td>
        <th class="pageCell" width="45%" align="left">
<?php
```

```
      echo $systemName;
?>
          </th>
          <th class="pageCell" width="45%" align="right">
<?php
  echo $pageName;
?>
          </th>
          <td width="5%"> </td>
      </tr>
      <tr>
          <td> </td>
          <td> </td>
          <td> </td>
          <td> </td>
      </tr>
</table>
<?php
}
?>
```

5.3.2   Updateable

As with the previous page type, the next type of page to be generated is also tabular in nature. However, unlike the previous example, this page allows for input beyond the navigation to the next page type. In a nutshell, here is our first chance to use the majority of the architecture functions, and, in a nutshell, here is where there is a big chance that things can go seriously wrong.

The big question is, just how can things go seriously wrong? Is it a flaw in the underlying concepts of Ajax? Nope, it is more of what I refer to as a "Homer Simpson Moment." These moments are caused by coding while the brain is on autopilot, and for me it usually manifests itself in the form of using the wrong event handler or forgetting an event handler altogether. Fortunately, by coding the submitForm() handler to deal with changes to HTML objects, I've managed to avoid one of my more common points of failure.

Alright, now with that out of the way, I feel less likely to screw up in the same old way. If I am going to screw up, I want it to be in an entirely new and original way. After all, in most cases, more can be learned from getting something wrong than by getting something right.

Now that we've covered the basics of what can go wrong when working with forms, let's put it into practice. Hmm, that didn't sound right. Okay, take two. Now that we've covered some of the potential pitfalls of working with forms, let's create a web page avoiding them. Whew!

The purpose of the next page that we are working with is to display the contents of the guest's virtual shopping cart. As with its real-world counterpart, shoppers will have several possible actions available to them. First, they can remove individual items from the cart just like they do in the real world; how else do you suppose frozen peas find their way to the cookie aisle? The next possible action is to change the quantity, either up (yeah!) or down (pout!). Oh, I should mention that decreasing an item's quantity to zero has the same end result as removing the item from the cart. Finally, shoppers will have the option of giving up and just abandoning their shopping cart.

This is a good time to point out that, unlike some virtual shopping carts where the contents are stored on the server, this one doesn't. Instead, I chose to follow the "why bother the server any more than absolutely necessary?" philosophy, so the shopping cart is cached in a hidden text box in a form on the visible frame as item-quantity pairs. Why? Because after being loaded, with the exception of the cloned form, the visible frame doesn't change. Although it sounds somewhat strange, it has the advantage of reducing server traffic. When the time comes to display the shopping cart, it can simply be coded into the URL, which, although it does have a 4K limit, should be more than enough for our purpose.

Although we already have a lot of the code necessary for this to work (the numeric input function and the CSS), several bits of code are needed. First, there is the JavaScript function that builds the URL for displaying the shopping cart (see Listing 5-20). In addition, there is the stored procedure and two stored functions to retrieve all the necessary information from the tables shown in Listing 5-21. Finally, there is the page itself in Figure 5-3 and Listing 5-22.

Listing 5-20   JavaScript Function That Builds the URL for Displaying the Shopping Cart

```
function displayCart() {
  if(document.getElementById('cartContents').value.length = 0)
    alert("Your shopping cart is empty.");
  else
    parent.frames['hidden_frame'].document.location =
'displayCart.php?cart=' + document.getElementById('cartContents').value;
}
```

Listing 5-21   The Stored Procedure and the Two Stored Functions

```
DELIMITER $$

DROP PROCEDURE IF EXISTS `ajax`.`shoppingCartSelect`$$
CREATE PROCEDURE `ajax`.`shoppingCartSelect`(
/*
```

```
      To display the contents of the shopping cart.
*/
itemIds LONGTEXT
)
BEGIN
  DECLARE work LONGTEXT;

  CREATE TEMPORARY TABLE search (
        id INTEGER(6) AUTO_INCREMENT NOT NULL,
        search_id INTEGER(6) NOT NULL,
     quantity INTEGER NOT NULL,
        PRIMARY KEY (id),
        UNIQUE id (id)
  );

  SET work = itemIds;

  WHILE INSTR(work,',') > 0 DO
    INSERT INTO search
                (search_id,
                 quantity)
    VALUES      (CAST(f_substringBefore(work,'-') AS UNSIGNED),
                 CAST(f_subStringAfter(work,'-') AS UNSIGNED));

    SET work = f_substringAfter(work,',');
  END WHILE;

  SELECT      s.id,
              i.item_name,
              i.item_description,
              i.item_price,
              s.quantity,
              i.item_price * s.quantity total_price
  FROM        search s
  INNER JOIN  guild_item_bridge b
  ON          s.search_id = b.guild_item_id
  INNER JOIN  item i
  ON          b.item_id = i.item_id
  ORDER BY    s.id ASC;

  DROP TEMPORARY TABLE search;
END$$

DELIMITER ;

DROP FUNCTION IF EXISTS `ajax`.`f_substringAfter`$$
CREATE FUNCTION `ajax`.`f_substringAfter`(
/*
  To return the text after a string.
*/
  stringOperand LONGTEXT,
  stringSearch LONGTEXT
```

continues

Listing 5-21   continued

```
) RETURNS longtext
BEGIN
  RETURN SUBSTRING(stringOperand,INSTR(stringOperand,stringSearch) + 1);
END$$

DELIMITER ;

DELIMITER $$

DROP FUNCTION IF EXISTS `ajax`.`f_substringBefore`$$
CREATE FUNCTION `ajax`.`f_substringBefore`(
/*
  To return the text before a string.
*/
  stringOperand LONGTEXT,
  stringSearch LONGTEXT
) RETURNS longtext
BEGIN
  RETURN SUBSTRING(stringOperand,1,INSTR(stringOperand,stringSearch) - 1);
END$$

DELIMITER ;
```

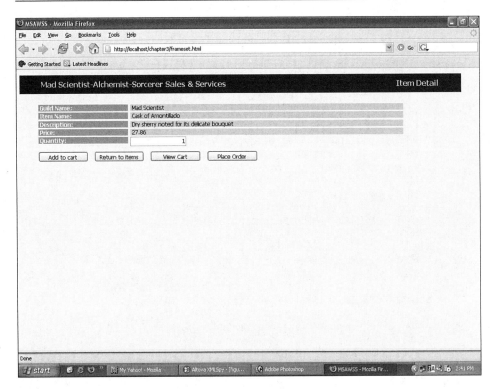

Figure 5-3   The shopping cart page

Listing 5-22   Code for the Shopping Cart Page

```
<!DOCTYPE HTML PUBLIC "-//W3C//DTD HTML 4.0 Transitional//EN">
<html>
<?php
include('common.php');

$title="Item Detail";
$id = substr(@$_SERVER['QUERY_STRING'],3);
$query = "CALL itemSelect(" . $id . ",NULL)";
$mysqli = new mysqli($server,$user,$password,$database);

if (mysqli_connect_errno())
{
  printf("Connect failed: %s\n", mysqli_connect_error());

  exit();
}

if(!$result = $mysqli->query($query))
{
  printf("Error: %s\n", $mysqli->error);

  exit();
}
?>
      <head>
            <link rel="stylesheet" type="text/css" href="common.css"/>
            <title><?php echo $title; ?></title>
            <script language="javascript" src="library.js"></script>
      </head>
      <body onload="initialize()">
            <form name="hidden_form" id="hidden_form" action="post.aspx">
<?php
pageHeader($system,$title);

$row = $result->fetch_array(MYSQLI_ASSOC);

$rowLabel ="<div class='rowHeader' style='position: absolute; left: 50px;
right: auto%; bottom: auto; width: 200px; top: ";
$rowData = "<div class='rowData' style='position: absolute; left: 255px;
right: auto; bottom: auto; width: 600px; top: ";

echo $rowLabel . "75px'> Guild Name:</div>";
echo $rowLabel . "92px'> Item Name:</div>";
echo $rowLabel . "110px'> Description:</div>";
echo $rowLabel . "127px'> Price:</div>";
echo $rowLabel . "144px'> Quantity:</div>";

printf($rowData . "75px'> %s</div>",$row["guild_name"]);
printf($rowData . "92px'> %s</div>",$row["item_name"]);
printf($rowData . "110px'> %s</div>",$row["item_description"]);
printf($rowData . "127px'> %s</div>",$row["item_price"]);
?>
```

continues

Listing 5-22   continued

```
            <input type='text' id='quantity' name='quantity' value=''
onkeyup='restrict(this,\'[0-9]\',\'gi\')' style='position: absolute; left:
255px; right: auto; bottom: auto; top: 144px; text-align: right'>
<?php
echo "<input type='button' value='Add to cart'
onclick='JavaScript:add2Cart(" . $row["guild_item_id"] . ")'
style='position: absolute; top: 175px; left: 50px; right: auto; bottom:
auto; height: 22px; width: 110px'>";
echo "<input type='button' value='Return to items'
onclick='JavaScript:itemsList()' style='position: absolute; top: 175px;
left: 175px; right: auto; bottom: auto; height: 22px; width: 110px'>";
echo "<input type='button' value='View Cart'
onclick='JavaScript:displayCart()' style='position: absolute; top: 175px;
left: 300px; right: auto; bottom: auto; height: 22px; width: 110px'>";
echo "<input type='button' value='Place Order'
onclick='JavaScript:itemsList()' style='position: absolute; top: 175px;
left: 425px; right: auto; bottom: auto; height: 22px; width: 110px'>";
?>
            </form>
        </body>
<?php
mysqli_close($mysqli);
?>
</html>
```

5.4   FORMS

This heading does say "Forms," which we briefly touched upon in the previous section, even if it was because we needed somewhere to cache information, such as the contents of the shopping cart. Because of this, and the fact that I don't like to code similar functions too often, much of the client-side JavaScript from the tabular web pages is reused here—or, if you're a friend of nature, recycled. See, not only is Ajax the wave of the future, it is also environmentally friendly.

5.4.1   Read Only

In my opinion, the classic read-only form on an e-commerce website has to be the shipping information page. In fact, it is so well known that the page doesn't even have to be coded as a form. It is perfectly acceptable to "fake it" using Cascading Style Sheets, or simply display the information in some kind of orderly fashion. The advantage of this is that we can avoid having to use the `disabled` and `readonly` attributes, which, in the case of the `disabled` attribute, tends to be a little hard on the eyes because the text is grayed out.

The approach that I've decided upon here is to simply display the information directly from the database. Also, because I'm feeling somewhat adventurous, I've used CSS positioning for content layout instead of the method that I normally employ. Just in case you're wondering, using HTML tables is my usual method of content layout, but I'm undergoing therapy to overcome this shortcoming.

Before going into detail about the SQL that defines the tables needed for this example, I want to clarify one thing again. I am by no means a DBA; I am, according to some, a mad scientist (or mad, at the very least). Any of these can be used as an explanation of why I did what I did when designing these tables. In short, I went a little bit overboard when normalizing.

There isn't a single table to contain information pertaining to a customer. There aren't two tables to contain the information pertaining to a customer, such as one for the address and one for everything else. I made three tables: one for the customer name, one for the address, and one for all other customer-related information. I'm pretty sure that if you look up the word *overkill*, this is definition number six, but it does have some advantages that we'll get into later when doing updates.

Now that my long-winded excuse is over, let's take a gander at the SQL that defines the tables and the associated stored procedure that retrieves the information. The SQL for this is shown in Listings 5-23 and 5-24, respectively.

Listing 5-23   SQL to Create MySQL Database Tables

```
CREATE TABLE address (
        address_id int(6) auto_increment NOT NULL,
        address_company varchar(255)  NULL,
        address_line1 varchar(255)  NOT NULL,
        address_line2 varchar(255)  NULL,
        address_city varchar(255)  NOT NULL,
        state_abbreviation varchar(2)  NOT NULL,
        address_postal varchar(10)  NOT NULL,
        names_id int(6) NULL,
        PRIMARY KEY (address_id),
        UNIQUE id (address_id)
);

CREATE TABLE country (
        country_id int(6) auto_increment NOT NULL,
        country_name varchar(255)  NOT NULL,
        PRIMARY KEY (country_id),
        UNIQUE id (country_id)
);

CREATE TABLE customer (
        customer_id int(6) auto_increment NOT NULL,
        customer_telephone varchar(10)  NULL,
```

continues

Listing 5-23   continued

```
      customer_email varchar(255)  NOT NULL,
      customer_credit_card varchar(16)  NOT NULL,
      customer_credit_pin varchar(6)  NULL,
      customer_expiration datetime NOT NULL,
      names_id int(6) NULL,
      address_id int(6) NULL,
      PRIMARY KEY (customer_id),
      UNIQUE id (customer_id),
      KEY names_key (names_id),
      KEY address_key (address_id)
);

CREATE TABLE names (
      names_id int(6) auto_increment NOT NULL,
      names_last varchar(255)  NOT NULL,
      names_first varchar(255)  NOT NULL,
      names_mi varchar(1)  NULL,
      PRIMARY KEY (names_id),
      UNIQUE id (names_id)
);

CREATE TABLE state (
      state_abbreviation varchar(2)  NOT NULL,
      state_name varchar(255)  NOT NULL,
      country_id int(6) NOT NULL,
      PRIMARY KEY (state_abbreviation),
      UNIQUE id (state_abbreviation),
      KEY country_key (country_id)
);
```

Listing 5-24   MySQL Stored Procedure to Select Address Information

```
DELIMITER $$

DROP PROCEDURE IF EXISTS `ajax`.`addressSelect`$$
CREATE PROCEDURE `ajax`.`addressSelect`(
email VARCHAR(255)
)
BEGIN
  SELECT      c.customer_id,
              n.names_last,
              n.names_first,
              n.names_mi,
              c.customer_telephone,
              c.customer_email,
              a.address_company,
              a.address_line1,
              a.address_line2,
              a.address_city,
```

```
                  a.state_abbreviation,
                  s.state_name,
                  a.address_postal,
                  y.country_name
   FROM           customer c
   INNER JOIN     names n
   ON             c.names_id = n.names_id
   INNER JOIN     address a
   ON             c.address_id = a.address_id
   INNER JOIN     state s
   ON             a.state_abbreviation = s.state_abbreviation
   INNER JOIN     country y
   ON             s.country_id = y.country_id
   WHERE          (email IS NULL OR c.customer_email = email);
END$$

DELIMITER ;
```

The thing that I always find amazing about stored procedures is that they have a tendency to reduce the amount of code needed on the web server. Consider the example that we're currently going over; the PHP merely formats the information returned by the stored procedure for the web browser, as Listing 5-25 illustrates.

Listing 5-25   *Customer Display*

```php
<!DOCTYPE HTML PUBLIC "-//W3C//DTD HTML 4.0 Transitional//EN">
<html>
<?php
include('common.php');

$title="Customer Display";
$email = substr(@$_SERVER['QUERY_STRING'],6);
$query = "CALL addressSelect(" . $email . ")";
$mysqli = new mysqli($server,$user,$password,$database);

if (mysqli_connect_errno())
{
  printf("Connect failed: %s\n", mysqli_connect_error());

  exit();
}

if(!$result = $mysqli->query($query))
{
  printf("Error: %s\n", $mysqli->error);

  exit();
}
```

continues

Listing 5-25   continued

```php
?>
      <head>
            <link rel="stylesheet" type="text/css" href="common.css"/>
            <title><?php echo $title; ?></title>
            <script language="javascript" src="library.js"></script>
      </head>
      <body onload="initialize()">
            <form name="hidden_form" id="hidden_form" action="post.aspx">
<?php
pageHeader($system,$title);

$row = $result->fetch_array(MYSQLI_ASSOC);
$rowLabel ="<div class='rowHeader' style='position: absolute; left: 50px;
right: auto%; bottom: auto; width: 200px; top: ";
$rowData = "<div class='rowData' style='position: absolute; left: 255px;
right: auto; bottom: auto; width: 600px; top: ";

echo $rowLabel . "75px'> Name:</div>";
echo $rowLabel . "92px'> Company:</div>";
echo $rowLabel . "110px'> Address Line 1:</div>";
echo $rowLabel . "127px'> Address Line 2:</div>";
echo $rowLabel . "144px'> City:</div>";
echo $rowLabel . "161px'> State:</div>";
echo $rowLabel . "178px'> Zip/Postal Code:</div>";
echo $rowLabel . "195px'> Country:</div>";
echo $rowLabel . "212px'> Telephone Number:</div>";
echo $rowLabel . "229px'> EMail Address:</div>";

echo $rowData . "75px'> " . $row["names_last"] . ', ' .
$row["names_first"] . ' ' . $row["names_mi"] . "</div>";
echo $rowData . "92px'> " . $row["address_company"] . "</div>";
echo $rowData . "110px'> " . $row["address_line1"] . "</div>";
echo $rowData . "127px'> " . $row["address_line2"] . "</div>";
echo $rowData . "144px'> " . $row["address_city"] . "</div>";
echo $rowData . "161px'> " . $row["state_name"] . "</div>";
echo $rowData . "178px'> " . $row["address_postal"] . "</div>";
echo $rowData . "195px'> " . $row["country_name"] . "</div>";
echo $rowData . "212px'> " . $row["customer_telephone"] . "</div>";
echo $rowData . "229px'> " . $row["customer_email"] . "</div>";

echo "<input type='button' value='Continue to items' onclick='itemsList()'
style='position: absolute; top: 250px; left: 50px; right: auto; bottom:
auto; height: 22px; width: 120px'>";

hidden($row,'customer_id');
hidden($row,'names_last');
hidden($row,'names_first');
hidden($row,'names_mi');
hidden($row,'customer_email');
hidden($row,'customer_id');
?>
```

```
            </form>
        </body>
<?php
mysql_close();
?>
```

5.4.2 Updateable

In the previous example, we covered the display of information from multiple tables, which was easy enough because there wasn't much happening on the client side. The server side was also rather easy; yeah, there were some inner joins, but it is hard to get all worked up about something that easy. There is, however, something that you might have missed—I know that I did.

Let's review my overzealous database normalization from a different point of view. First, customer information is spread across three tables. Second, the customer table contains the information that specifies how to find the related information in the other two tables. Third, retrieving the information is merely a matter of using inner joins. So we know what the data looks like and how to get it out of the tables, but the big question is, how do I get it in?

On the bright side, I know how the guy who spent years building a sailboat in his basement felt when his wife said, "Nice, but how are you going to get it out of the basement?" Whoops, didn't think that far ahead. What he ended up doing was supporting the floor joists along one outside basement wall, digging a ramp from the outside to that position, and knocking out a boat-sized hole. It worked, but I want a little more elegant solution. In fact, I want one so elegant that you might think that my earlier screw-up was intentional so that I could demonstrate some really cool features of MySQL.

All my current issues arise from the fact that data in three different tables needs to be updated. Seems simple enough—just use a transaction. Unfortunately, I forgot to mention that during my earlier fit of normalization, I wrote two stored procedures, shown in Listings 5-26 and 5-27, that I want to use. Waste not, want not.

Listing 5-26   Stored Procedure to Insert Names

```
DELIMITER $$

DROP PROCEDURE IF EXISTS `ajax`.`namesInsert`$$
CREATE PROCEDURE `ajax`.`namesInsert`(
  IN nameLast VARCHAR(255),
  IN nameFirst VARCHAR(255),
  IN nameMI VARCHAR(1),
  OUT namesId INTEGER(6)
```

continues

Listing 5-26   continued

```
)
BEGIN
  INSERT INTO names
               (names_last,
                names_first,
                names_mi)
  VALUES       (nameLast,
                nameFirst,
                nameMI);

  SET namesID = LAST_INSERT_ID();
END$$

DELIMITER ;
```

Listing 5-27   MySQL Stored Procedure to Insert Customer Address Information

```
DELIMITER $$

DROP PROCEDURE IF EXISTS `ajax`.`addressInsert`$$
CREATE PROCEDURE `ajax`.`addressInsert`(
  IN addressCompany VARCHAR(255),
  IN addressLine1 VARCHAR(255),
  IN addressLine2 VARCHAR(255),
  IN addressCity VARCHAR(255),
  IN stateAbbreviation VARCHAR(255),
  IN addressPostal VARCHAR(10),
  IN namesId INTEGER(6),
  OUT addressId INTEGER(6)
)
BEGIN
  INSERT INTO  address
               (address_company,
                address_line1,
                address_line2,
                address_city,
                state_abbreviation,
                address_postal,
                names_id)
  VALUES       (addressCompany,
                addressLine1,
                addressLine2,
                addressCity,
                stateAbbreviation,
                addressPostal,
                namesId);

  SET addressId = LAST_INSERT_ID();
END$$

DELIMITER ;
```

Alright, if I have it straight and haven't painted myself into another corner, what is needed is a way to tie these stored procedures together. I suppose that I could somehow stick them together using PHP, but that seems too much like making the sailboat out of duct tape, and that solution is a little too Red Green for me. I ended up writing a third stored procedure (see Listing 5-28) that uses transactions and calls the other two stored procedures.

Listing 5-28 MySQL Stored Procedure That Calls Other Stored Procedures

```
DELIMITER $$

DROP PROCEDURE IF EXISTS `ajax`.`customerInsert`$$
CREATE PROCEDURE `ajax`.`customerInsert`(
  IN namesLast VARCHAR(255),
  IN namesFirst VARCHAR(255),
  IN namesMI VARCHAR(1),
  IN customerTelephone VARCHAR(10),
  IN customerEmail VARCHAR(255),
  IN customerCreditCard VARCHAR(16),
  IN customerCreditPin VARCHAR(6),
  IN customerExpiration DATETIME,
  IN addressCompany VARCHAR(255),
  IN addressLine1 VARCHAR(255),
  IN addressLine2 VARCHAR(255),
  IN addressCity VARCHAR(255),
  IN stateAbbreviation VARCHAR(2),
  IN addressPostal VARCHAR(10),
  OUT customerId INTEGER(6)
)
BEGIN
  DECLARE errorInd INTEGER DEFAULT 0;
  DECLARE namesId INTEGER(6);
  DECLARE addressId INTEGER(6);
  DECLARE CONTINUE HANDLER FOR SQLEXCEPTION SET errorInd = 1;

  START TRANSACTION;

  CALL namesInsert(namesLast,
                   namesFirst,
                   namesMI,
                   namesId);

  CALL addressInsert(addressCompany,
                     addressLine1,
                     addressLine2,
                     addressCity,
                     stateAbbreviation,
                     addressPostal,
                     namesId,
                     addressId);
```

continues

Listing 5-28   continued

```
INSERT INTO  customer
             (customer_telephone,
              customer_email,
              customer_credit_card,
              customer_credit_pin,
              customer_expiration,
              names_id,
              address_id)
    VALUES   (customerTelephone,
              customerEmail,
              customerCreditCard,
              customerCreditPin,
              customerExpiration,
              namesId,
              addressId);

  IF errorInd = 0 THEN
    COMMIT;

    SET customerId = LAST_INSERT_ID();
  ELSE
    ROLLBACK;

    SET customerId = 0;
  END IF;
END$$

DELIMITER ;
```

Now that the sailboat is out of the basement, the remaining task is simply a matter of putting all the pieces together, as shown in Listing 5-29 and Figure 5-4.

Listing 5-29   Customer Display Page

```php
<!DOCTYPE HTML PUBLIC "-//W3C//DTD HTML 4.0 Transitional//EN">
<html>
<?php
include('common.php');

$title="Customer Display";
$email = substr(@$_SERVER['QUERY_STRING'],6);
$query = "CALL addressSelect('" . $email . "')";
$mysqli = new mysqli($server,$user,$password,$database);

if (mysqli_connect_errno())
{
  printf("Connect failed: %s\n", mysqli_connect_error());

  exit();
```

```
  }

  if(!$result = $mysqli->query($query))
  {
    printf("Error: %s\n", $mysqli->error);

    exit();
  }
?>
      <head>
            <link rel="stylesheet" type="text/css" href="common.css"/>
            <title><?php echo $title; ?></title>
            <script language="javascript" src="library.js"></script>
      </head>
      <body onload="initialize()">
            <form name="hidden_form" id="hidden_form"
action="customerInput.php">
<?php
pageHeader($system,$title);

$row = $result->fetch_array(MYSQLI_ASSOC);
$rowLabel ="<div class='rowHeader' style='valign: center; height: 20px;
width: 200px;'> %s</div>";
$rowData = "<div class='rowData' style='position: absolute; left: 255px;
right: auto; bottom: auto; width: 600px; top: ";

?>
<table border="0" width="980px" id="Table1" border="1" cellpadding="2"
cellspacing="2">

<?php
echo "<tr><th class='rowHeader' width='20%' align='left'> First
Name:</th>";
printf("<td class='rowData'> <input type='text' name='names_first'
id='names_first' size='50' maxlength='255' value='%s'
onchange='changeEvent(this)'></td></tr>",$row["names_first"]);
echo "<tr><th class='rowHeader' align='left'> Middle Initial:</th>";
printf("<td class='rowData'> <input type='text' name='names_mi'
id='names_mi' size='2' maxlength='1' value='%s'
onchange='changeEvent(this)'></td></tr>",$row["names_mi"]);
echo "<tr><th class='rowHeader' align='left'> Last Name:</th>";
printf("<td class='rowData'> <input type='text' name='names_last'
id='names_last' size='50' maxlength='255' value='%s'
onchange='changeEvent(this)'></td></tr>",$row["names_last"]);
echo "<tr><th class='rowHeader' align='left'> Address Line 1:</th>";
printf("<td class='rowData'> <input type='text' name='address_line1'
id='address_line1' size='50' maxlength='255' value='%s'
onchange='changeEvent(this)'></td></tr>",$row["address_line1"]);
echo "<tr><th class='rowHeader' align='left'> Address Line 2:</th>";
printf("<td class='rowData'> <input type='text' name='address_line2'
id='address_line2' size='50' maxlength='255' value='%s'
onchange='changeEvent(this)'></td></tr>",$row["address_line2"]);
echo "<tr><th class='rowHeader' align='left'> City:</th>";
```

continues

Listing 5-29   continued

```php
printf("<td class='rowData'> <input type='text' name='address_city'
id='address_city' size='50' maxlength='255' value='%s'
onchange='changeEvent(this)'></td></tr>",$row["address_city"]);
echo "<tr><th class='rowHeader' align='left'> State:</th><td
class='rowData'>";
stateSelect($server,$user,$password,$database,$row['state_abbreviation']);
echo "</td></tr><tr><th class='rowHeader' align='left'> Postal
Code:</th>";
printf("<td class='rowData'> <input type='text' name='address_postal'
id='address_postal' size='50' maxlength='10' value='%s'
onchange='changeEvent(this)'></td></tr>",$row["address_postal"]);
echo "<tr><th class='rowHeader' align='left'> Telephone
Number:</th>";
printf("<td class='rowData'> <input type='text'
name='customer_telephone' id='customer_telephone' size='50' maxlength='10'
value='%s'
onchange='changeEvent(this)'></td></tr>",$row["customer_telephone"]);
echo "<tr><th class='rowHeader' align='left'> E-Mail Address:</th>";
printf("<td class='rowData'> <input type='text' name='customer_email'
id='customer_email' size='50' maxlength='255' value='%s'
onchange='changeEvent(this)'></td></tr>",$row["customer_email"]);
?>
</table>
<?php
echo "<input type='button' value='Place Order' onclick='submitForm()'>";
?>
            </form>
        </body>
<?php
mysqli_close($mysqli);

function stateSelect($server,$user,$password,$database,$value)
{
    $query = "CALL stateSelect(null)";
    $mysqli = new mysqli($server,$user,$password,$database);

    if (mysqli_connect_errno())
    {
      printf("Connect failed: %s\n", mysqli_connect_error());

      exit();
    }

    if(!$result = $mysqli->query($query))
    {
      printf("Error: %s\n", $mysqli->error);

      exit();
    }
```

```
        echo "<select id='state_abbreviation' name='state_abbreviation'
onchange='changeEvent(this)'>";

        while($row = $result->fetch_array(MYSQLI_ASSOC))
        {
            if($row['state_abbreviation'] == $value)
                printf("<option value='%s'
selected='true'>%s</option>",$row[state_abbreviation],$row[state_name]);
            else
                printf("<option
value='%s'>%s</option>",$row[state_abbreviation],$row[state_name]);
        }

        echo "</select>";

        mysqli_close($mysqli);
}
?>
```

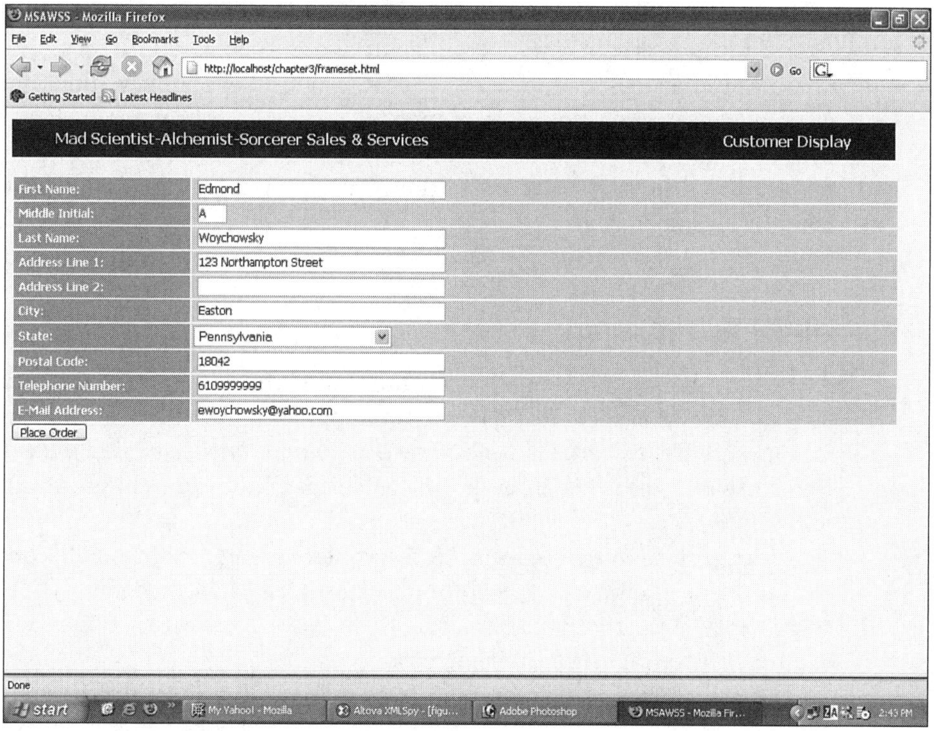

Figure 5-4   Customer display page

5.5   ADVANTAGES AND DISADVANTAGES

The major advantage to developing an application using this technique is that there are very few browsers for which this method does not work, including older browsers. In fact, the only thing that some web developers might consider out of the ordinary is the use of hidden frames. Nevertheless, it works, which is all that really matters when developing an application.

Unfortunately, problems begin to arise when an inexperienced developer attempts to maintain an application developed using this technique. In fact, several years ago, I developed an application that used hidden frames for an insurance company. It was one of the few applications for which I received calls after leaving the company. It was explained to me that there wasn't anything wrong with the application—in fact, it worked wonderfully—but the new developers couldn't quite grasp how it worked. To the new developers, the application was a classic black box; information went in and information came out, but what happened to it in the box was a complete mystery.

The final problem with this technique is that it really isn't Ajax; it only offers a similar look and feel. Think of it as a kind of primitive ancestor to Ajax or, if you prefer, as flexing our mental muscles getting ready for the main event. So now that we're all warmed up, let's push the knuckle-walking ancestor out the door and move on to the next chapter and something that everybody will agree is Ajax.

5.6   SUMMARY

Although the technique is somewhat old-fashioned, it demonstrates, to a degree, how processing flows in an Ajax application. In addition, the "dark art" of communicating information between frames was covered. However, two items of note from this chapter will be carried into later chapters: JavaScript and MySQL stored procedures.

Regardless of any opinion to the contrary, JavaScript has become essential in the development of web applications that feel more like GUI applications. And even though some shortcuts may have been taken with these examples, they do serve their purpose.

The inclusion of stored procedures in MySQL was a purely personal decision on my part. Originally, I considered using straight SQL; however, it has been several years since I created any kind of nontrivial application using anything but stored procedures. In addition, because the topic of stored procedures in MySQL is so new, trying to find examples is pretty much like looking for a unicorn. So I thought, why not include a few examples here? And as you've probably determined by now, I like examples.

CHAPTER 6

XML

What can I say about XML that somebody before me hasn't already said? One little Google search is enough to learn that XML whitens whites and brightens brights. In short, name an ill that plagues today's world, and there is probably someone out there who has written an article about it and how XML can fix it.

Alright, I admit it, I'm stretching the truth a little to get my point across. However, it does give something of the feel of the aura that surrounds XML—well, at least from an outsider's perspective. XML is another one of those "I don't know what it is, but I want it" type of things.

The format of this chapter goes along the following lines:

☞ Elements
☞ Attributes
☞ Handling Verboten Characters
☞ Comments
☞ Document description
☞ XML declarations
☞ Processing instructions
☞ XML Data Islands

In its simplest form, XML is nothing more than a text file containing a single well-formed XML document. Come to think of it, the same is pretty much true in its most complex form as well. Looking past all the hype surrounding XML, it is easy to see that XML is merely the text representation of self-describing data in a tree data structure. When you understand this, all that is left are the nitty-gritty little details, as in "What's a tree data structure?" and "How exactly does data describe itself?"

A tree data structure is built of nodes, with each node having only one node connected above it, called a *parent* node. The sole exception to this rule is the *root* node, which has no parent node. Nodes can also have other nodes connected below; these are called *child* nodes. In addition, nodes that are on the same level as the same parent node are called children. Figure 6-1 is a graphical representation of a tree data structure. If you are thinking to yourself, "I've seen this before," you're right—we also used this example in Chapter 2, "Introducing Ajax."

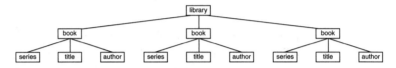

Figure 6-1   An XML document as a tree

The diagram in Figure 6-1 can also be represented as the XML document shown in Listing 6-1. We used this listing in Chapter 2 as well. But it doesn't hurt to reiterate the points here.

Listing 6-1   An XML Document as Text

```
<?xml version="1.0" encoding="UTF-8" standalone="yes"?>
<library>
        <book>
                <series/>
                <title/>
                <author/>
        </book>
        <book>
                <series/>
                <title/>
                <author/>
        </book>
        <book>
                <series/>
                <title/>
                <author/>
        </book>
</library>
```

6.1 ELEMENTS

The nodes shown in Listing 6-1 are called *elements,* and they closely resemble HTML tags. And like HTML tags, start tags begin with < and end tags begin with </. However, unlike HTML tags, all XML tags must either have a closing tag or be self-closing or empty elements. Self-closing tags are recognizable by the ending />. If the forward slash was omitted, the document would not be a *well-formed* XML document. In addition to all elements being either closed or self-closing, the tags must always match up in order. This means that the XML document in Listing 6-2 is well formed, whereas the XML document in Listing 6-3 is not well formed.

Listing 6-2 A Well-Formed XML Document

```
<?xml version="1.0" encoding="UTF-8" standalone="yes"?>
<one>
      <two>
            <three>
                  <four/>
            </three>
      </two>
</one>
```

Listing 6-3 A Document That Is Not Well Formed

```
<?xml version="1.0" encoding="UTF-8" standalone="yes"?>
<one>
      <two>
            <three>
                  <four/>
      </two>
            </three>
</one>
```

So far, we have covered elements that contain either other elements or empty elements, leaving the question of what elements that contain actual data look like. Using the XML from Listing 6-1 as a starting point, you can see that the answer is not very different. Listing 6-4 shows what elements that contain text data look like.

Listing 6-4 An XML Document with Text Data

```
<?xml version="1.0" encoding="UTF-8" standalone="yes"?>
<library>
      <book>
            <series>The Lord of the Rings</series>
            <title>The Fellowship of the Ring</title>
            <author>J.R.R. Tolkien</author>
      </book>
      <book>
            <series>The Lord of the Rings</series>
```

continues

Listing 6-4   continued

```
            <title>The Two Towers</title>
            <author>J.R.R. Tolkien</author>
      </book>
      <book>
            <series>The Lord of the Rings</series>
            <title>The Return of the King</title>
            <author>J.R.R. Tolkien</author>
      </book>
</library>
```

One thing to remember is that elements aren't limited to containing either other elements or text data; they can do both at the same time. In fact, there is even a way for empty elements to contain text data through the use of *attributes*.

6.2   ATTRIBUTES

Attributes are a name-value pair that is contained in an element's start tag. The name portion of an attribute is separated from the value by an equals sign, and the value is enclosed in either single or double quotes. Elements can have multiple attributes, separated from one another by whitespace, usually one or more spaces. It is not unusual for XML documents to use a combination of container elements and attributes. Listing 6-5 shows what the XML document in Listing 6-4 would look like using attributes.

Listing 6-5   An XML Document with Attributes

```
<?xml version="1.0" encoding="UTF-8" standalone="yes"?>
<library>
      <book series="The Lord of the Rings" title="The Fellowship of the
Ring" author="J.R.R. Tolkien"/>
      <book series="The Lord of the Rings" title="The Two Towers"
author="J.R.R. Tolkien"/>
      <book series="The Lord of the Rings" title="The Return of the King"
author="J.R.R. Tolkien"/>
</library>
```

Before proceeding any further, I want to cover the three rules for the naming of elements and attributes; these rules are only slightly more complex than the rules for the addressing of cats. The first rule is that only alphanumeric (a–z, 0–9) characters, the underscore (_), the hyphen/dash (-), and the colon (:) are permissible in names. The second rule is that names can begin only with an alpha, underscore, or hyphen character. The third and final rule is that names are case sensitive, so `Mistoffelees` is a different animal than `MISTOFFELEES`, and `mistoffelees` is yet another animal. Think of these rules as a practical guide, and you won't have any problems with names.

6.3   HANDLING VERBOTEN CHARACTERS

Occasionally when dealing with XML documents, you will encounter certain characters that will cause a document to be not well formed. For example, imagine an element that contains a JavaScript function, such as the one shown in Listing 6-6. Examined from a JavaScript perspective, the function looks like it works, but when examined from an XML point of view, there is one big glaring error. Here is a hint: Look at the `for` loop.

Listing 6-6   A Script Element That Is Not Well Formed

```
            <script language="JavaScript">
function hello(intTimes) {
      for(var i=0;i < intTimes;i++)
            alert('Hello, World!');
}
            </script>
```

XML interprets the less-than (<) operator as the beginning of a new element, and from an XML viewpoint, the new tag is not well formed. Fortunately, you can use one of two methods to get around this issue: entities or CDATA sections. Each of these methods is suited to a different purpose, so let's examine each to determine which better suits our problem.

6.3.1   Entities

Entities. A part of me just likes to say the word *entities*. It's just a fun word to say, especially to a manager who is unfamiliar with XML. Just imagine someone's reaction when being told that the XML contains *entities*. Talk about your flashbacks to late-night horror movies! Of course, there is always the alternative: being fitted for a jacket with wraparound sleeves. Either way, you've gotten the manager's attention.

XML has five predefined entities whose purpose it to avoid well-formedness issues when encountering select common characters. Table 6-1 defines these five entities, and later topics cover how to define additional entities.

Table 6-1   Entities

Character	Entity	Description
<	<	Less than
>	>	Greater than
'	'	Apostrophe/single quote
"	&qout;	Double quote
&	&	Ampersand

The JavaScript in Listing 6-6 can be made well formed by replacing the character < by its corresponding entity <. Unfortunately, although the use of entities would correct the issue from an XML point of view, from a JavaScript perspective, there is a world of difference between < and <. To make both XML and JavaScript happy, it is necessary to use a CDATA section.

6.3.2   CDATA Sections

A CDATA section is the XML equivalent of "Pay no attention to that man behind the curtain," from *The Wizard of Oz*. However, there is no pesky little girl with a little dog to mess things up. Because of this, XML totally ignores whatever is within a CDATA section's tags, <![CDATA[*and*]]>, as shown in Listing 6-7.

Listing 6-7   A Well-Formed Script Element

```
            <script language="JavaScript">
<![CDATA[
function hello(intTimes) {
      for(var i=0;i < intTimes;i++)
            alert('Hello, World!');
}
]]>
            </script>
```

6.4   COMMENTS

From an XML point of view, Listing 6-7 is well formed; unfortunately, some web browsers would have an issue with it as part of a web page. A method is needed to hide the JavaScript from XML, and the CDATA section tags from both the browser and the browser's JavaScript interpreter. This can be accomplished with XML comment tags, which, by the way, are identical to the comment tags from HTML. Because the JavaScript interpreter has problems only with the CDATA section's closing tag, a // is enough to make the browser look the other way. The end result is the node shown in Listing 6-8.

Listing 6-8   A Well-Formed Cross-Browser Script Element

```
            <script language="JavaScript">
<!-- <![CDATA[
function hello(intTimes) {
      for(var i=0;i < intTimes;i++)
            alert('Hello, World!');
}
// ]]> -->
            </script>
```

6.5 EXPECTATIONS

When the Rolling Stones sang "You Can't Always Get What You Want," they were telling only half of the story. The other half is, "You Don't Always Want What You Get." Yeah, it doesn't roll off of the tongue the same way, and I don't sing anything like Mick Jagger; in fact, my children would prefer it if I didn't sing at all. So when I sing, they're both not getting something they want and getting something that they don't want. They'll get over it, but how would XML handle getting something expected and getting something unexpected?

6.5.1 Namespaces

Dealing with both the expected and the unexpected is what namespaces in XML are all about. A namespace is used to describe vocabularies because in some instances the same element name could have two different meanings, which is an unexpected occurrence often with undesirable results.

   To put it in nontechnical terms, imagine that you have a shipment of cotton that you want to ship from India to England. Let's say that you want it to be sent on a particular ship that sails in November. Seems clear, doesn't it? Well, now imagine that there is another ship with the same name that sets sail in December. See the problem? Simply using the name isn't enough because it can have more than one meaning.

   Namespaces are a URI that is used to get around this type of problem by providing what in law would be called a "meeting of the minds." It is a way to ensure that when the elements and attribute have the same names, the correct meaning is used. This is a good way to avoid conflict. The only alternative would be to guess, which was done in the previous example from the mid-1800s. In case you were wondering, they guessed wrong.

6.5.2   DTD

A Document Type Definition is used to describe and validate an XML document. Essentially, you spell out exactly what to expect in a particular XML document, to avoid confusion. Consider the XML document shown in Listing 6-9, basically a short list of monsters and where they've appeared.

Listing 6-9   An Example XML Document

```
<?xml version="1.0" encoding="UTF-8"?>
<monsters >
      <monster name="Dracula" books="yes" plays="yes" movies="yes"/>
      <monster name="Alien" books="yes" plays="no" movies="yes"/>
      <monster name="The Thing" books="yes" plays="no" movies="yes"/>
      <monster name="Sweeny Todd" books="yes" plays="yes" movies="no"/>
</monsters>
```

If confusion concerning names were a possibility, a DTD like the one in Listing 6-10 would then be used.

Listing 6-10   The DTD for Listing 6-9

```
<!ELEMENT monster EMPTY>
<!ATTLIST monster
      name CDATA #REQUIRED
      books CDATA #REQUIRED
      plays CDATA #REQUIRED
      movies CDATA #REQUIRED
>
<!ELEMENT monsters (monster+)>
```

All that then would be left to do would be to save it in a folder called namespace on the C: drive and assign the DTD by inserting the following before the first element:

```
<!DOCTYPE monsters SYSTEM "C:\namespace\sample.dtd">
```

Just in case you haven't noticed something strange about Document Type Definitions, I want to point out that they are not XML. However, there is an XML equivalent to Document Type Definitions called schemas.

6.5.3   Schema

Schemas have the advantages of being XML and being able to provide greater validation than DTDs. The reason for this is that a schema can describe complex data types beyond the basic dateTime, decimal, integer, and string available with DTDs. This essentially means that it is possible to describe complex types, as shown in Listing 6-11.

Listing 6-11   Schema for Listing 6-9

```xml
<?xml version="1.0" encoding="UTF-8" standalone="yes"?>
<!--W3C Schema generated by XMLSpy v2006 sp2 U (http://www.altova.com)-->
<xs:schema xmlns:xs="http://www.w3.org/2001/XMLSchema"
elementFormDefault="qualified">
    <xs:complexType name="monsterType">
        <xs:attribute name="name" use="required">
            <xs:simpleType>
                <xs:restriction base="xs:string">
                    <xs:enumeration value="Alien"/>
                    <xs:enumeration value="Dracula"/>
                    <xs:enumeration value="Sweeny Todd"/>
                </xs:restriction>
            </xs:simpleType>
        </xs:attribute>
        <xs:attribute name="books" use="required">
            <xs:simpleType>
                <xs:restriction base="xs:string">
                    <xs:enumeration value="no"/>
                    <xs:enumeration value="yes"/>
                </xs:restriction>
            </xs:simpleType>
        </xs:attribute>
        <xs:attribute name="plays" use="required">
            <xs:simpleType>
                <xs:restriction base="xs:string">
                    <xs:enumeration value="no"/>
                    <xs:enumeration value="yes"/>
                </xs:restriction>
            </xs:simpleType>
        </xs:attribute>
        <xs:attribute name="movies" use="required">
            <xs:simpleType>
                <xs:restriction base="xs:string">
                    <xs:enumeration value="no"/>
                    <xs:enumeration value="yes"/>
                </xs:restriction>
            </xs:simpleType>
        </xs:attribute>
    </xs:complexType>
    <xs:element name="monsters">
        <xs:complexType>
            <xs:sequence>
                <xs:element name="monster" type="monsterType"
maxOccurs="unbounded"/>
            </xs:sequence>
        </xs:complexType>
    </xs:element>
</xs:schema>
```

Yes, it is longer, but it also better describes the XML document in greater detail than the DTD ever could. This leaves only the "how to assign it?" question, which Listing 6-12 answers.

Listing 6-12   The Document with the Schema Applied

```
<?xml version="1.0" encoding="UTF-8"?>
<monsters xmlns:xsi="http://www.w3.org/2001/XMLSchema-instance"
xsi:noNamespaceSchemaLocation="C:\namespace\sample.xsd">
        <monster name="Dracula" books="yes" plays="yes" movies="yes"/>
        <monster name="Alien" books="yes" plays="no" movies="yes"/>
        <monster name="Sweeny Todd" books="yes" plays="yes" movies="no"/>
</monsters>
```

6.6   XML DECLARATION

Before proceeding any further, I want to explain a little about the stuff between the <? and the ?>. It is called the XML declaration, which is an example of a META data tag that appears at the beginning of an XML document. Its purpose is to specify the version of XML, the character encoding, and whether there is an external markup declaration.

Determining whether the XML document has an external markup declaration (standalone="no") or not (standalone="true") is based upon three rules. An XML document has an external markup declaration if attributes have default values, there are entities used other than the five default entities, or either elements or attributes are subject to whitespace nominalization.

6.7   PROCESSING INSTRUCTIONS

In addition to the XML declaration META tag, there is something called a processing instruction that also uses the <? and ?>. At first glance, processing instructions appear to be the same as the XML declaration, but they have different capabilities and serve a different purpose. For example, unlike an XML declaration, a processing instruction can appear anywhere in an XML document. Also, processing instructions are used to pass information to an application that can read the XML document.

6.8   XML DATA ISLANDS

For readers who are unfamiliar with the term *XML Data Islands,* they refer to the real estate that is usually purchased with the profits from one's first book.

You know, the kind of real estate that isn't there when the tide is in. Oops, my mistake: wrong definition.

Take two!

For those readers who are unfamiliar with the term *XML Data Islands*, they are XML that is embedded with the body of an HTML document. Although this sounds simple enough, there is a little more to it than that; Microsoft Internet Explorer hides the XML, whereas Firefox and other Gecko-based web browsers do not.

6.8.1 Internet Explorer

Because Microsoft Internet Explorer has built-in support for XML data islands, it is simply a matter of embedding the XML in a web page, as described in more detail in Chapter 8. Binding the XML to the HTML is merely a matter of defining the `datasrc` and the `datafld`, where the `datasrc` is the ID from the XML element and the `datafld` is either an element or an attribute. The idea is that because the HTML is bound to the XML, changes in one are reflected in the other, which can be a real timesaver when developing a web application.

6.8.2 Firefox

With Gecko-based web browsers such as Firefox, Flock, Netscape, or Mozilla XML, data islands require a bit more work to pull off. Let's look at an example of a Cascading Style Sheet shown here in Listing 6-13. Its purpose is to prevent the XML data island from being rendered, which solved only part of the problem.

Listing 6-13 CSS to Hide XML

```
xml
{
display: none;
font-size: 0px
}
```

The rest of the problem, the binding, was resolved using JavaScript and HTML as originally shown in Listing 4-7 and again is shown in Listing 6-14.

Listing 6-14 Cross-Browser Binding XML

```
<html>
    <head>
            <title>XML Data Island Test</title>
            <style type="text/css">
```

continues

Listing 6-14   continued

```
xml
{
     display: none;
     font-size: 0px
}
            </style>
            <script language="JavaScript">
var _IE = (new RegExp('internet explorer','gi')).test(navigator.appName);


/*
    Function:     _bind
    Programmer: Edmond Woychowsky
    Purpose:    Handle the logic necessary to bind HTML elements
to XML nodes.  Note that in some instances this
binding is a two-way street.  For example, if the value in
a text box should change the corresponding value in the
XML data island will also change.
*/
function _bind() {
  if(arguments.length == 0) {
    doBind(document.body.getElementsByTagName('div'));
    doBind(document.body.getElementsByTagName('input'));
    doBind(document.body.getElementsByTagName('select'));
    doBind(document.body.getElementsByTagName('span'));
    doBind(document.body.getElementsByTagName('textarea'));
  } else {
    applyChange(arguments[0],arguments[1]);
    _bind();                                   //  Re-bind
  }

  /*
       Function:   doBind
       Programmer: Edmond Woychowsky
       Purpose:    To handle data-binds for specific nodes
  based upon HTML element type and browser type.
  */
  function doBind(objects) {
    var strTag;                        //  HTML tag
    var strDI;                         //  XML data island id
    var strNode;                       //  XML node name
    var strValue;                      //  XML node value

    for(var i=0;i < objects.length;i++) {
      strTag = objects[i].tagName;
      strDI = objects[i].getAttribute('xmldi');
      strNode = objects[i].getAttribute('xmlnode');

      if(_IE)
        strValue =
document.getElementById(strDI).XMLDocument.selectNodes('//' +
strNode).item(i).text;
      else
```

```
                   strValue =
document.getElementById(strDI).getElementsByTagName(strNode)[i].innerHTML;

        switch(strTag) {
          case('DIV'):
          case('SPAN'):
              objects[i].innerHTML = strValue;

              break;
          case('INPUT'):
              switch(objects[i].type) {
                  case('text'):
                  case('hidden'):
                  case('password'):
                      objects[i].value = strValue;
                      objects[i].onchange = new Function("_bind(this," +
i.toString() + ")");

                      break;
                  case('checkbox'):
                      if(objects[i].value == strValue)
                          objects[i].checked = true;
                      else
                          objects[i].checked = false;

                      objects[i].onclick = new Function("_bind(this," +
i.toString() + ")");

                      break;
                  case('radio'):
                      if(_IE)
                          strValue =
document.getElementById(strDI).XMLDocument.selectNodes('//' +
strNode).item(0).text;
                      else
                          strValue =
document.getElementById(strDI).getElementsByTagName(strNode)[0].innerHTML;

                      if(objects[i].value == strValue)
                          objects[i].checked = true;
                      else
                          objects[i].checked = false;

                      objects[i].onclick = new Function("_bind(this,0)");

                      break;
              }

              break;
          case('SELECT'):
          case('TEXTAREA'):
              objects[i].value = strValue;
```

continues

Listing 6-14   continued

```
            objects[i].onchange = new Function("_bind(this," +
i.toString() + ")");

            break;
      }
    }
  }

  /*
      Function:    applyChange
      Programmer: Edmond Woychowsky
      Purpose:    To handle changes to the bound HTML elements and apply
                  those changes to the appropriate XML node.
  */
  function applyChange(obj,index) {
    var strDI = obj.getAttribute('xmldi');
    var strNode = obj.getAttribute('xmlnode');
    var strValue = obj.value;

    if(obj.type == 'checkbox')
        if(obj.checked)
            strValue = obj.value;
        else
            strValue = '';

    if(_IE)
        document.getElementById(strDI).XMLDocument.selectNodes('//' +
strNode).item(index).text = strValue;
    else

document.getElementById(strDI).getElementsByTagName(strNode)[index].innerH
TML = strValue;
  }
}
            </script>
      </head>
      <body onload="_bind()">
            <xml id="xmlDI">
                <a>
                <b>
                    <c>one</c>
                </b>
                <b>
                    <c>two</c>
                </b>
                <b>
                    <c>three</c>
                </b>
                </a>
            </xml>
            <b>XML Data Island Test</b>
            <br />
```

```
            <div xmldi="xmlDI" xmlnode="c"></div>
            <br />
            <div xmldi="xmlDI" xmlnode="c"></div>
            <br />
            <div xmldi="xmlDI" xmlnode="c"></div>
            <br />
            <input type="text" xmldi="xmlDI" xmlnode="c" value="" />
            <br />
            <input type="text" xmldi="xmlDI" xmlnode="c" value="" />
            <br />
            <input type="text" xmldi="xmlDI" xmlnode="c" value="" />
            <br />
    </body>
</html>
```

Essentially, the code in this listing searches the HTML document for tags of the type that can be bound to the XML. As they are encountered, the next value from the XML is used and a change event handler is attached to the HTML. This way, when the visitor changes the value, the XML Data Island is updated.

Talk about lazy! No need to code-change event handlers by hand. This leads to the possibility of simply refreshing the XML Data Island from the server and rebinding to display updates. Pretty useful when the user requests another page of information, not only the next page or the previous page, but maybe even a search.

6.9   SUMMARY

This chapter covered some of the basics of XML, including the differences between elements and attributes. It also delved into what makes an XML document well formed and not well formed. In addition, I covered how to make script elements in XHTML from both an XML and JavaScript point of view, as well as entities.

The subject of namespaces was covered along with their purpose. This included a brief look at both Document Type Definitions and schemas, and the role that they play in validation. Finally, this chapter covered the role that XML Data Islands can play within an HTML document.

CHAPTER 7

XMLHttpRequest

Several years ago, I worked for a company that had a reputation for conceiving incredible ideas. Unfortunately, the company also had a reputation for being unable to either recognize the value of those ideas or market a product using those ideas. Such was the case with the XMLHttpRequest object, originally created by Microsoft for use with one of the products in its Office Suite. It languished unused until outsiders discovered it in Internet Explorer.

These unknown intrepid developers knew immediately that the XMLHttpRequest object was a solution in search of a problem. The only real question was in finding the problem. And although I can't speak for anyone else, the problem that I chose was a shopping cart application described in Chapter 2, "Introducing Ajax." Remember the "mockup" that wasn't a mockup and didn't "blink"? After that particular incident, I was considerably more careful in my selection of applications—or, at least, in my selection of attendees at my demonstrations.

In fact, at times I was so careful in selecting where to use the XMLHttpRequest object that it was necessary to examine the code to see exactly how it worked. I started by choosing applications in which it appeared that the information was cached on the client side: the dreaded HTML select whose contents are based upon another HTML select, which, in turn, is based upon another HTML select. As long as nobody ever looked at the code, which nobody ever did, the web page wouldn't appear any different from the hundreds of others in the system. That is, it wouldn't appear different unless you take into account speed. Without all the cached information, the initial load was considerably faster.

In retrospect, looking back upon several of those "mad scientist" applications, I realize now that not all of them could be considered Ajax. This is because Ajax is shorthand for Asynchronous JavaScript and XML, and some of these applications were coded to be synchronous. And whoever heard of Sjax?

Nevertheless, because the XMLHttpRequest object can be used both synchronously and asynchronously, both are covered. Moreover, we cover the following topics in this chapter:

☞ Synchronous

☞ Asynchronous

☞ Microsoft Internet Explorer

☞ XML Document Object Model

☞ RSS

☞ Web Services

7.1 SYNCHRONOUS

Although not nearly as cool as coding an asynchronous client-side application, a synchronous client-side application is nothing to look down at. In fact, it beats the pants off the average web application—figuratively speaking, of course, because web applications don't wear pants. Thinking about it, using the XMLHttpRequest object synchronously is actually a good way to expose yourself, also figuratively, to some of the basics.

One of the interesting things about the basics of the XMLHttpRequest object is that these basics are actually basic. Only a few parameters and a few lines of code separate the synchronous from the asynchronous. When you understand that, not much is required to change a synchronous application into an asynchronous application. Don't believe me? Take a look at the XMLHttpRequest object's properties and methods shown in Table 7-1.

Table 7-1 XMLHttpRequest Object Properties and Methods

Method/Property	Description
abort()	Terminates the previous outstanding request.
getAllResponseHeaders()	Returns all response headers, labels, and values, as a string.
getResponseHeader("label")	Returns the value for the provided label.
open("method","url", asynchronous,"username", "password")	Opens/assigns a method: GET or POST and, optionally, an asynchronous indicator.
send(content)	Sends the request with optional content. This content can be either a string or DOM data.
setRequestHeader ("label","value")	Sets a request header label/value pair.

Method/Property	Description
onreadystatechange	Event handler for asynchronous requests; fires on each change to the readyState property.
readyState	Status of the request as an integer. 0 = uninitialize 1 = loading 2 = loaded 3 = interactive 4 = complete
responseText	String returned from the server.
responseXML	XML document returned from the server.
status	HTTP response code returned from the server.
statusText	String message associated with the HTTP a.

Right now, the XMLHttpRequest object might seem like a pile of unrelated parts, but when the individual parts are assembled in the correct sequence, things are different. To prove my point, let's take a look at the JavaScript that uses XMLHTTP to synchronously get a file from the server in Gecko-based browsers such as Firefox, Mozilla, and Flock (see Listing 7-1).

Listing 7-1 Getting a File Synchronously

```
var objXMLHTTP = new XMLHttpRequest();

objXMLHTTP.open('GET', 'books.xml', false);
objXMLHTTP.send(null);

var objXML = objXMLHTTP.responseXML;
```

The first step is to create an instance of the XMLHttpRequest object using the JavaScript new operator. Next, the open method is invoked using the request method, GET, a destination URL, and a Boolean indicating that the request is not asynchronous. The third and final step is to invoke the send method and assign the responseXML, an XML document, to a variable. And if you're not interested in using XML, there is always the responseText property.

7.2 ASYNCHRONOUS

On the surface, what's required to change the request from synchronous to asynchronous appears to be simply changing the false parameter to true for the open method. Unfortunately, although that would make the request asynchronous, it would have some issues with the responseXML property. This is because the request is asynchronous; instead of waiting for a response from the send method, processing just continues on its merry way. This means that the responseXML property is undefined, which is not exactly what we're looking for or expecting.

Fortunately, there is a way to correct this issue, but it requires creating an event handler to, er, handle changes to the readyState property. With the XMLHttpRequest object, the value of the readyState property changes every time something changes with the response to the request. This change fires the handler defined by the onreadystatechange property. Let's take a look at the example shown in Listing 7-2.

Listing 7-2   Example of Creating an Event Handler to Correct the Problem

```
var objXMLHTTP = new XMLHttpRequest();
var objXML;

objXMLHTTP.onreadystatechange = asyncHandler;
objXMLHTTP.open('GET', 'books.xml', true);
objXMLHTTP.send(null);

function asyncHandler() {
  if(objXMLHTTP.readyState == 4)
    objXML = objXMLHTTP.responseXML;
}
```

In this example, the function asyncHandler is assigned as an event handler using the onreadystatechange property. This means that the asyncHandler function fires each time the readyState property changes. Because it fires every time the property changes, it is necessary to verify that the response is actually complete before doing anything with the response. The if statement in the asyncHandler function takes care of this issue; a readyState equal to 4 means that everything is fine and we're done. But what if everything isn't fine?

Anyone who has ever played any of the Mech Assault campaigns knows that something always goes wrong. What fun would it be if everything worked all the time? Thinking about it, please disregard my last statement as the ramblings of a sick mind. Nevertheless, the universe is perverse, so bad things happen to good people, countries, cities, and web applications. Because of this, it is sometimes necessary to code defensively, to handle the unexpected. Note that I said *defensively,* not *offensively.* Don't go looking for problems; like a mad cat with charged PPCs, they'll find you soon enough.

You can handle this potential problem in several ways. The first possible method involves hoping and wishing. Unfortunately, management has a tendency to frown upon this method of error handling. Possibly this is because mangers aren't a particularly hopeful group of people. Maybe because their heads are on the chopping block right next to our own.

A better method of handling potential problems, at least from a job longevity point of view, is to consider what could go wrong. The way that I see it, things can go wrong in two possible ways. The first of these is getting basic bad information back from the server. During development, this can be handled by an alert and the `responseText` property. Beyond the development phase, however, this would probably scare away the non–mad scientists. At these times, you might want to inform the user that an error has taken place and use the `XMLHttpRequest` object to tell development about it. A more common, and much harder to handle, error is a timeout.

A timeout, for those who have been watching *Star Gate SG-1* instead of reading about web development, occurs when an application either doesn't respond at all or doesn't respond in a reasonable amount of time. Who defines "reasonable"? You do. Big believer in the 7-second rule? Then use 7 seconds. Like the *Hitchhiker's Guide to the Galaxy*? Then use 42 seconds. In short, use whatever time period seems appropriate. After you decide this, all that is necessary is to figure out how to handle it.

Personally, I'm fond of using the `setTimeout` method with a variable set to the result from the method. If the response is received within the specified time limit, `clearTimeout` can be used to prevent the timeout function from executing. Otherwise, the function specified by the `setTimeout` method will execute and any problems can be dealt with then. All in all, using the `setTimeout` method is a rather elegant solution to a potentially fatal problem.

This leaves really only one issue: What to do with those individuals who, for some reason, choose to use Microsoft Internet Explorer? Keep it clean! Yes, we have to accommodate those people in some way, beyond the Click Here to Download option.

7.3   MICROSOFT INTERNET EXPLORER

Unlike most other web browsers, Microsoft Internet Explorer uses something called ActiveX, which is a holdover from an earlier age when object libraries where new, untried, and obscure. Because of this, ActiveX is like the bowels of a ship: Sometimes nasty things are down there. In the case of ActiveX, the ship is a spaceship named Nostromo. However, this isn't a "knock Internet Explorer" session. You'll find enough of those online today.

Unlike most cross-browser differences encountered when developing web applications, this one doesn't require a lot of code. In fact, the single line of code shown here is enough to do the deed, from an Internet Explorer point of view. This JavaScript creates in Microsoft Internet Explorer an ActiveX object that is the XMLHttpRequest object:

```
var objXMLHTTP = new ActiveXObject('Microsoft.XMLHTTP');
```

So now that we've got a potential source of XML, the big question is how to handle it.

7.4 XML DOCUMENT OBJECT MODEL

The majority of web developers are familiar with the HTML DOM, but unless they're used to XML development, they might not even realize that the XML DOM exists. In fact, even if they are aware that there is a Document Object Model for use with XML, they might not know that there is a difference between the XML and the HTML DOM. For example, the HTML DOM is geared more toward the various HTML elements, whereas the XML Document Object Model is somewhat more generic.

The XML Document Object Model is a common API for dealing with XML. It provides a standard interface for accessing, modifying, and creating the various parts of an XML document. Let's take a look at the XML document shown in Listing 7-3 as a starting point, and you'll see what I mean.

Listing 7-3   An XML Document

```
<?xml version="1.0"?>
<garden>
  <plant>
    <name>Foxglove</name>
    <use>heart</use>
    <part>root</part>
  </plant>
  <plant>
    <name>Mandrake</name>
    <use>impotency</use>
    <part>root</part>
  </plant>
  <plant>
    <name>Trillium</name>
    <use>poison</use>
    <part>leave</part>
  </plant>
  <plant>
    <name>Wolfsbane</name>
    <use>werewolf repellent</use>
    <part>flower</part>
  </plant>
```

```
<plant>
  <name>Meadowsweet</name>
  <use>cramps</use>
  <part>leave</part>
</plant>
</garden>
```

After the requisite browser-specific JavaScript is executed and the XML document from Listing 7-3 is loaded into a variable—say, myXML—it is time to try out the DOM. Let's say, for instance, that we're interested in getting all the plant nodes in a node set. Using the DOM, we could code the following:

```
var myNodeset = myXML.getElementsByTagName('plant');
```

Pretty slick, isn't it?

But there's more to the XML Document Object Model than the getElementsByTagName method. In fact, an entire slew of properties and methods is available by using the XML DOM interfaces in JavaScript. However, to use these properties and methods, it is necessary to know the various interfaces available in JavaScript, as outlined in Table 7-2.

Table 7-2 JavaScript Interfaces Relevant to Using the XML DOM

Interface Name	Description
DOMException	Exception raised by a DOM method when the requested action cannot be completed
ExceptionCode	Integer that indicates the type of error raised by a DOMException
DOMImplementation	Provides methods that are independent of any implementation of the XML Document Object Model
DocumentFragment	A lightweight XML document, often used to hold portions of an XML document
Document	Used to hold an entire XML document
Node	Represents a single node of an XML document
NodeList	An indexed list of nodes
NamedNodeMap	A collection of nodes that are accessed either by name or by index
CharacterData	Extends the Node interface by adding character-specific properties and methods
Attr	Represents the attributes for individual elements

continues

Table 7-2   continued

Interface Name	Description
Element	Extends the Node interface by adding methods for accessing and adding attributes
Text	Represents the text content of an Element
Comment	Represents an XML comment, the text between <!-- and -->
CDATASection	Interface used to escape text that would normally be parsed as XML
DocumentType	Used to define the document type
Notation	Represents a notation declared in the Document Type Definition (DTD)
Entity	Interface used to represent an XML entity, which can be either parsed or unparsed
EntityReference	Interface that contains a reference to an XML entity
ProcessingInstruction	Interface that contains a text-processing instruction

Each of these interfaces has a number of properties and methods that can be used to manipulate an XML document. Table 7-3 lists the various properties and methods, along with their associated interfaces.

Table 7-3   Properties and Methods for Various Interfaces

Property/Method	Interface	Description
hasFeature(feature,version)	DOMImplementation	Returns a Boolean indicating whether the feature is supported.
Doctype	Document	The DTD associated with this XML document.
Implementation	Document	The DOMImplementation for this document.
documentElement	Document	The document's root element.
createElement(tagName)	Document	Creates the specified element.
createDocumentFragment()	Document	Creates an empty document fragment.
createTextNode(data)	Document	Creates a Text element using the data provided.
createComment(data)	Document	Creates a Comment node using the data provided.

Property/Method	Interface	Description
`createCDATASection(data)`	`Document`	Creates a `CDATASection` node using the data provided.
`createProcessingInstruction` `(target,data)`	`Document`	Creates a `ProcessingInstruction` node.
`createAttribute(name)`	`Document`	Creates an `Attribute`.
`createEntityReference(name)`	`Document`	Creates an `EntityReference`.

`getElementsByTagName` `(tagname)`	`Document`
	`Node`
	`CharacterData`
	`Attr`
	`Element`
	`Text`
	`Comment`
	`CDATASection`
	`DocumentType`
	`Notation Entity`
	`EntityReference`
	`ProcessingInstruction`
		Returns a node set consisting of elements with matching tag names.

`nodeName`	`Document`
	`Node`
	`CharacterData`
	`Attr`
	`Element`
	`Text`
	`Comment`
	`CDATASection`
	`DocumentType`
	`Notation Entity`
	`EntityReference`
	`ProcessingInstruction`
		The name of the node.

`nodeValue`	`Document`
	`Node`
	`CharacterData`
	`Attr`
	`Element`
	`Text`
	`Comment`
	`CDATASection`
	`DocumentType`
	`Notation Entity`
	`EntityReference`
	`ProcessingInstruction`
		The value of the node.

continues

Table 7-3   continued

Property/Method	Interface	Description
nodeType	Document Node CharacterData Attr Element Text Comment CDATASection DocumentType Notation Entity EntityReference ProcessingInstruction	The type of the node. See Table 7-4 for accepted values.
parentNode	Document Node CharacterData Attr Element Text Comment CDATASection DocumentType Notation Entity EntityReference ProcessingInstruction	The parent of the current node.
childNodes	Document Node CharacterData Attr Element Text Comment CDATASection DocumentType Notation Entity EntityReference ProcessingInstruction	A node set consisting of the child nodes of the current node. Note that the node set may be empty.
firstChild	Document Node CharacterData Attr Element Text Comment CDATASection DocumentType Notation Entity EntityReference ProcessingInstruction	The first child node of the current node.

Property/Method	Interface	Description
lastChild	Document Node CharacterData Attr Element Text Comment CDATASection DocumentType Notation Entity EntityReference ProcessingInstruction	The last child of the current node.
previousSibling	Document Node CharacterData Attr Element Text Comment CDATASection DocumentType Notation Entity EntityReference ProcessingInstruction	The previous child of the current node's parent.
nextSibling	Document Node CharacterData Attr Element Text Comment CDATASection DocumentType Notation Entity EntityReference ProcessingInstruction	The next child of the current node's parent.
Attributes	Document Node CharacterData Attr Element Text Comment CDATASection DocumentType Notation Entity EntityReference ProcessingInstruction	A collection consisting of the attributes for the current node.

continues

Table 7-3   continued

Property/Method	Interface	Description
ownerDocument	Document Node CharacterData Attr Element Text Comment CDATASection DocumentType Notation Entity EntityReference ProcessingInstruction	The Document associated with the current element.
insertBefore(new,reference)	Document Node the CharacterData Attr Element Text Comment CDATASection DocumentType Notation Entity EntityReference ProcessingInstruction	Inserts the new child node before reference child node.
replaceChild(new,old)	Document Node CharacterData Attr Element Text Comment CDATASection DocumentType Notation Entity EntityReference ProcessingInstruction	Replaces the old child node with the new child node.
removeChild(old)	Document Node CharacterData Attr Element Text Comment CDATASection DocumentType Notation Entity EntityReference ProcessingInstruction	Removes the old child node.

Property/Method	Interface	Description
appendChild(new)	Document Node CharacterData Attr Element Text Comment CDATASection DocumentType Notation Entity EntityReference ProcessingInstruction	Appends the new child node as the last child.
hasChildNodes()	Document Node CharacterData Attr Element Text Comment CDATASection DocumentType Notation Entity EntityReference ProcessingInstruction	Returns a true if child nodes exist and a false if child nodes do not exist.
cloneNode(deep)	Document Node CharacterData Attr Element Text Comment CDATASection DocumentType Notation Entity EntityReference ProcessingInstruction	Duplicates the specified node. The Boolean parameter deep is used to indicate a deep copy, which states whether the children should be copied.
Length	NodeList NamedNodeList CharacterData	The number of items in the collection or the length of the character data.
item(index)	NodeList NamedNodeList	Returns a single node from a collection based upon the index.
getNamedItem(name)	NamedNodeMap	Returns a single node based upon the node name.
setNamedItem(node)	NamedNodeMap	Adds a single node.

continues

Table 7-3   continued

Property/Method	Interface	Description
removeNamedItem(name)	NamedNodeMap	Removes a node based upon the node name.
Data	CharacterData Text Comment CDATASection ProcessingInstruction	The character data for the node.
substringData(offset,length)	CharacterData Text Comment CDATASection	Extracts a substring from the character data for the node.
appendData(string)	CharacterData Text Comment CDATASection	Appends the string to the end of the node's character data.
insertData(offset,string)	CharacterData Text Comment CDATASection	Inserts the string into the node's character data at the offset.
deleteData(offset,length)	CharacterData Text Comment CDATASection	Deletes the number of characters specified by the length, starting at the offset.
replaceData (offset,length,string)	CharacterData Text Comment CDATASection	Replaces the number of characters specified by the length, starting at the offset with the specified string.
Name	Attr DocumentType	The attribute name or the DTD name, in the case of the DocumentType.
Specified	Attr	A Boolean indicating whether the attribute has a value in the original document.
Value	Attr	The string value of the attribute.
tagName	Element	The tag name of the Element.

Property/Method	Interface	Description
getAttribute(name)	Element	Returns the value of an attribute based upon name.
setAttribute(name,value)	Element	Creates an attribute and sets its value.
removeAttribute(name)	Element	Removes an attribute by name.
getAttributeNode(name)	Element	Retrieves an Attr node by name.
setAttributeNode(name)	Element	Adds an Attr node by name.
removeAttributeNode(name)	Element	Removes an Attr node by name.
normalize()	Element	Normalizes the specified element and children of the specified element.
splitText(offset)	Text	Splits the Text node into two Text nodes at the specified offset.
Entities	DocumentType	A NamedNodeMap containing the entities declared in the DTD.
Notations	DocumentType	A NamedNodeMap containing the notations declared in the DTD.
publicId	Notation Entity	The public identifier for this notation, or a null if no public identifier is specified.
systemId	Notation Entity	The system identifier for this notation, or a null if no system identifier is specified.
notationName	Entity	The name of the notation for this entity if the entity is unparsed. If the entity is parsed, the result is null.
Target	ProcessingInstruction	The target for this processing instruction.

Table 7-4   The Node Types

Node Type	Value	Interface
ELEMENT_NODE	1	Element
ATTRIBUTE_NODE	2	Attr
TEXT_NODE	3	Text
CDATA_SECTION_NODE	4	CDATASection
ENTITY_REFERENCE_NODE	5	EntityReference
ENTITY_NODE	6	Entity
PROCESSING_INSTRUCTION_NODE	7	ProcessingInstruction
COMMENT_NODE	8	Comment
DOCUMENT_NODE	9	Document
DOCUMENT_TYPE_NODE	10	DocumentType
DOCUMENT_FRAGMENT_NODE	11	DocumentFragment
NOTATION_NODE	12	Notation

By using these interfaces, it is possible to manipulate an XML document without really having to mess around too much. The only real issue is the vast array of properties and methods available. They can be rather overwhelming. But personally, I find myself using a narrow range of properties and methods to perform any task that is needed. This narrow range includes methods such as `getElementsByTagname` and attributes.

7.5   RSS

Really Simple Syndication, or RSS, is a dialect of XML that is commonly used for providing news-related content. Things such as news headlines are the realm of RSS. The only issue is that because RSS is XML, it doesn't appear as pretty as HTML does in a web browser. Consider the RSS shown in Listing 7-4 as an example.

Listing 7-4   RSS Example

```
<?xml version="1.0"?>
<rss version="2.0">
  <channel>
    <title>NEWS!</title>
    <link>http://overlord.gov/</link>
    <description>Latest news</description>
    <language>en-us</language>
    <pubDate>Tue, 29 Nov 2005 03:00:00 GMT</pubDate>
```

```
<lastBuildDate>Tue, 29 Nov 2005 03:07:00 GMT</lastBuildDate>
<docs>http://blogs.overlord.gov/rss</docs>
<generator>My Generator</generator>
<managingEditor>Bob@gol.com</managingEditor>
<webMaster>webmaster@gol.com</webMaster>

<item>
  <title>Galactic Overlord Resigns</title>
  <link>http://overlord.gov/news/2005/news-resign.aspx</link>
  <description>
   The much despised Galactic Overlord has announced
   his resignation as the Blorf fleet entered
    orbit.
   </description>
  <pubDate>Tue, 29 Nov 2005 03:07:00 GMT</pubDate>
  <guid>http://overlord.gov/news/2005/11/28.html#item1</guid>
</item>
<item>
  <title>Earth's Moon Stolen</title>
  <link>http://overlord.gov/news/2005/news-moon.aspx</link>
  <description>
   Luna, the often photographed natural satellite of
   Earth, has been reported stolen.  According to a
   UN spokesperson, at this moment, there are no
    suspects.
   </description>
  <pubDate>Tue, 29 Nov 2005 05:28:00 GMT</pubDate>
  <guid>http://overlord.gov/news/2005/11/28.html#item2</guid>
</item>
</channel>
</rss>
```

Not very pretty, is it? There are, however, ways to prettify it. (Wow, who would have thought that *prettify* was a word? Oops, off the subject matter.) Using JavaScript and the DOM methods and properties, it is possible to extract only the headlines from the RSS shown. For example, the getElementsByTagname or the getNamedItem properties could be used to obtain the title elements. The content of these elements could then be displayed on the page as a hyperlink. Clicking on the link could then fire a JavaScript handler that would display the description element.

The purpose of this side trip into the wonderful world of Really Simple Syndication was to merely show some of the possibilities of XML. When information is available as XML, it can at times be treated as something like a database. In essence, XML is not only the data itself, but also the source of subsets of that data.

7.6 WEB SERVICES

Regardless of where you look, web services are a hot subject, and not just on resumés. Something of a mystique surrounds web services; like the latest hot video game, everybody wants one, even if nobody is quite sure what one is. Ah, to be a kid again, wanting something just because I want it. Who am I kidding? I'm still that way, obsessing over games such as *Stargate: The Alliance* for XBox, and books such as *Practical Guide to Red Hat Linux: Fedora Core and Red Hat Enterprise Linux*. However, unlike businesses, my pockets aren't full of much other than lint, which means that I have to wait, whereas businesses can just whip out the checkbook.

7.6.1 What Is a Web Service?

Alright, because everybody wants a web service, there are only two questions. The first question is, what is a web service? And the second question is, how does a web service work? Let's start by answering the first question: What is a web service?

A web service is a piece of software designed to respond to requests across either the Internet or an intranet. In essence, it is a program that executes when a request is made of it, and it produces some kind of result that is returned to the caller. This might sound a lot like a web page, but there is a significant difference: With a web page, all the caller is required to know about the page is the URI. With a web service, the caller needs to know both the URI and at least one of the web service's public methods. Consider, for example, the C# web service shown in Listing 7-5. Knowing the URI, which, incidentally, is http://localhost/AJAX4/myService.asmx, isn't enough. It is also necessary to know that the public method is called `monster`.

Listing 7-5 Web Service Example

```
using System;
using System.Collections;
using System.ComponentModel;
using System.Data;
using System.Diagnostics;
using System.Web;
using System.Web.Services;

namespace AJAX4
{
  public class myService : System.Web.Services.WebService
  {
    public myService()
    {
```

```
      InitializeComponent();
   }

   #region Component Designer generated code

   //Required by the Web Services Designer
   private IContainer components = null;

   /// <summary>
   /// Required method for Designer support - do not modify
   /// the contents of this method with the code editor.
   /// </summary>
   private void InitializeComponent()
   {
   }

   /// <summary>
   /// Clean up any resources being used.
   /// </summary>
   protected override void Dispose( bool disposing )
   {
     if(disposing && components != null)
     {
       components.Dispose();
     }
     base.Dispose(disposing);
   }

   #endregion

   [WebMethod]
   public string monster()
   {
     return "Grrr!";
   }
 }
}
```

Great, now we have a web service—whoopee, we're done, right? Wrong! Having a web service is only part of the battle; it falls into the same category as having a swimming pool and not knowing how to swim. Yeah, it is impressive, but deep down, there is a nagging feeling of feeling stupid for the unnecessary expense. What is needed is the knowledge of how to invoke the web service.

Impressive word, *invoke*; it conjures up images of smoke, candles, pentagrams, and demons, the kind that could rip a soul from a body and torment it for eternity—or, at least, during the annual performance evaluation. As with invoking a demon, invoking a web service is all a matter of how things are phrased, knowing both what to ask and how to ask. In both cases, mistakes can lead to, um, undesirable results.

7.6.2 SOAP

Unlike demonology, which requires the use of Latin (of the Roman variety, not the swine variety), invoking a web service requires the use of a dialect of XML called SOAP. And as with everything even remotely computer related, SOAP is an acronym standing for Simple Object Access Protocol. Fortunately, with SOAP, the little elves who name things didn't lie: It is actually simple, and who would have thought it?

The basic structure of a SOAP request is an envelope, which is also a pretty good analogy of not only what it is, but also what it does. It serves as a wrapper around the request and any parameters being passed to the web service. Consider the example of SOAP shown in Listing 7-6, whose purpose is to invoke the web service from Listing 7-5.

Listing 7-6   SOAP to Invoke the Web Service

```
<?xml version="1.0" encoding="utf-8"?>
<soap:Envelope xmlns:xsi="http://www.w3.org/2001/XMLSchema-instance"
xmlns:xsd="http://www.w3.org/2001/XMLSchema"
xmlns:soap="http://schemas.xmlsoap.org/soap/envelope/">
  <soap:Body>
    <monster xmlns="http://tempuri.org/" />
  </soap:Body>
</soap:Envelope>
```

Doesn't look like much does it? All that the SOAP envelope does is specify the method, `monster`, along with a namespace—which, in this case, is the default, basically a placeholder. If the method requires any parameters, they would be passed as children of that method. For example, let's add the method shown in Listing 7-7 to the web service from Listing 7-5.

Listing 7-7   Method to Add to the Web Service

```
[WebMethod]
public string echo(string text)
{
  return text;
}
```

Beyond changing the method from `monster` to `echo`, there is the little problem of the parameter named `text`. Because of the parameter, it is necessary to change the body of the SOAP request to the one shown in Listing 7-8..

Listing 7-8   The New SOAP Request

```
<?xml version="1.0" encoding="utf-8"?>
<soap:Envelope xmlns:xsi="http://www.w3.org/2001/XMLSchema-instance"
```

```
xmlns:xsd="http://www.w3.org/2001/XMLSchema"
xmlns:soap="http://schemas.xmlsoap.org/soap/envelope/">
  <soap:Body>
    <echo xmlns="http://tempuri.org/">
      <text>Dijon Ketchup</text>
    </echo>
  </soap:Body>
</soap:Envelope>
```

Now that we've got the basics down of the SOAP envelope (yes, there is more) let's consider how to deliver it to the web service. Unfortunately, FedEx and UPS are both out of the question, although it might be fun to call and ask the rates for delivering a SOAP envelope to a web service—at least, until they got a restraining order. This leaves the XMLRequest object as the best available resource: neither rain, nor snow, and all that stuff.

Everything necessary to deliver the SOAP envelope is already in there, so the only issue is how to send our SOAP envelope—after all, there are no mailboxes with little red flags. Fortunately, we have a good chunk of the code down already, including the SOAP envelope itself. Instead of beating around the bush, Listing 7-9 shows the client-side JavaScript necessary to invoke the monster method of our web service.

Listing 7-9   JavaScript to Invoke the monster Method

```
try {
  objXMLHTTP = new XMLHttpRequest();
}
catch(e) {
  objXMLHTTP = new ActiveXObject('Microsoft.XMLHTTP');
}

objXMLHTTP.onreadystatechange = asyncHandler;

objXMLHTTP.open('POST', 'http://localhost/AJAX4/myService.asmx', true);
objXMLHTTP.setRequestHeader('SOAPAction','http://tempuri.org/monster');
objXMLHTTP.setRequestHeader('Content-Type','text/xml');
objXMLHTTP.send(soap);

function asyncHandler() {
  if(objXMLHTTP.readyState == 4)
    alert(objXMLHTTP.responseText);
}
```

The first noticeable change from the earlier asynchronous request (refer to Listing 7-2) is that the method has been changed from GET to POST; this is because it is necessary to post the SOAP envelope to the web service. This leads to the second change; the URI in the open method is now the address of the web service instead of a filename.

Perhaps the biggest changes are the addition of two setRequestHeader methods. The first one sets the SOAPAction to the web service's namespace and the method to be invoked. It is important to note that it is absolutely necessary for the SOAPAction header to be identical to the method in the SOAP envelope. If they aren't identical, it won't work. Personally, I spent a lot of time chasing my tail trying to figure out what was wrong whenever the methods were different, but, then, I was raised by wolves and have a strong tendency to chase my tail.

The second setRequestHeader is the easy one; all that it does is set the Content-type to text/xml. As if we'd be doing anything else. But this raises the question of what the response from the web service will look like, beyond being XML.

Well, there are essentially two possible responses; either it worked or it didn't. If it worked, it will look a lot like the response shown in Listing 7-10. However, there could be some differences. For instance, it could be an XML document instead of the "Grrr!", but this is only an example, so why strain ourselves?

Listing 7-10   The Response

```
<?xml version="1.0" encoding="utf-8"?>
<soap:Envelope xmlns:soap="http://schemas.xmlsoap.org/soap/envelope/"
xmlns:xsi="http://www.w3.org/2001/XMLSchema-instance"
xmlns:xsd="http://www.w3.org/2001/XMLSchema">
  <soap:Body>
    <monsterResponse xmlns="http://tempuri.org/">
      <monsterResult>Grrr!</monsterResult>
    </monsterResponse>
  </soap:Body>
</soap:Envelope>
```

The second possible response is broken into two parts. The first part is called a SOAP fault. Basically, it means that something is wrong with the request, such as the methods not being identical. Listing 7-11 shows a SOAP fault that was created when I changed the SOAPAction in the request header to xxxx when it should have been monster.

Listing 7-11   A SOAP Fault

```
<?xml version="1.0" encoding="utf-8"?>
<soap:Envelope xmlns:soap="http://schemas.xmlsoap.org/soap/envelope/"
xmlns:xsi="http://www.w3.org/2001/XMLSchema-instance"
```

```
xmlns:xsd="http://www.w3.org/2001/XMLSchema">
  <soap:Body>
    <soap:Fault>
      <faultcode>soap:Client</faultcode>
      <faultstring>
        System.Web.Services.Protocols.SoapException: Server
        did not recognize the value of HTTP Header
        SOAPAction: http://tempuri.org/xxxx.
    at
System.Web.Services.Protocols.Soap11ServerProtocolHelper.RouteRequest()
    at System.Web.Services.Protocols.SoapServerProtocol.Initialize()
    at System.Web.Services.Protocols.ServerProtocol.SetContext(Type type,
HttpContext context, HttpRequest request, HttpResponse response)
    at System.Web.Services.Protocols.ServerProtocolFactory.Create(Type
type, HttpContext context, HttpRequest request, HttpResponse response,
Boolean&amp; abortProcessing)
</faultstring>
        <detail/>
      </soap:Fault>
    </soap:Body>
</soap:Envelope>
```

The final two possible responses also cover errors. For example, there could be errors that are not handled correctly in the web service. This could result in the web service returning text concerning the error instead of either a SOAP response or a SOAP fault. It is important to take this into consideration when creating a web service.

Although the language C# was used here for writing the web services, it is important to remember that these techniques can be applied to a whole slew of languages. In the end, the choice of language is yours, or it belongs to the powers-that-be, or somewhere in the hierarchy.

7.7 SUMMARY

This chapter covered the object essential to Ajax, the XMLHttpRequest object in both Gecko-based browsers and Microsoft Internet Explorer. In addition, the differences between synchronous and asynchronous requests were described, along with the care and feeding of both types of requests. The question of how to handle the XML retrieved was described through the use of the XML Document Object Model.

The ever-present Really Simple Syndication was then covered as a potential source of XML. Finally, the ultimate source of XML (one which you might already have), web services, was described along with SOAP.

Ajax Using XML and XMLHttpRequest

Unlike the previous chapter, which was sort of "mad scientist stuff" with training wheels, here the training wheels come off. We're free to either fly like the wind or remove large amounts of skin from various body parts. Based upon my personal experience as a web developer, we'll probably do some of both. From this chapter forward, nobody, regardless of their personal feelings, can deny that what we do in this chapter falls under the definition of Ajax.

Up to this point, the only part of Ajax that we've really seen is the JavaScript. Feels like a rip-off, doesn't it?

Don't worry, we're building up to it. It would not do to have the monster rise off the slab in the beginning of Chapter 1, would it? Alright, I, too have a tendency to fast-forward to the good parts. For example, I don't care how SG-1 got to Antarctica; I just want to see the ship-to-ship battle over the pole and the battle in space. Come to think of it, *Stargate SG-1* should be required watching for mad scientists because two of the regular characters could be classified as mad scientists themselves.

The mad scientist stuff covered in this chapter is the basic building block of Ajax applications, the XMLHttpRequest object and how to determine what's actually going on. Along with this object is XML, including how to deal with it on the client and some of the ways to deal with it, such as SOAP (basically, a way to package XML for transport to and from the server). The final item covered is what to do with the XML on the client, such as put it in an XML Data Island. To skip ahead a little, because mad scientists like to describe their diabolical plans, XML Data Islands are one of the methods that can be used to both embed and bind HTML controls and data. The best part is, if you change one, the other changes.

8.1 TRADITIONAL VERSUS AJAX WEBSITES

Before we go any further, this is a good time to review how the average website works, if only to see the contrast between it and Ajax websites. With a traditional website, it isn't unusual for the same page to go through the unload/reload cycle several times before progressing to the next logical page. A number of valid reasons explain why these unload/reload cycles occur, ranging from HTML select objects whose contents are based on other select objects to simply bad input caught on the server side. In the end, the result looks quite a lot like Figure 8-1.

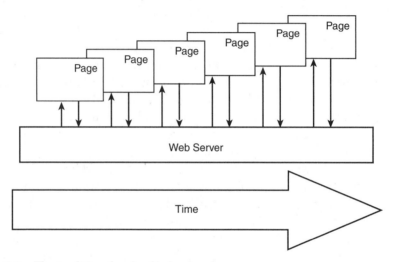

Figure 8-1   The traditional unload/reload cycle

Even in the early days, when the paint wasn't yet fully dry on the World Wide Web, the unload/reload cycle got old pretty quick, especially at dial-up speeds. Now with the improved bandwidth available, things are different; it is old right from the start. For example, several years ago, I worked as a consultant for a company that was trying to get a handle on the whole "web thing," as they referred to it. Their approach was to wave a magic wand, and, "Poof!"—a CICS programmer was now a web developer. Although this approach worked, after a fashion, it led to some rather interesting web development standards.

Their standard went pretty much along the lines of trying to make web pages as much like the mainframe CICS pages as possible. These standards were a combination of the weird and the scary. An example of the weird was that initially all scrolling, regardless of the direction, was forbidden because it was thought to be unprofessional. This meant that it was necessary to break up tabular web pages into single page–sized chunks and provide the user with some means of navigation.

On the other hand, some of the scary things were really scary. For example, they believed that there was nothing wrong with giving scripts write permission to the web server. Let's say, for instance, that a shopping cart for the web application was needed. Following the local standards, it was perfectly acceptable for the "temporary" shopping cart to be written to the web server. The rationale was that it was easier to work with flat files than to store information either on the client side or in a database table. Time permitting, they also could write a "batch job" to clean up the web server of abandoned shopping carts.

The shopping cart was actually coded in the manner that I described, but, thankfully, it was an absolute pig. It was both slow and temperamental, with items both appearing and disappearing seemingly at random in the shopping cart. In fact, my wife would probably say that it was like shopping with me: "Where did those Parmesan Goldfish and Double-Stuff Oreos come from?"

I still shudder whenever I think that there was actually a chance of that page making it into a production environment and that management thought it was a perfectly acceptable design. Fortunately, the individual who developed that application was needed to fix a mainframe production problem, so I was assigned the task of making it work. I spent maybe a total of 10 minutes attempting to determine what was going wrong before deciding to try a somewhat more modern approach.

The initial concept was to make the client work for a living and to pad my resumé with a whole bunch of things that I had only played with in the past, such as the XMLHttpRequest object. The result was a separation between the presentation layer and the web server; it was easily ten times faster than any of their existing web pages. It could have been faster yet, but, unfortunately, I was unable to bypass the draconian rules that were in place regarding stored procedures. Stored procedures were, in a word, forbidden, being considered as both too confusing to write and of no use. Argh! I was one step away from a three-tiered architecture.

Regardless of the frustration that I felt at the time, I did achieve something wonderful by stumbling upon what was years later to be named Ajax. The shopping cart application was both similar to and different from the site's existing pages. The similarity to the existing applications was akin to the similarity between a soufflé and scrambled eggs. Many of the ingredients are the same; the real differences come from the technique used in putting the ingredients together. Probably the easiest way to illustrate this difference is to use a picture, such as the one shown in Figure 8-2.

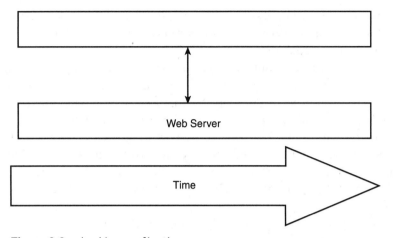

Figure 8-2   An Ajax application

Very different from Figure 8-1, isn't it? Instead of a page seemingly unloading and reloading forever, the single page communicates directly with the web server. This greatly reduces the need for the unload/reload cycle, which has a lot of overhead. Think of it in terms of a trip to the moon. What if the Apollo astronauts needed to bring every necessity with them? Air, water, food, and anything else that was required had to be trucked along with them from the Earth to the moon. Now imagine for a moment that the moon had a breathable atmosphere and McDonald's. All of a sudden, a trip to the moon becomes almost as easy as a trip to Florida.

Ajax does something similar by establishing an infrastructure on the client side. This infrastructure can be as simple or as complex as you want. In fact, now is a good time to see what goes into building our Ajax infrastructure. So queue the storm sound effects and put on the lab coat, and let's get our hands dirty.

8.2   XML

As you're aware, if only from the cameo appearance in Chapter 2, "Introducing Ajax," XML stands for eXtensible Markup Language, but other than the purpose of padding resumés, you're probably not aware of why XML is used so much. Basically, there are three main reasons for the popularity of XML, not including the air of mystery surrounding anything with an *X* in it. (Don't believe me about the air of mystery? What about *The X-Files* and *X-Men*?)

Literally tons has been written about XML—well, at least when hard copy is taken into account. As for electronic editions, I can't say because my notebook seems to weigh the same, regardless of the free space available. For this reason, I won't bore you with the history of XML and how it is the best thing since sliced bread, or how it cures baldness, because it would be either redundant or an outright lie. Anyone who has ever developed an application that uses XML knows that there is a good chance of pulling out one's own hair when attempting to explain XML to fellow developers who still haven't grasped the software equivalent of the concept of fire. However, I should at least hit the highlights and point out some of the more useful and obscure topics.

8.2.1   Well Formed

Alright, the concept that XML has to be well formed is not obscure, but it does fall well into the useful bucket. You'd be surprised at the number of times that I've had to explain the concept of "well formed" to a particular project leader with mainframe roots. Or, come to think of it, maybe you wouldn't. Let's just say that, like the Creature from the Black Lagoon, the XML challenged walk among us, and you don't even need to travel to the now-closed Marineland in Florida to find them. For this reason, it is time for XML 101.

An XML document is well formed when the follow conditions have been met:

☞ All opening tags either have a closing tag or are self-closing.

☞ All attributes have values.

☞ All the values for the attribute are enclosed in either quotes or apostrophes. I should point out, however, that they need to be consistent. This means no mixing and matching; if a quotation mark is used on the left side of a value, a quotation mark must be used on the right side.

☞ Beware of entities! Wow, that sounds spooky, doesn't it? Entities are special characters that need to be handled with respect because, without special handling, they can be mistaken as something other than content.

That was relatively easy, wasn't it? I recommend quoting it verbatim whenever it is necessary to explain the concept to a clueless project leader. But you need to remember to make your eyes big when saying "Beware of entities!" because they like that.

Alright, now that you're (hopefully) open to XML, the big question is, where does it come from? Well, that depends on both your web server and database environments; some have built-in methods for producing XML directly from the result of SQL SELECT statements or stored procedures. If your environment doesn't support that, there is always the possibility of "rolling" your own XML. Because XML is human readable—essentially, text—with a little work, it is possible to create XML, even where XML isn't supported.

Take, for example, MySQL. Although both Oracle and SQL Server can produce XML directly from a stored procedure, a little more effort is required to produce XML from MySQL. First, a stored function is required to build the individual nodes by concatenating the node name and value, as in Listing 8-1. Next, a function is needed that uses a cursor to step through the results of a query and build the XML using the aforementioned stored function. Listing 8-2 contains a sample stored procedure to do just that.

Listing 8-1 Concatenating a Stored Function

```
DELIMITER $$

DROP FUNCTION IF EXISTS `ajax`.`f_xmlNode`$$
CREATE FUNCTION `ajax`.`f_xmlNode`(
/*
  To produce the text representation of an XML node.
*/
  nodeName VARCHAR(255),  /*  XML node name                    */
  nodeValue LONGTEXT,  /*  XML node value                 */
  escape BOOLEAN  /*  Apply XML entity escaping        */
) RETURNS longtext
BEGIN
  DECLARE xml LONGTEXT;  /*  XML text node/value combination    */

  IF nodeValue IS NULL OR LENGTH(nodeValue) = 0 THEN
    SET xml = CONCAT('<',nodeName,' />');
  ELSE
    IF escape THEN
      SET xml =
CONCAT('<',nodeName,'>',REPLACE(REPLACE(REPLACE(REPLACE(REPLACE(nodeValue,
'&','&amp;'),'>','&gt;'),'<','&lt;'),'''','&apos;'),'"','&quot;'),'</',nod
eName,'>');
    ELSE
      SET xml = CONCAT('<',nodeName,'>',nodeValue,'</',nodeName,'>');
    END IF;
  END IF;

  RETURN xml;
END$$

DELIMITER ;
```

Listing 8-2 XML Producing a Stored Procedure

```
DELIMITER $$

DROP PROCEDURE IF EXISTS `ajax`.`itemSelectXML`$$
CREATE PROCEDURE `ajax`.`itemSelectXML`(
guildItemId INTEGER,
guildId INTEGER
)
```

```
BEGIN
  DECLARE done BOOLEAN DEFAULT FALSE;
  DECLARE xml LONGTEXT DEFAULT '<items>';
  DECLARE cGuildItemId INTEGER(6);
  DECLARE cGuildId INTEGER(6);
  DECLARE cGuildName VARCHAR(255);
  DECLARE cItemName VARCHAR(255);
  DECLARE cItemDescription VARCHAR(255);
  DECLARE cItemPrice DECIMAL(10,2);
  DECLARE itemCursor CURSOR FOR SELECT      b.guild_item_id,
                                            b.guild_id,
                                            g.guild_name,
                                            i.item_name,
                                            i.item_description,
                                            i.item_price
                               FROM         guild_item_bridge b
                               INNER JOIN guild g
                               ON           b.guild_id =
                                            g.guild_id
                               INNER JOIN item i
                               ON           b.item_id = i.item_id
                               WHERE        (guildItemId IS NULL
                                            OR guildItemId =
                                            b.guild_item_id)
                               AND          (guildId IS NULL
                                            OR guildId =
                                            b.guild_id);
  DECLARE CONTINUE HANDLER FOR SQLSTATE '02000' SET done = TRUE;

  OPEN itemCursor;

  FETCH itemCursor INTO cGuildItemId,
                        cGuildId,
                        cGuildName,
                        cItemName,
                        cItemDescription,
                        cItemPrice;

  REPEAT
    SET xml =
CONCAT(xml,'<item><guild_item_id>',cGuildItemId,'</guild_item_id>');
    SET xml = CONCAT(xml,'<guild_id>',cGuildId,'</guild_id>');
    SET xml =
CONCAT(xml,'<guild_item_name>',REPLACE(REPLACE(REPLACE(REPLACE(REPLACE(cGu
ildName,'&','&amp;'),'>','&gt;'),'<','&lt;'),'''','&apos;'),'"','&quot;'),
'</guild_item_name>');
    SET xml = CONCAT(xml,f_xmlString('item_name',cItemName));
    SET xml =
CONCAT(xml,'<item_description>',REPLACE(REPLACE(REPLACE(REPLACE(REPLACE(cI
temDescription,'&','&amp;'),'>','&gt;'),'<','&lt;'),'''','&apos;'),'"','&q
uot;'),'</item_description>');
```

continues

Listing 8-2   continued

```
   SET xml =
CONCAT(xml,'<item_price>',cItemPrice,'</item_price></item>');

   FETCH itemCursor INTO cGuildItemId,
                         cGuildId,
                         cGuildName,
                         cItemName,
                         cItemDescription,
                         cItemPrice;
  UNTIL done END REPEAT;

  SET xml = CONCAT(xml,'</items>');

  SELECT xml;

  CLOSE itemCursor;
END$$

DELIMITER ;
```

Here's how it works: The stored procedure shown in listing 8-2 retrieves the result of a query, builds an XML string containing the opening root element, and then performs the following steps for each row retrieved:

1. If the item is numeric, concatenate it, wrapped in the appropriate XML tags, to the XML string.
2. If the item is alpha or alphanumeric, the stored function shown in Listing 8-1 is invoked to handle any entities and wrap the information in appropriate XML tags. The result of this stored function is then concatenated to the XML string.

After all the rows have been processed, the closing root element is appended to the XML string and the process is complete. Now that we have a reliable source of XML, let's examine how we can use it in a web browser.

8.2.2   Data Islands for Internet Explorer

The official party line about XML Data Islands is that they are a "Microsoft-only" technology and, therefore, will not work with any other browser. Yeah, right. However, before altering the fabric of reality as only a mad scientist can, let's take a closer look at what XML data islands are and how they work.

As foreboding as the term *XML Data Island* is, according to the official definition, it is nothing more than XML embedded somewhere in an HTML document. Not too bad—sounds about as scary as a bowl of goldfish. In fact, Listing 8-3 is a basic HTML page with XML embedded smack in the middle of it, with Figure 8-3 showing what it looks like in Microsoft Internet Explorer.

Listing 8-3   HTML with Embedded XML

```html
<html>
  <head>
    <title>XML Data Island Test</title>
  </head>
  <body>
    <xml id="di">
      <states>
        <state>
            <abbreviation>NJ</abbreviation>
          <name>New Jersey</name>
          </state>
          <state>
            <abbreviation>NY</abbreviation>
            <name>New York</name>
          </state>
          <state>
            <abbreviation>PA</abbreviation>
            <name>Pennsylvania</name>
          </state>
        </states>
      </xml>
      <b>XML Data Island Test</b>
  </body>
</html>
```

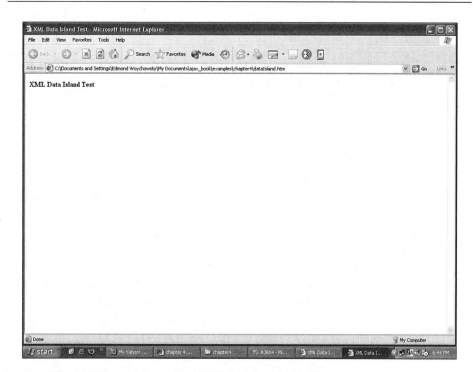

Figure 8-3   HTML with embedded XML in Internet Explorer

Piece of cake, isn't it? Right up to the point that somebody opens it in Firefox, as Figure 8-4 illustrates.

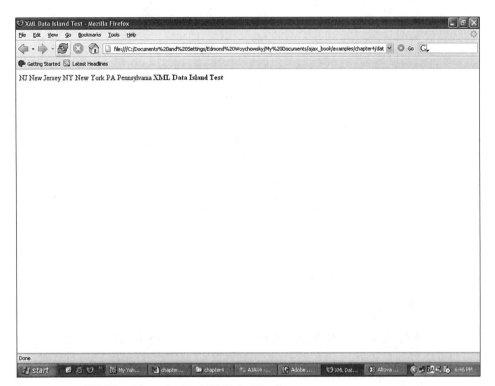

Figure 8-4   HTML with embedded XML in Firefox

8.2.3   Data Islands for All!

Right about now, if you're anything like me, you're leaning a little bit toward despair. And why not? A bunch of ugly stuff is embedded in the middle of the web page, but remember, just because something is there does not mean it has to be visible. Multiple methods exist for hiding information on a web page, such as sticking it in the value of a hidden input box or Cascading Style Sheets (CSS), or using white-out.

Hmm, thinking about it, I'd ignore the first option because, although it will work, it will also be extremely cumbersome. I'd also ignore the third option as being either too permanent or just plain stupid. This leaves only the second option, Cascading Style Sheets.

The great part about using CSS is that not only is it an elegant solution, but it is also cross-browser friendly. So let's make a minor modification to the previous web page—namely, adding the style sheet shown in Listing 8-4, and take another look at the page (see Figure 8-5).

Listing 8-4   CSS to Hide XML

```
xml
{
display: none;
font-size: 0px
}
```

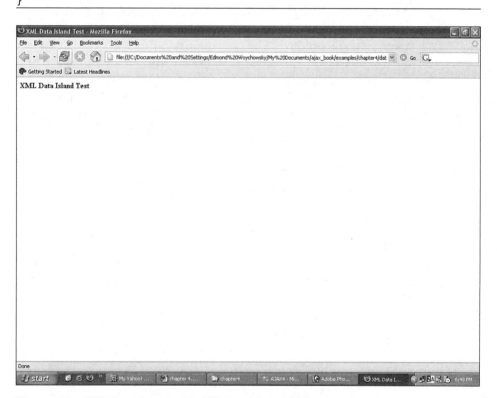

Figure 8-5   HTML with embedded XML with CSS in Firefox

Okay, now that we have both the XML Data Island and a workable cloaking device for said XML Data Island, we still need a way to use it. Because with the exception of a "Doomsday Device," something that isn't being used is essentially useless, and I'm pretty sure that demanding "One million dollars in uncut flawless diamonds or I use my XML Data Island" wouldn't get much of a response—unless, of course, you count the nice people with the butterfly nets and jackets with wrap-around sleeves as a response.

The big question is, now that we have it, how do we use it? This is a good although somewhat broad question that, unfortunately, ignores some of the technical issues yet to be addressed. Perhaps it would be better to break the single question into two separate questions—for instance, "Now that we have an XML data island, how do we find it on the page?" and "How can it be incorporated into the page?"

The first one is easy. Remember the transverse function from Chapter 5, "Ajax Using HTML and JavaScript"? It was the one that essentially walked through the HTML DOM. Something similar would work. I, however, prefer the more direct route and would use either the `getElementById` method or the `getElementsByName` method. The `getElementById` method, which we've used in earlier examples, has the advantage of returning a single object. However, if for some unforeseen reason the object doesn't exist, an error will be thrown. On the other hand, the `getElementsByName` method returns an array consisting of those nodes with a particular name. This requires a little more typing than the other method. The syntax for both of these methods is shown here:

```
document.getElementById('xmldi')

document.getElementsByTagName('xml')
```

The next question is, "How can it be incorporated into the page?" As with the previous question, there are several different means to an end. For instance, if you're interested in only replacing existing XHTML objects with new XHTML objects, you can use `getElementById`, as the page in Listing 8-5 shows.

Listing 8-5   Using `getElementById`

```
<html>
    <head>
        <title>XML Data Island Test - Version 2</title>
        <style type="text/css">
xml
{
    display: none;
    font-size: 0px
}
        </style>
        <script language="javascript">
/*
    Replace one input textbox with another one from an XML
    data island.  In addition, the button that invoked this
```

```
    function is hidden.
*/
function doReplace() {
     document.getElementById('here').innerHTML =
document.getElementById('xmldi').innerHTML;
     document.getElementById('replace').style.display = 'none';
}
            </script>
        </head>
        <body>
            <xml id="xmldi">
                    <input type="text" id="new" name="new"
value="Hello, World!" />
            </xml>
            <b>XML Data Island Test - Version 2</b>
            <br />
            <div id="here">
                    <input type="text" id="old" name="old"
value="Goodbye, cruel world!" />
            </div>
            <br />
            <input type="button" id="replace" name="replace"
 value="Replace" onclick="doReplace()" />
        </body>
</html>
```

As neat and nifty as this is, essentially, it is only a variation on the DHTML methods that have been used for the last several years. To turn heads, what is needed is a way to update the page's content dynamically. Fortunately, a number of approaches can be taken to accomplish this task, which we cover later. The only question is how much of a tolerance you have for "mad scientist stuff."

8.2.4 Binding

To those of you with impure thoughts about this heading, I'd like to say, "Shame on you!" It simply refers to the act of binding XML to a web page's HTML. Get your minds out of the gutter. If you've never used this technique, there are a number of reasons to consider using it. First, when you get the syntax down, it is relatively easy to understand. Another reason is that, for all of its power, it is quite compact, yet it separates content from presentation. Finally, it sounds really kinky, and how often do we get to use something that sounds kinky?

Binding XML to HTML is usually considered a Microsoft Internet Explorer–only kind of thing. In Internet Explorer, each bound HTML element identifies both the XML data island's ID and the individual node that is being bound, as shown in Listing 8-6.

Listing 8 -6   XML Binding in Internet Explorer

```
<html>
    <head>
            <title>XML Data Island Test</title>
            <style type="text/css">
xml
{
    display: none;
    font-size: 0px
}
            </style>
    </head>
    <body>
            <xml id="xmlDI">
                <plugh>
                  <magic>xyzzy</magic>
                </plugh>
            </xml>
            <b>XML Data Island Test</b>
            <br />
            <input type="text" name="test" datasrc="#xmlDI"
datafld="magic" value="" />
    </body>
</html>
```

Each HTML tag to be bound, the input tags in the example above, has both a datasrc to identify the XML Data Island and a datafld that identifies the specific node. It is important to realize that changes made to the contents of the text box are reflected in the XML Data Island itself. So type plover over xyzzy, and the text in the magic node is plover. This is a fine, although somewhat flakey, solution if the visitor is using Microsoft Internet Explorer, but what if they're using Firefox?

The simple answer is to fake it. Using client-side JavaScript, a number of functions add the same functionality to Firefox, right down to using the same tags. The interesting thing about most of these tools is that they're usually more stable than Internet Explorer's own built-in binding. In an effort to work around IE's flakey-ness, I wrote the page shown in Listing 8-7. In addition, I renamed the datasrc attribute xmldi and the datafld attribute xmlnode to avoid having Internet Explorer use its own binding.

Listing 8-7   Cross-Browser XML Binding

```
<html>
    <head>
            <title>XML Data Island Test</title>
            <style type="text/css">
xml
```

```
    {
        display: none;
        font-size: 0px
    }
                </style>
                <script language="JavaScript">
    try {
      var x = new DOMParser();
      var _IE = false;
    }
    catch(e) { var _IE = true; };

    /*
        Handle the logic necessary to bind HTML elements to XML
        nodes.  Note that in some instances this binding is a two-way
        street.  For example, if the value in a text box should
        change the corresponding value in the XML data island will
        also change.
    */
    function _bind() {
      if(arguments.length == 0) {
        doBind(document.body.getElementsByTagName('div'));
        doBind(document.body.getElementsByTagName('input'));
        doBind(document.body.getElementsByTagName('select'));
        doBind(document.body.getElementsByTagName('span'));
        doBind(document.body.getElementsByTagName('textarea'));
      } else {
        applyChange(arguments[0],arguments[1]);
        _bind();                                    //  Re-bind
      }

      /*
          To handle data-binds for specific nodes based upon HTML
          element type and browser type.
      */
      function doBind(objects) {
        var strTag;                     //   HTML tag
        var strDI;                      //   XML data island id
        var strNode;                    //   XML node name
        var strValue;                   //   XML node value

        for(var i=0;i < objects.length;i++) {
          strTag = objects[i].tagName;
          strDI = objects[i].getAttribute('xmldi');
          strNode = objects[i].getAttribute('xmlnode');

          if(_IE)
            strValue =
document.getElementById(strDI).XMLDocument.selectNodes('//' +
strNode).item(i).text;
          else
```

continues

Listing 8-7   continued

```
            strValue =
document.getElementById(strDI).getElementsByTagName(strNode)[i].innerHTML;

        switch(strTag) {
          case('DIV'):
          case('SPAN'):
              objects[i].innerHTML = strValue;

              break;
          case('INPUT'):
              switch(objects[i].type) {
                  case('text'):
                  case('hidden'):
                  case('password'):
                      objects[i].value = strValue;
                      objects[i].onchange = new Function("_bind(this," +
i.toString() + ")");

                      break;
                  case('checkbox'):
                      if(objects[i].value == strValue)
                          objects[i].checked = true;
                      else
                          objects[i].checked = false;

                      objects[i].onclick = new Function("_bind(this," +
i.toString() + ")");

                      break;
                  case('radio'):
                      if(_IE)
                          strValue =
document.getElementById(strDI).XMLDocument.selectNodes('//' +
strNode).item(0).text;
                      else
                          strValue =
document.getElementById(strDI).getElementsByTagName(strNode)[0].innerHTML;

                      if(objects[i].value == strValue)
                          objects[i].checked = true;
                      else
                          objects[i].checked = false;

                      objects[i].onclick = new Function("_bind(this,0)");

                      break;
              }

              break;
          case('SELECT'):
          case('TEXTAREA'):
              objects[i].value = strValue;
```

```
                objects[i].onchange = new Function("_bind(this," +
        i.toString() + ")");

                break;
            }
        }
    }

    /*
        To handle changes to the bound HTML elements and apply
        those changes to the appropriate XML node.
    */
    function applyChange(obj,index) {
      var strDI = obj.getAttribute('xmldi');
      var strNode = obj.getAttribute('xmlnode');
      var strValue = obj.value;

      if(obj.type == 'checkbox')
          if(obj.checked)
              strValue = obj.value;
          else
              strValue = '';

      if(_IE)
          document.getElementById(strDI).XMLDocument.selectNodes('//' +
strNode).item(index).text = strValue;
      else

document.getElementById(strDI).getElementsByTagName(strNode)[index].innerH
TML = strValue;
      }
}
                </script>
        </head>
        <body onload="_bind()">
            <xml id="xmlDI">
                <a>
                <b>
                    <c>one</c>
                </b>
                <b>
                    <c>two</c>
                </b>
                <b>
                    <c>three</c>
                </b>
            </a>
            </xml>
            <b>XML Data Island Test</b>
            <br />
            <div xmldi="xmlDI" xmlnode="c"></div>
            <br />
```

continues

Listing 8-7   continued

```
        <div xmldi="xmlDI" xmlnode="c"></div>
        <br />
        <div xmldi="xmlDI" xmlnode="c"></div>
        <br />
        <input type="text" xmldi="xmlDI" xmlnode="c" value="" />
        <br />
        <input type="text" xmldi="xmlDI" xmlnode="c" value="" />
        <br />
        <input type="text" xmldi="xmlDI" xmlnode="c" value="" />
        <br />
    </body>
</html>
```

The bind() function retrieves all the div, input, select, span, and textarea elements using the DOM. Next, the ID of the data island and the elements' names are retrieved from HTML using the xmldi and xmlnode attributes. The XML node values are then copied to the HTML. Finally, an event handler is set for each HTML element affected. The purpose of this event handler is to update the XML when the visitor modifies the HTML value, for instance, by changing the value in an input box.

8.3   THE XMLHTTPREQUEST OBJECT

As interesting as the previous section may have been, remember that it was only an appetizer. Now the time has come for the entrée: the XMLHttpRequest object. If you've never used the XMLHttpRequest object, it is, as described previously, an object that gives web browsers the capability to communicate directly with the server, without the unload/reload cycle—or "blink," as the peasants call it.

8.3.1   Avoiding the Unload/Reload Cycle

The best analogy that I can think of to the XMLHttpRequest object is the transporter from any of the various incarnations of *Star Trek*. With the transporter, only the personnel essential to a particular mission need go down to the planet's surface. The alternative would be to either land the Starship, if it were capable of planetary landings, or send a shuttlecraft. In either case, there would be a lot of unnecessary equipment and personnel being moved about at great expense, as opposed to the "move only what you need" philosophy of the transporter.

The XMLHttpRequest object is the web equivalent of the transporter. Why transmit an entire web page when all that is really needed is the data itself?

The HTML and JavaScript for presentation are already there, so just change the data and we're good to go. I should point out that although the data being beamed from the server to the client doesn't necessarily have to be XML, in all these examples, it is XML.

8.3.2   Browser Differences

Before describing the actual syntax necessary to use XMLHTTP, I recommend that you sit down because I don't want to shock you or anything. Sitting down? Good. The syntax used for the XMLHttpRequest object is different in Microsoft Internet Explorer than from every other browser that supports it. In fact, from Microsoft's perspective, somewhere on the surface of Charon, not even the World Wide Web Consortium got it right. As a matter of fact, they made exactly the same mistake as Firefox. Fortunately, because the error is consistent among all non–Internet Explorer browsers all that is necessary is to code for IE and everybody else. Mmm, I wonder if maybe…nah!

The first thing is to create an instance of the XMLHttpRequest object in the following manner:

```
try {

   var x = new DOMParser();
   var _IE = false;

}

catch(e) { var _IE = true; };
var _XMLHTTP;

if(_IE)
    _XMLHTTP = new ActiveXObject('Microsoft.XMLHTTP');
else
    _XMLHTTP = new XMLHttpRequest();
```

Before proceeding any further, a couple of decisions must be made that involve just how we'd like the page to work.

Synchronous or asynchronous?

GET or POST?

The choice of synchronous or asynchronous is a relatively big one, but it boils down to waiting for a response or being notified when there is a response. As long as you remember to specify a state change handler for responses to asynchronous requests, things should work. The GET or POST question is also an important decision. Fortunately, it is the same decision that has been around ever since the introduction of HTML forms, so as long as we follow the same rules, everything will be alright.

Let's say, for instance, that we want to retrieve the XML file of states and provinces shown in Listing 8-8 from the server. The first thing that is needed is to determine the browser—basically, Microsoft Internet Explorer and everyone else. The next task is to create an instance of the XMLHttpRequest object, followed by setting the event handler, for asynchronous requests. Finally, the XMLHttpRequest object is opened with three parameters:

☞ GET or POST

☞ The URL for the request

☞ Either true for asynchronous or false for synchronous

However, you must remember one thing about coding a state change handler. It is a state *change* handler, not an "I'm *finished*" handler. There are other states than "complete"; we're interested in 4, which indicates that the request is complete. Listing 8-9 shows a page that retrieves the XML from Listing 8-8, storing it in an XML Data Island and binding it for display purposes.

Listing 8-8   Sample XML Document

```
<states>
     <state>
          <state_abbreviation>AB</state_abbreviation>
          <state_name>Alberta</state_name>
          <country_id>3</country_id>
     </state>
     <state>
          <state_abbreviation>AK</state_abbreviation>
          <state_name>Alaska</state_name>
          <country_id>1</country_id>
     </state>
     <state>
          <state_abbreviation>AL</state_abbreviation>
          <state_name>Alabama</state_name>
          <country_id>1</country_id>
     </state>
     <state>
          <state_abbreviation>AR</state_abbreviation>
          <state_name>Arkansas</state_name>
          <country_id>1</country_id>
     </state>
     <state>
          <state_abbreviation>AS</state_abbreviation>
          <state_name>American Samoa</state_name>
          <country_id>1</country_id>
     </state>
     <state>
          <state_abbreviation>AZ</state_abbreviation>
          <state_name>Arizona</state_name>
          <country_id>1</country_id>
     </state>
</states>
```

Listing 8-9   HTML Document Using an XML Data Island

```
<html>
    <head>
            <title>XML Data Island Test</title>
            <style type="text/css">
xml
{
     display: none;
     font-size: 0px
}
            </style>
            <script language="JavaScript">
try {
  var x = new DOMParser();
  var _IE = false;
}
catch(e) { var _IE = true; };
var _URL = 'http://localhost/chapter4/states.xml';
var _XMLHTTP;

/*
    Perform page initialization.
*/
function initialize() {
    if(_IE)
        _XMLHTTP = new ActiveXObject('Microsoft.XMLHTTP');
    else
        _XMLHTTP = new XMLHttpRequest();

    _XMLHTTP.onreadystatechange = stateChangeHandler;

    _XMLHTTP.open('GET',_URL,true);     // Asynchronous (true)
    _XMLHTTP.send(null);
}

/*
    Handle the asynchronous response to a XMLHttpRequest,
    including the loading of the XML Data Island.
*/
function stateChangeHandler() {
  if(_XMLHTTP.readyState == 4) {
    var strHTML = '';
    var nodeCount;

    if(_IE) {

document.getElementById('xmlDI').XMLDocument.load(_XMLHTTP.responseXML);
      nodeCount =
document.getElementById('xmlDI').XMLDocument.getElementsByTagName('state_n
ame').length;
```

continues

Listing 8-9   continued

```
    } else {
      document.getElementById('xmlDI').innerHTML = _XMLHTTP.responseText;
      nodeCount = document.body.getElementsByTagName('state_name').length;
    }

      try {
          _XMLHTTP.close();                    //  Close XMLHttpRequest
      }
      catch(e) {}

      for(var i=0;i < nodeCount;i++)
        strHTML += '<div xmldi="xmlDI" xmlnode="state_name"></div>';

      document.getElementById('show').innerHTML = strHTML;

      _bind();                                 //  Bind XML and HTML
  }
}

/*
   Handle the logic necessary to bind HTML elements to XML
   nodes.  Note that in some instances this binding is a two-way
   street.  For example, if the value in a text box should
   change the corresponding value in the XML data island will
   also change.
*/
function _bind() {
  if(arguments.length == 0) {
    doBind(document.body.getElementsByTagName('div'));
    doBind(document.body.getElementsByTagName('input'));
    doBind(document.body.getElementsByTagName('select'));
    doBind(document.body.getElementsByTagName('span'));
    doBind(document.body.getElementsByTagName('textarea'));
  } else {
    applyChange(arguments[0],arguments[1]);
    _bind();                                   //  Re-bind
  }

  /*
     To handle data-binds for specific nodes based upon HTML
     element type and browser type.
  */
  function doBind(objects) {
    var strTag;                      //  HTML tag
    var strDI;                       //  XML data island id
    var strNode;                     //  XML node name
    var strValue;                    //  XML node value

    for(var i=0;i < objects.length;i++) {
      strTag = objects[i].tagName;
      strDI = objects[i].getAttribute('xmldi');
      strNode = objects[i].getAttribute('xmlnode');
```

```
        if(strDI != null && strNode != null) {
          if(_IE)
              strValue =
document.getElementById(strDI).XMLDocument.selectNodes('//' +
strNode).item(i).text;
          else
              strValue =
document.getElementById(strDI).getElementsByTagName(strNode)[i].innerHTML;

        switch(strTag) {
            case('DIV'):
            case('SPAN'):
                objects[i].innerHTML = strValue;

                break;
            case('INPUT'):
                switch(objects[i].type) {
                    case('text'):
                    case('hidden'):
                    case('password'):
                        objects[i].value = strValue;
                        objects[i].onchange = new Function("_bind(this," +
i.toString() + ")");

                        break;
                    case('checkbox'):
                        if(objects[i].value == strValue)
                            objects[i].checked = true;
                        else
                            objects[i].checked = false;

                        objects[i].onclick = new Function("_bind(this," +
i.toString() + ")");

                        break;
                    case('radio'):
                        if(_IE)
                            strValue =
document.getElementById(strDI).XMLDocument.selectNodes('//' +
strNode).item(0).text;
                        else
                            strValue =
document.getElementById(strDI).getElementsByTagName(strNode)[0].innerHTML;

                        if(objects[i].value == strValue)
                            objects[i].checked = true;
                        else
                            objects[i].checked = false;

                        objects[i].onclick = new
Function("_bind(this,0)");
```

continues

Listing 8-9   continued

```
                          break;
                  }

                  break;
              case('SELECT'):
              case('TEXTAREA'):
                  objects[i].value = strValue;
                  objects[i].onchange = new Function("_bind(this," +
i.toString() + ")");

                  break;
          }
      }
    }
  }

  /*
      To handle changes to the bound HTML elements and apply
      those changes to the appropriate XML node.
  */
  function applyChange(obj,index) {
    var strDI = obj.getAttribute('xmldi');
    var strNode = obj.getAttribute('xmlnode');
    var strValue = obj.value;

    if(obj.type == 'checkbox')
        if(obj.checked)
            strValue = obj.value;
        else
            strValue = '';

    if(_IE)
        document.getElementById(strDI).XMLDocument.selectNodes('//' +
strNode).item(index).text = strValue;
    else

document.getElementById(strDI).getElementsByTagName(strNode)[index].
innerHTML = strValue;
  }
}
            </script>
        </head>
        <body onload="initialize()">
              <xml id="xmlDI">
              </xml>
              <b>XML Data Island Test</b>
              <br />
              <div id="show"></div>
        </body>
</html>
```

Essentially, the JavaScript in Listing 8-9 makes an asynchronous XML-HTTP request. This entails, beyond the usual "which browser is it?" stuff, creating an instance of the XMLHttpRequest object, setting an event handler for the response, and making the request using the request type, the URL, and true for asynchronous. The state change handler, er, handles the response from the server. If you look closely, you'll see a condition testing the readyState property to see if it is equal to 4, which is complete. The reason for testing the readyState property is that this handler fires multiple times for different reasons, ranging from the equivalent of "I'm sitting here" to "Hey, I'm getting a response."

The previous example illustrated how to use the XMLHttpRequest object to asynchronously obtain an XML document from a file located on the server. Think of it as something along the lines of a proof of concept because the odds are against the XML document needed sitting in a folder on the web server. Instead, there will probably be some script version of Igor sitting around watching Oprah, waiting for some real work to do.

Several different methods exist for getting data to and from our virtual Igor, ranging from a simple custom approach to slightly more complex XML-based standards. One of the standards that can be used to get the virtual Igor moving is called XML Remote Procedure Calling, or XML-RPC, for short. In a nutshell, XML-RPC is a World Wide Web Consortium Recommendation that describes a request/response protocol. A request is posted to the web server, and the web server acts upon the request and returns a response. This entire process might sound rather complex, but it really isn't any more difficult than what we've already accomplished. The only differences are that instead of a GET, we'll be doing a POST, and the request needs to be in XML, as shown in Listing 8-10 and the response in Listing 8-11.

Listing 8-10   XML-RPC Request

```
<?xml version="1.0"?>
<methodCall>
      <methodName>igor.getGuildName</methodName>
      <params>
           <param>
                   <value>
                           <int>1</int>
                   </value>
           </param>
      </params>
</methodCall>
```

Listing 8-11   XML-RPC Response

```
<?xml version="1.0"?>
<methodResponse>
    <params>
        <param>
            <value>
                <string>Mad Scientist</string>
            </value>
        </param>
    </params>
</methodResponse>
```

As you've probably deduced from this, the structure of the XML document goes along the lines of methodCall, params, param, value, and, finally,
data type (integer, in this instance). The rule for the structure goes along the
lines of one methodResponse, one params, and at least one param. In addition,
each param can have only one value—no more, no less. Values, in turn, have a
single node that both describes and holds the data. Table 8-1 shows the valid
data types for XML-RPC.

Table 8-1   XML-RPC Data Types

Type	Description
int	4-byte signed integer
i4	4-byte signed integer
boolean	True = 1 and false = 0
sting	Character string
double	Double-precision floating point
dateTime.iso8601	Date/time
base64	Base 64 binary

Of course, communicating a single item of information as shown is pretty
rare. More common are more complex data structures, such as arrays or the
record-line structs. Both arrays and structs work pretty much along the same
lines as the simpler example earlier. Listing 8-12 shows an example of an
array, and Listing 8-13 shows an example of a struct.

Listing 8-12   XML-RPC Array

```
<?xml version="1.0"?>
<array>
    <data>
        <value>
```

```
                        <int>5</i4>
            </value>
            <value>
                    <string>Lab Coat</string>
            </value>
            <value>
                    <double>29.95</double>
            </value>
        </data>
</array>
```

Listing 8-13   XML-RPC Struct

```
<?xml version="1.0"?>
<struct>
    <member>
            <name>name_last</name>
            <value>
                    <string>Woychowsky<//>
            </value>
    </member>
    <member>
            <name>name_first</name>
            <value>
                    <string>Edmond</string>
            </value>
    </member>
    <member>
            <name>purpose</name>
            <value>
                    <int>42</int>
            </value>
    </member>
</struct>
```

The array example shown is merely an elaboration of the earlier simple XML document, but the struct example is more complex. Along with specifying the parameter type and value, it specifies the name of the parameter. This might not seem like much, but it is useful in applications with so many parameters that it becomes difficult to keep their relative positions straight.

This leads us to the question, what does the response look like when the relative positions aren't kept straight? That's simple enough; a fault like the one in Listing 8-14 is returned.

Listing 8-14   XML-RPC Fault

```
<?xml version="1.0"?>
<methodResponse>
      <fault>
            <value>
                  <struct>
                        <member>
                              <name>faultCode</name>
                              <value>
                                    <int>86</int>
                              </value>
                        </member>
                        <member>
                              <name>faultString</name>
                              <value>
                                    <string>
                                          Invalid data type.
                                    </string>
                              </value>
                        </member>
                  </struct>
            </value>
      </fault>
</methodResponse>
```

Now that we know what the request looks like ordinarily, the next step is to modify the previous example, in which the XSLT was retrieved through the XMLHttpRequest object and a GET to use XML-RPC. This time, however, we skip the examples and progress directly to what is considered by some the protocol of choice when creating web services: SOAP.

8.3.3   Cleaning Up with SOAP

Other than being something for cleaning, SOAP is an acronym for Simple Object Access Protocol, a protocol used to communicate between web browsers and web servers. SOAP is probably one of the more difficult subjects to research on the web, if for no other reason than the multiple websites that deal with the original SOAP. Nevertheless, when searching, you eventually will obtain the desired results and discover that SOAP is nothing more than a wrapper for XML.

XML-RPC was designed to provide a standard structure. However, with SOAP, a slightly different approach was used. Instead of the strict params-param-value used by XML-RPC, which rigidly ties the information with the wrapper, SOAP uses a more flexible envelope method. As with a physical envelope, a SOAP envelope both identifies the recipient and contains the message

within. The only real difference between a SOAP envelope and a physical
envelope is that the message contained by a SOAP envelope must be well
formed, like the one shown in Listing 8-15.

Listing 8-15   SOAP Request

```xml
<?xml version="1.0" encoding="utf-8"?>
<soap:Envelope xmlns:xsi="http://www.w3.org/2001/XMLSchema-instance"
xmlns:xsd="http://www.w3.org/2001/XMLSchema"
xmlns:soap="http://schemas.xmlsoap.org/soap/envelope/">
  <soap:Body>
    <getItems xmlns="http://tempuri.org/">
      <guild_item_id>string</guild_item_id>
      <guild_id>string</guild_id>
    </getItems>
  </soap:Body>
</soap:Envelope>
```

As with the XML-RPC example, there are two possible responses to a
SOAP request. Either the web service worked and returned a SOAP response,
as shown in Listing 8-16, or some kind of error occurred, and the request failed
and a SOAP fault was returned. Listing 8-17 contains an example of a SOAP
fault.

Listing 8-16   SOAP Response

```xml
<?xml version="1.0" encoding="utf-8"?>
<soap:Envelope xmlns:xsi="http://www.w3.org/2001/XMLSchema-instance"
xmlns:xsd="http://www.w3.org/2001/XMLSchema"
xmlns:soap="http://schemas.xmlsoap.org/soap/envelope/">
  <soap:Body>
    <getItemsResponse xmlns="http://tempuri.org/">
      <getItemsResult>xml</getItemsResult>
    </getItemsResponse>
  </soap:Body>
</soap:Envelope>
```

Listing 8-17   SOAP Fault

```xml
<soap:Envelope xmlns:xsi="http://www.w3.org/2001/XMLSchema-
instance"xmlns:xsd="http://www.w3.org/2001/XMLSchema"xmlns:soap="http://sc
hemas.xmlsoap.org/soap/envelope/">
  <soap:Body>
    <soap:Fault>
      <faultcode>soap:MustUnderstand</faultcode>
      <faultstring>Mandatory Header error.</faultstring>
      <faultactor>http://localhost/AJAX4/chapter4.asmx</faultactor>
```

continues

Listing 8-17   continued

```
    <detail>Web Service coffee break.</detail>
  </soap:Fault>
 </soap:Body>
</soap:Envelope>
```

8.4   A PROBLEM REVISITED

Now that we have covered some of the necessary background material for using XML, SOAP, and XMLHTTP, let's apply it to the e-commerce site. As you might recall, the objective of the site is to provide materials for the often-over-looked market of mad scientists, alchemists, and sorcerers. In Chapter 5, we created pages using a primitive ancestor of Ajax; now let's give it a shot using the real thing. This doesn't mean that it is entirely necessary to completely abandon hidden frames. If you decide that you need them, then by all means, use them; we abandon hidden frames from here on, however.

In addition, we change server-side languages from PHP to C#. The reason for this change isn't that PHP can't be used to develop web services; it is actually the fact that I'm more comfortable using C# for developing web services. To those of you who question the presence of C# in an open source book, I have one word for you: Mono.

No, not the Mono that everybody came down with in high school, college, or, in my case, Bell Labs—the Mono that is the open source implementation of the .NET Framework. You haven't lived until you've seen a C# application running under Linux. It doesn't feel wrong; it feels more like when Lieutenant Commander Worf said: "Assimilate this!" in *Star Trek First Contact*.

Listing 8-18 contains the web service that will handle the server-side requirements for the remainder of this chapter.

Listing 8-18   A Web Service

```
using System;
using System.Collections;
using System.ComponentModel;
using System.Data;
using System.Diagnostics;
using System.IO;
using System.Web;
using System.Web.Services;
using System.Web.Services.Protocols;
using System.Xml;
using MySql.Data.MySqlClient;
using MySql.Data.Types;
```

```
namespace AJAX
{
  /// <summary>
  /// Summary description for msas.
  /// </summary>
  public class msas : System.Web.Services.WebService
  {
    const string CONNECTION_STRING =
      "Persist Security
Info=False;database=ajax;server=localhost;username=root;password=wyvern";

    public msas()
    {
      InitializeComponent();
    }

    #region Component Designer generated code

    //Required by the Web Services Designer
    private IContainer components = null;

    /// <summary>
    /// Required method for Designer support - do not modify
    /// the contents of this method with the code editor.
    /// </summary>
    private void InitializeComponent()
    {
    }

    /// <summary>
    /// Clean up any resources being used.
    /// </summary>
    protected override void Dispose( bool disposing )
    {
      if(disposing && components != null)
      {
        components.Dispose();
      }
      base.Dispose(disposing);
    }

    #endregion

    [WebMethod]
    public XmlDocument getState(string state_abbreviation)
    {
      MySqlConnection connection =
      new MySqlConnection(CONNECTION_STRING);
      MySqlDataAdapter adapter = new MySqlDataAdapter();
      DataSet dataSet = new DataSet();
      XmlDocument xml = new XmlDocument();
```

continues

Listing 8-18   continued

```
    string query = "CALL stateSelect(NULL)";

    if(state_abbreviation.Length != 0)
      query = "CALL stateSelect('" + state_abbreviation + "')";

    adapter.SelectCommand =
    new MySqlCommand(query, connection);
    adapter.Fill(dataSet);
    xml.LoadXml(dataSet.GetXml());

    connection.Close();

    return(xml);
  }

  [WebMethod]
  public XmlDocument getXML(string name)
  {
    XmlDocument xml = new XmlDocument();

    try
    {
      xml.Load(Server.MapPath(name));
    }
    catch(Exception e)
    {
      StringWriter writer = new StringWriter();
      Server.UrlEncode(name, writer);
      String encodedName = writer.ToString();
      XmlNode node =
      xml.CreateNode(XmlNodeType.CDATA,"detail","");

      node.Value = encodedName;

      throw(new
SoapException(e.Message,SoapException.ClientFaultCode,"",node));
    }

    return(xml);
  }

  [WebMethod]
  public XmlDocument getItems(string guild_item_id,string guild_id)
  {
    MySqlConnection connection =
    new MySqlConnection(CONNECTION_STRING);
    MySqlDataAdapter adapter = new MySqlDataAdapter();
    DataSet dataSet = new DataSet();
    XmlDocument xml = new XmlDocument();
    string query;

    if(guild_item_id.Length == 0)
```

```
        if(guild_id.Length == 0)
          query = "CALL itemSelect(NULL,NULL)";
        else
          query = "CALL itemSelect(NULL," + guild_id + ")";
      else
        if(guild_id.Length == 0)
          query = "CALL itemSelect(" + guild_item_id + ",NULL)";
        else
          query = "CALL itemSelect(" + guild_item_id + "," + guild_id +
")";

      adapter.SelectCommand =
      new MySqlCommand(query, connection);
      adapter.Fill(dataSet);
      xml.LoadXml(dataSet.GetXml());

      connection.Close();

      return(xml);
    }
  }
}
```

I'd like to point out that the web service shown handles several different jobs. First, if necessary, it performs database queries against a MySQL database. Immediately following the queries, it builds the XHTML required to display the page; finally, it creates a node that contains a line of JavaScript. All this is then incorporated into a single XML document, which is then sent to the client. Although this might seem a wee bit strange, there is a method to my madness. As with the hidden frames example, there will be a single HTML document that also has several different jobs to perform.

8.5 TABULAR INFORMATION AND FORMS

With the server side taken care of, there are three ways to proceed with developing on the client side. The first is to continue developing the way that we've been developing, hand-coding every function. Although this would give us a really good understanding of how the application works, it would take forever to develop anything useful.

The second approach is to get online and find a suitable Ajax library, download it, and proceed with developing. Currently, quite a number of them are out there, such as Sarissa and JSON (pronounced "Jason"). (However, if memory serves, Jason was the leader or the Argonauts, whereas Ajax was a hero of the Trojan War.)

The third possibility is to write our own Ajax library—or, rather, use one that I've already written. This approach is useful for several reasons, the first being that I'll (hopefully) know exactly how the library works. The second reason is that I can dissect them in a later chapter so that we'll know exactly how they work. The final reason is that it will help to pad the page count—eh, I mean, to increase the depth of these examples. Table 8-2 briefly describes the classes in the library, along with their associated methods and properties.

Table 8-2   Ajax Library Classes

Name	Parent Class	Type	Description
XMLHttpRequest	—	Class	Constructor
action	XMLHttpRequest	Property	GET, POST, or HEAD
asynchronous	XMLHttpRequest	Property	true or false
envelope	XMLHttpRequest	Property	SOAP envelope
readyState	XMLHttpRequest	Method	Returns the document readyState
getResponseHeader	XMLHttpRequest	Method	Returns a single HTTP response header
getAllResponseHeaders	XMLHttpRequest	Method	Returns all HTTP response headers
responseText	XMLHttpRequest	Method	Returns the SOAP response as text
responseXML	XMLHttpRequest	Method	Returns the SOAP response as an XML document
stateChangeHandler	XMLHttpRequest	Method	Dummy state change handler
setRequestHeader	XMLHttpRequest	Method	Sets an HTTP response header
removeRequestHeader	XMLHttpRequest	Method	Removes a previously set HTTP response header
Send	XMLHttpRequest	Method	Sends the XMLHttpRequest
Cache	—	Class	Constructor
insert	Cache	Method	Inserts a name/value pair
retrieve	Cache	Method	Retrieves a value
purge	Cache	Method	Purges one or more name/value pairs

Name	Parent Class	Type	Description
names	Cache	Method	Returns an array of names
XMLDocument	—	Class	Constructor
Load	XMLDocument	Method	Loads an\ XML document
serialize	XMLDocument	Method	Serializes an XML document to text
DOMDocument	XMLDocument	Method	Returns an XML document
readyState	XMLDocument	Method	Returns the document readyState
setRequestHeader	XMLDocument	Method	Sets an HTTP response header
getResponseHeader	XMLDocument	Method	Returns a single HTTP response header
getAllResponseHeaders	XMLDocument	Method	Returns all HTTP response headers
setEnvelope	XMLDocument	Method	Sets the envelope for an XMLHttpRequest
selectNodes	XMLDocument	Method	Returns an array of XML nodes
SOAPEnvelope	—	Class	Constructor
envelope	SOAPEnvelope	Method	SOAP envelope

Now that the foundations of the application architecture have been covered, albeit lightly, this is a good time to see what the HTML page built upon that architecture looks like. Figure 8-6 shows what it looks like in a browser, and Listing 8-19 shows the HTML and JavaScript.

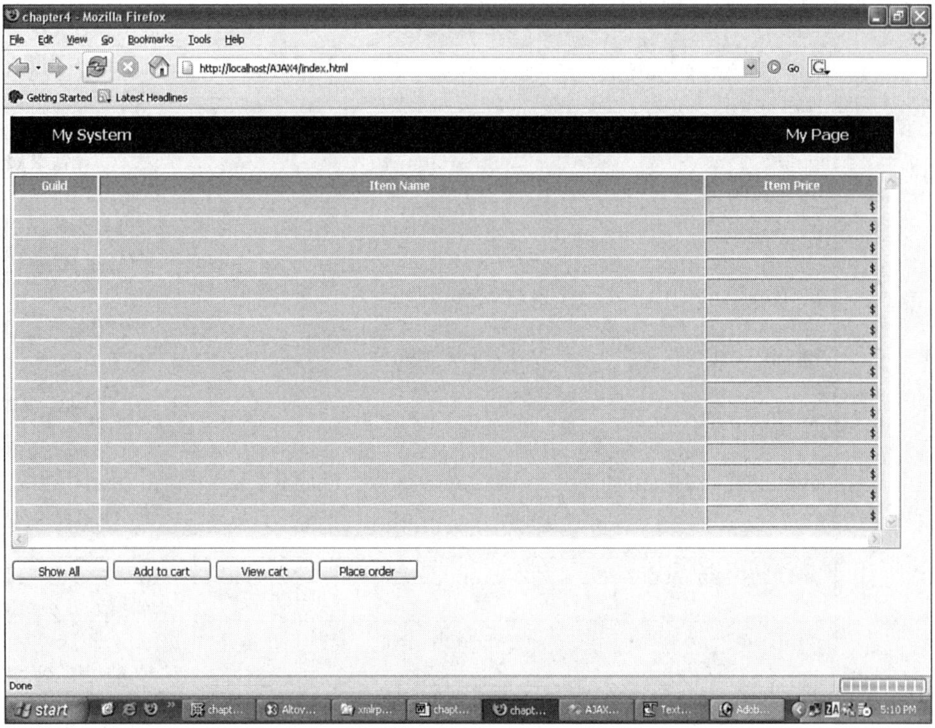

Figure 8-6   Ajax page

Listing 8-19   Ajax Page

```html
<html>
  <head>
    <title>chapter4</title>
    <link rel="stylesheet" type="text/css" href="common.css"/>
    <script language="JavaScript" src="Cache.js"></script>
    <script language="JavaScript" src="XMLHTTPRequest.js"></script>
    <script language="JavaScript" src="XMLDocument.js"></script>
    <script language="JavaScript" src="SOAPEnvelope.js"></script>
    <script language="javascript">
<!-- <![CDATA[
try {var x = new DOMParser(); var _IE = false; } catch(e)
{ var _IE = true; };
var xml = new XMLDocument();
var soap = new SOAPEnvelope();
var pageName = 'Items';
var itemsXHTMLStart = '<table width="960px" border="1" cellpadding="2"
cellspacing="2"><tr class="rowHeader">
<th width="10%">Guild</th><th width="70%">Item Name</th><th>
Item Price</th></tr>';
var itemsXHTMLEnd = '</table>';
```

```
var itemsInnerXHTML = '<tr class="rowData" id="data">
<td align="center"><a href="javascript:pageLoad(\'Items\',@guild)"
xmldi="xmlDI" xmlnode="guild_name"></a></td><td align="left">
<a href="javascript:pageLoad(\'Detail\',@item)"><div id="value"
xmldi="xmlDI" xmlnode="item_name"></div></a></td>
<td class="numeric">$<span xmldi="xmlDI"
xmlnode="item_price"></span></td></tr>';
var detailXHTML = '<div><div class="rowHeader" style="position: absolute;
left: 50px; right: auto%; bottom: auto; width: 200px; top: 75px"> Guild
Name:</div><div class="rowHeader" style="position: absolute; left: 50px;
right: auto%; bottom: auto; width: 200px; top: 92px"> Item Name:</div><div
class="rowHeader" style="position: absolute; left: 50px; right: auto%;
bottom: auto; width: 200px; top: 110px"> Description:</div><div
class="rowHeader" style="position: absolute; left: 50px; right: auto%;
bottom: auto; width: 200px; top: 127px"> Price:</div><div
class="rowHeader" style="position: absolute; left: 50px; right: auto%;
bottom: auto; width: 200px; top: 144px"> Quantity:</div><div
class="rowData" style="position: absolute; left: 255px; right: auto;
bottom: auto; width: 600px; top: 75px" xmldi="xmlDI"
xmlnode="guild_name"></div><div class="rowData" style="position: absolute;
left: 255px; right: auto; bottom: auto; width: 600px; top: 92px"
xmldi="xmlDI" xmlnode="item_name"></div>
<div class="rowData" style="position: absolute; left: 255px; right: auto;
bottom: auto; width: 600px; top: 110px" xmldi="xmlDI"
xmlnode="item_description"></div><div class="rowData" style="position:
absolute; left: 255px; right: auto; bottom: auto; width: 600px; top:
127px">$<span  xmldi="xmlDI" xmlnode="item_price"></span></div><input
type="text" id="quantity" name="quantity" value=""
onkeyup="restrict(this,\'[0-9]\',\'gi\')" class="rowData" style="position:
absolute; left: 255px; right: auto; bottom: auto; width: 600px; top:
144px; text-align: right"></div>';

function setEvents() {
  pageLoad();
}

function pageLoad(name,parm) {
  switch(true) {
    case(arguments.length == 0):
      soap.content = '<guild_item_id/><guild_id/>';
    case(name == 'Items'):
      if(arguments.length != 0)
        soap.content =
        '<guild_item_id/><guild_id>' + parm + '</guild_id>';

      soap.operator = 'getItems';
      xml.setEnvelope(soap.envelope());
      xml.setRequestHeader('SOAPAction','http://tempuri.org/getItems');
      xml.setRequestHeader('Content-Type','text/xml');
      xml.load('http://localhost/AJAX4/chapter4.asmx');
```

continues

Listing 8-19   continued

```
      window.setTimeout('pageWait()',10);

      pageName = 'Items';

      break;
   case(name == 'Detail'):
     soap.content =
     '<guild_item_id>' + parm + '</guild_item_id><guild_id/>';

     soap.operator = 'getItems';
     xml.setEnvelope(soap.envelope());
     xml.setRequestHeader('SOAPAction','http://tempuri.org/getItems');
     xml.setRequestHeader('Content-Type','text/xml');
     xml.load('http://localhost/AJAX4/chapter4.asmx');

     window.setTimeout('pageWait()',10);

     pageName = name;

     break;
   default:
     alert(name);
  }
}

function pageWait() {
  if(xml.readyState() == 4) {
    var xhtml = itemsXHTMLStart;
    var input =
document.getElementById('buttons').getElementsByTagName('input');

    if(_IE)

document.getElementById('xmlDI').XMLDocument.loadXML(xml.selectSingleNode(
'//NewDataSet').serialize());
    else
      document.getElementById('xmlDI').innerHTML =
xml.selectSingleNode('//NewDataSet').serialize();

    switch(pageName) {
      case('Items'):
        for(var i=0;i < xml.selectNodes('//Table').length;i++) {
          var reGuild = new RegExp('@guild','i');
          var reItem = new RegExp('@item','i');
          var guild =
xml.selectNodes('//guild_id')[i].serialize().replace(new
RegExp('<[^<]{0,}>','g'),'');
          var item =
xml.selectNodes('//guild_item_id')[i].serialize().replace(new
RegExp('<[^<]{0,}>','g'),'');

          xhtml +=
itemsInnerXHTML.replace(reGuild,guild).replace(reItem,item);
```

```
            }

            document.getElementById('formBody').innerHTML = xhtml +
        itemsXHTMLEnd;

            break;
          case('Detail'):
            document.getElementById('formBody').innerHTML = detailXHTML;

            break;
      }

      window.setTimeout('_bind()',10);
    } else
      window.setTimeout('pageWait()',10);
}

function _bind() {
  if(arguments.length == 0) {
    doBind(document.body.getElementsByTagName('a'));
    doBind(document.body.getElementsByTagName('div'));
    doBind(document.body.getElementsByTagName('input'));
    doBind(document.body.getElementsByTagName('select'));
    doBind(document.body.getElementsByTagName('span'));
    doBind(document.body.getElementsByTagName('textarea'));
  } else {
    applyChange(arguments[0],arguments[1]);
    _bind();                                // Re-bind
  }

  /*
        Function:    doBind
        Programmer: Edmond Woychowsky
        Purpose:     To handle data-binds for specific nodes based
                     upon HTML element type and browser type.
  */
  function doBind(objects) {
    var strTag;                    // HTML tag
    var strDI;                     // XML data island id
    var strNode;                   // XML node name
    var strValue;                  // XML node value
    var index = new Object();      // Object to store information

    for(var i=0;i < objects.length;i++) {
      strTag = objects[i].tagName;
      strDI = objects[i].getAttribute('xmldi');
      strNode = objects[i].getAttribute('xmlnode');

      if(strDI != null && strNode != null) {
        if(typeof(index[strNode]) == 'undefined')
          index[strNode] = -1;
```

continues

Listing 8-19   continued

```
        ++index[strNode];

        if(_IE) {
            strValue =
document.getElementById(strDI).XMLDocument.selectNodes('//' +
strNode).item(index[strNode]).text;
        } else {
            strValue =
document.getElementById(strDI).getElementsByTagName(strNode)[index[strNode
]].innerHTML;
        }

        switch(strTag) {
            case('A'):
            case('DIV'):
            case('SPAN'):
                objects[i].innerHTML = strValue;

                break;
            case('INPUT'):
                switch(objects[i].type) {
                    case('text'):
                    case('hidden'):
                    case('password'):
                        objects[i].value = strValue;
                        objects[i].onchange = new Function("_bind(this," +
i.toString() + ")");

                        break;
                    case('checkbox'):
                        if(objects[i].value == strValue)
                            objects[i].checked = true;
                        else
                            objects[i].checked = false;

                        objects[i].onclick = new Function("_bind(this," +
i.toString() + ")");

                        break;
                    case('radio'):
                        if(_IE)
                            strValue =
document.getElementById(strDI).XMLDocument.selectNodes('//' +
strNode).item(0).text;
                        else
                            strValue =
document.getElementById(strDI).getElementsByTagName(strNode)[0].innerHTML;

                        if(objects[i].value == strValue)
                            objects[i].checked = true;
                        else
                            objects[i].checked = false;
```

```
                                objects[i].onclick = new
Function("_bind(this,0)");

                              break;
                    }

                  break;
              case('SELECT'):
              case('TEXTAREA'):
                  objects[i].value = strValue;
                  objects[i].onchange = new Function("_bind(this," +
i.toString() + ")");

                  break;
          }
        }
      }
    }
}

/*
  Function:  restrict
  Programmer:  Edmond Woychowsky
  Purpose:  Restrict keyboard input for the provided object
            using the passed regular expression and option.
*/
function restrict(obj,rex,opt) {
  var re = new RegExp(rex,opt);
  var chr = obj.value.substr(obj.value.length - 1);

  if(!re.test(chr)) {
    var reChr = new RegExp(chr,opt);

    obj.value = obj.value.replace(reChr,'');
  }
}

/*
  Function:   add2Cart
  Programmer: Edmond Woychowsky
  Purpose:    To add an item/quantity pair to an XML Data
              Island that represents a shopping cart.
*/
function add2Cart() {
  var item =
xml.selectSingleNode('//guild_item_id').serialize().replace(new
RegExp('<[^<]{0,}>','g'),'');
  var quantity = document.getElementById('quantity').value;
  var re = new RegExp('<item><id>' + item +
'</id><quantity>[^<]{1,}</quantity></item>','g');

  if(re.test(document.getElementById('cart').innerHTML))
```

continues

Listing 8-19   continued

```
    document.getElementById('cart').innerHTML =
document.getElementById('cart').innerHTML.replace(re,'');

  document.getElementById('cart').innerHTML += '<item><id>' + item +
'</id><quantity>' + quantity + '</quantity></item>';

  alert('Item added to cart.');
}
// ]]> —>
    </script>
  </head>
  <body onload="setEvents()">
    <table border="0" height="60px" width="975px" cellpadding="0"
cellspacing="0" ID="Table1">
      <tr class="pageHeader" height="40px">
        <td width="5%"> </td>
        <th id="systemName" class="pageCell" width="45%" align="left">My
System</th>
        <th id="pageName" class="pageCell" width="45%" align="right">My
Page</th>
        <td width="5%"> </td>
      </tr>
      <tr>
        <td> </td>
        <td> </td>
        <td> </td>
        <td> </td>
      </tr>
    </table>
  <xml id="cart"></xml>
  <xml id="xmlDI"></xml>
    <div id="formBody" style="color: #000000; background-color: F0F8FF;
font-family: tahoma; font-size: 12px; border: solid 1px gray; height:
400px; width: 980px; overflow: scroll"></div>
    <p />
    <div id="buttons">
      <input id="show_all" type="button" value="Show All"
onclick="javascript:pageLoad()" style="height: 22px; width: 110px" />
      <input id="add_to_cart" type="button" value="Add to cart"
onclick="add2Cart()" style="height: 22px; width: 110px" />
      <input id="view_cart" type="button" value="View cart"
onclick="javascript:pageLoad('displayCart')" style="height: 22px; width:
110px" />
      <input id="place_order" type="button" value="Place order" onclick=""
style="height: 22px; width: 110px" />
    </div>
  </body>
</html>
```

Just as in the earlier HTML examples, Listing 8-19 has bound XML data islands and an asynchronous XMLHTTP request. The biggest differences are that the XML comes from a web service and that the request is made using SOAP. This means that although all the code that you see here is custom for this book, there is absolutely no reason why an Ajax front end cannot be written for existing web services. It's like General Patten said: "Never pay twice for the same real estate."

Please take note of the HTML DIV tag with the id attribute; there is something special about it. As you've probably deduced from the style attribute, both its height and its width are static. This is to keep the buttons along the bottom from moving around. In addition, it provides someplace to display the information returned from the server, without having to worry about the buttons. An alternative would be to put the buttons on the top of the page, but scrolling up to find the buttons would get old really quickly. With the underlying architecture around 90 percent complete, let's revisit the page that displays the items available for purchase on our site.

8.5.1   Read Only

Again, the purpose of the read-only page is to display our wares to visitors. On the surface, it is just rows and rows of items that are available for sale. Behind the scenes, however, is a different story. This is a web service delivering a SOAP response to a request for information—in this instance, the information relating to the items for sale.

Upon receiving the request, the web service obtains the necessary information from the database, which is the same MySQL database from the previous chapters. When it has the information, it programmatically builds the XHTML required to fill the scrollable div. Updates are not permitted on this page, so only the XHTML is being sent to the client. Hey, conserve bandwidth wherever you can.

Unfortunately, there is more to it than that. For instance, the page's onload event handler needs to send the SOAP request so that the previous method is invoked. In addition, buttons need to be activated or deactivated, clicks need to be handled, and, in short, there is more work to do.

Starting with the handler for the page onload event, we need to build a SOAP request, send the request to the web service, and activate the appropriate buttons. In addition, eventually the web service will get back to the page with its response, which will have to be dealt with. Sound like enough? Let's break it down into a little more detail.

1. Create a global instance of XMLDocument().
2. Build a SOAP request describing the URI of the web service, the method, the namespace, and the parameters being sent.

3. Send the SOAP request using the `XMLHttpRequest` that is incorporated into the `XMLDocument` class.

4. Wait for the SOAP response from the web service.

5. Active the appropriate buttons.

6. Populate the page.

Sound pretty easy? Well, it is easy, after the first time. The first time, however, it is kind of difficult to figure out what is what and what goes where. The first time that I did this, I stumbled a bit on steps 2 and 4. The problem that I had with step 2 was simply a matter of what goes where; a look at the code will explain everything. Dealing with step 4 is merely a matter of using `window.setTimeout` in JavaScript to repeatedly call a function after a suitable number of milliseconds to check the `readyState` of the `XMLHttpRequest`. If the `readyState` is 4, it is complete. Table 8-3 shows the possible `readyState` values and their meanings.

Table 8-3   `readyState` Values

readyState	Description
0	Uninitialized
1	Loading
2	Loaded
3	Interactive
4	Complete

Probably the hardest thing to get used to with Ajax is the ratio of client-side JavaScript to HTML. With traditional web development, the number of lines of HTML far exceeds the number of lines of JavaScript. With Ajax development, it is the other way around, with more JavaScript than HTML. Fortunately, with a halfway decent library of objects and functions, Ajax development doesn't usually need a lot of custom code. For example, Listing 8-20 shows the custom JavaScript for our page listing the items available, and Figure 8 -7 shows what it looks like in the browser.

Listing 8-20   Items Available

```
soap.content =

'<guild_item_id>' + parm + '</guild_item_id><guild_id/>';

soap.operator = 'getItems';
xml.setEnvelope(soap.envelope());
xml.setRequestHeader('SOAPAction','http://tempuri.org/getItems');
xml.setRequestHeader('Content-Type','text/xml');
```

```
xml.load('http://localhost/AJAX4/chapter4.asmx');

window.setTimeout('pageWait()',10);

pageName = name;


function pageWait() {
  if(xml.readyState() == 4) {
    var xhtml = itemsXHTMLStart;
    var input =
document.getElementById('buttons').getElementsByTagName('input');

    if(_IE)

document.getElementById('xmlDI').XMLDocument.loadXML(xml.selectSingleNode(
'//NewDataSet').serialize());
    else
      document.getElementById('xmlDI').innerHTML =
xml.selectSingleNode('//NewDataSet').serialize();

    switch(pageName) {
      case('Items'):
        for(var i=0;i < xml.selectNodes('//Table').length;i++) {
          var reGuild = new RegExp('@guild','i');
          var reItem = new RegExp('@item','i');
          var guild =
xml.selectNodes('//guild_id')[i].serialize().replace(new
RegExp('<[^<]{0,}>','g'),'');
          var item =
xml.selectNodes('//guild_item_id')[i].serialize().replace(new
RegExp('<[^<]{0,}>','g'),'');

          xhtml +=
itemsInnerXHTML.replace(reGuild,guild).replace(reItem,item);
        }

        document.getElementById('formBody').innerHTML = xhtml +
itemsXHTMLEnd;

        break;
      case('Detail'):
        document.getElementById('formBody').innerHTML =
        detailXHTML;

        break;
    }

    window.setTimeout('_bind()',10);
  } else
    window.setTimeout('pageWait()',10);
}
```

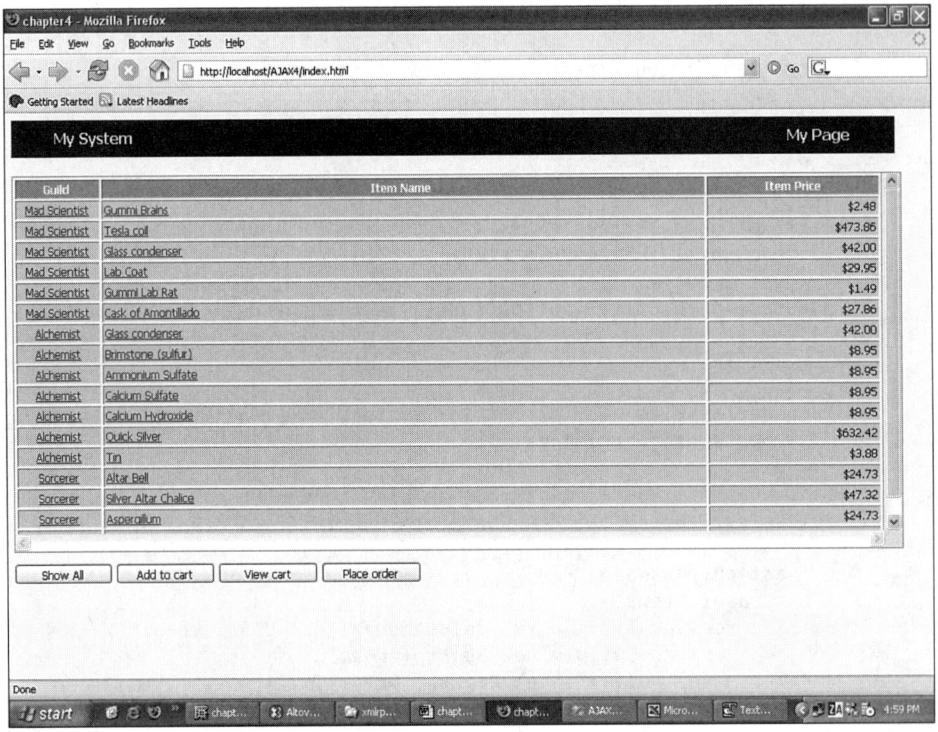

Figure 8-7   Items available

The `pageWait()` function shown here might seem somewhat formidable, but its sole purpose is to dynamically build the HTML necessary for the bound table in the page. This is a somewhat slick trick, but really nothing that hasn't been done for the last five years, although usually for different reasons.

8.5.2   Updateable

Because we've worked out the underlying architecture, an updateable page is merely a variant of the read-only page shown in the previous example. There are essentially two differences, the first being that, instead of using SPAN or DIV tags, the bound tags are things such as INPUT and SELECT. The second difference is that eventually it will be necessary to send an entire XML data island to the server. The interesting thing about this is that it doesn't have to be the XML Data Island that is bound to the HTML, although it could be.

Remember the shopping cart from earlier in the book? Well, instead of using the funky item id-dash-quantity in a text box, now the shopping is itself an XML Data Island. Unfortunately, this means that I can't be lazy and recycle the function from Chapter 5. Alas, it was necessary to write the function shown in Listing 8-21. It's not anything fancy; in fact, it treats the XML as text. Not only is that a valid option, but it also works in a cross-browser environment.

Listing 8-21 Add to Shopping Cart Function

```
/*
   To add an item/quantity pair to an XML Data Island that
   represents a shopping cart.
*/
function add2Cart() {
  var item =
xml.selectSingleNode('//guild_item_id').serialize().replace(new
RegExp('<[^<]{0,}>','g'),'');
  var quantity = document.getElementById('quantity').value;
  var re =
new RegExp('<item><id>' + item +
'</id><quantity>[^<]{1,}</quantity></item>','g');

  if(re.test(document.getElementById('cart').innerHTML))
    document.getElementById('cart').innerHTML =
document.getElementById('cart').innerHTML.replace(re,'');

  document.getElementById('cart').innerHTML += '<item><id>' + item +
'</id><quantity>' + quantity + '</quantity></item>';

  alert('Item added to cart.');
}
```

The end result of this is the page that was shown in Listing 8-21 and Figures 8-7 and 8-8. It works roughly the same as the pageWait() function from Listing 8-20. The difference is that, instead of adding elements to the HTML document based upon an XML document, elements are added to the embedded XML document based upon the actions of the visitor. The page shown in Figure 8-7 lists the items available for purchase, and Figure 8-8 handles the add to the shopping cart.

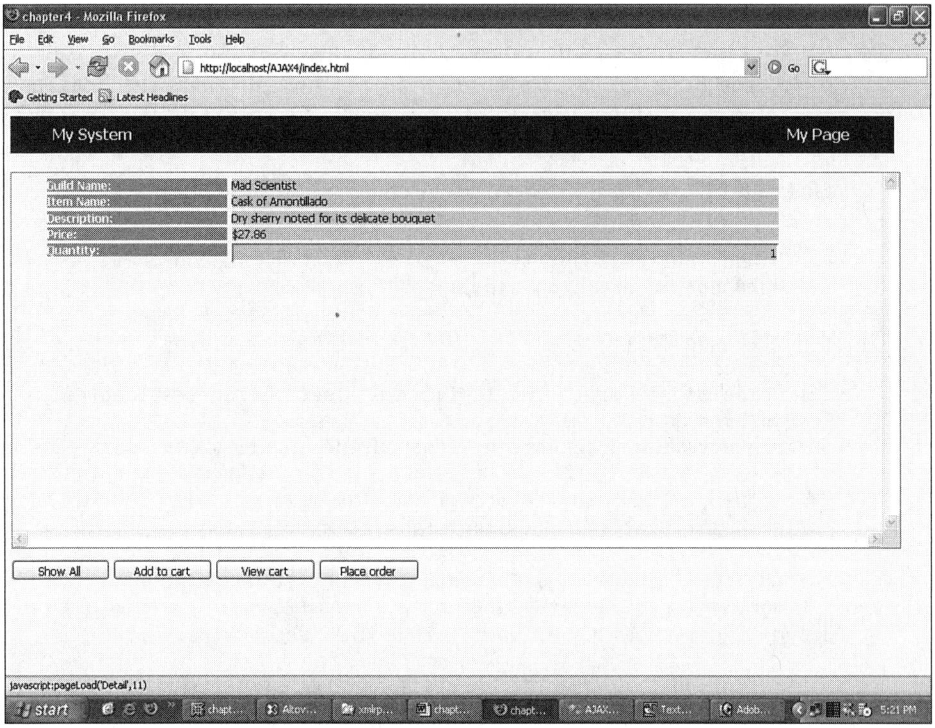

Figure 8-8   Item added to the shopping cart

8.6   ADVANTAGES AND DISADVANTAGES

At the risk of repeating myself, and everyone else who has ever uttered a word about Ajax, the advantage of Ajax is that a web application has the look and feel of a Windows or Linux application. No more does the visitor have to click and wait for the entire unload/reload cycle to complete. Instead, only the parts of the page that actually change are updated, which significantly cuts down on the time required for a page update.

On the other hand, Ajax requires additional work on the often-ignored client side; also, this technique is extremely browser dependent. Some people will be left out, including developers who fail to recognize that we are like deep-water sharks; we either continuously move forward or we begin to die. Some users will also be left behind, such as those who have not upgraded since they purchased their computer in 1995 and those who are so paranoid that they've disabled JavaScript. But from some points of view, that could be an advantage: The first group won't buy anything, and the second group is interested in only aluminum-foil hats.

8.7 SUMMARY

With a couple side trips into the magical worlds of XML, XML-RPC, SOAP, and MySQL stored functions and procedures, we've touched upon every part of Ajax as it stands at the time of this writing. Alright, maybe the MySQL part doesn't directly apply to Ajax because it would work perfectly well without it, but it does illustrate some of the possibilities that exist. As a matter of fact, both Oracle and SQL Server have XML support built in, so why shouldn't we "fake it" in MySQL?

Unarguably, what does directly apply to Ajax is the use of the `XMLHttpRequest` object, without which the examples shown in this chapter would be impossible.

CHAPTER 9

XPath

Just what is XPath? Briefly stated, XPath is to XML what an SQL SELECT is to a relational database. This might at first sound like an oversimplification, but it is essentially true. XPath can be used to locate and navigate the various parts of an XML document. Unfortunately, as with every other language under the sun, a number of unique terms should be defined before you can start understanding it. These concepts and terms might at first seem overwhelming, but they are essential to both querying XML and keeping us employed.

Although you can choose to fluff over these terms, I actually don't recommend it, if only for the purpose of job security. Several years ago, I used my understanding of terms to extend a contract when the client, who is widely known for being frugal, wanted to save money by having their employee mainframe programmers support a web application. During the turnover process, I described how the site worked using the precise web and XML terms. To make a long story short, the contract was extended for another two years.

The first concept is that, even with all the hoopla surrounding all things XML, it is essentially nothing more than data represented in a tree data structure. Looking at XML from an XPath perspective, XML consists of only seven types of nodes:

- ☞ The root node—only one per XML document. All other nodes are child nodes of the root node.
- ☞ Element nodes.
- ☞ Text nodes.
- ☞ Attribute nodes.
- ☞ Comment nodes.
- ☞ Processing instruction nodes.
- ☞ Namespace nodes.

Note that DTDs (Data Type Definitions), CDATA sections, and entity references are not included in this list of node types, each for different reasons. Because a DTD is not an XML document, XPath is incapable of addressing it. CDATA, on the other hand, is a part of XML but, by design, is ignored by XPath, as are entity references.

In addition, it is important to note that the root element and the root node are not different terms for the same thing. Using the XML document shown in Listing 9-1, an XML document's root node contains both the processing instruction, `<?xml version="1.0" encoding="UTF-8"?>`, and the root element, `<library>`.

Listing 9-1   Example XML Document

```
<?xml version="1.0" encoding="UTF-8"?>
<library>
      <book publisher="Del Rey">
            <series/>
            <title>Way Station</title>
            <author>Clifford D. Simak</author>
      </book>
      <book publisher="Del Rey">
            <series>The Lord of the Rings</series>
            <title>The Fellowship of the Ring</title>
            <author>J.R.R. Tolkien</author>
      </book>
      <book publisher="Del Rey">
            <series>The Lord of the Rings</series>
            <title>The Two Towers</title>
            <author>J.R.R. Tolkien</author>
      </book>
      <book publisher="Del Rey">
            <series>The Lord of the Rings</series>
            <title>The Return of the King</title>
            <author>J.R.R. Tolkien</author>
      </book>
      <book publisher="Ace">
            <series>Lord Darcy</series>
            <title>Too Many Magicians</title>
            <author>Randall Garrett</author>
      </book>
      <book publisher="Ace">
            <series>Lord Darcy</series>
            <title>Murder and Magic</title>
            <author>Randall Garrett</author>
      </book>
      <book publisher="Ace">
            <series>Lord Darcy</series>
            <title>The Napoli Express</title>
            <author>Randall Garrett</author>
      </book>
```

```
<book publisher="Ace">
    <series>Lord Darcy</series>
    <title>Lord Darcy Investigates</title>
    <author>Randall Garrett</author>
</book>
</library>
```

9.1   LOCATION PATHS

For all its power and flexibility, the location path is probably the easiest type of XPath to start with. Using the XML document in Listing 9-1 as a starting point, let's say that we want to get the root node. This can be accomplished by using the following XPath:

```
/
```

That's all there is to it. Remembering that there is a difference between the root node and the root element, the root element can be obtained by either of the two following XPath statements:

```
/library
```

```
/*
```

The first example implicitly specifies the root element by name. The second example uses a wildcard (*). Wildcards can be used to increase the flexibility of the XPath by making it unnecessary to know the individual node names. All that is required is the knowledge that we want the root element.

Before going any further, I'd like to introduce one of those pesky new concepts called a node set. A node set is a collection of nodes returned by an XPath statement; think SQL and SELECT with multiple rows returned, and you get the idea. With this in mind, let's say that we want the book elements from the XML document in Listing 9-1. This can be accomplished by any of the following XPath statements:

```
/library/book
```

```
/*/book
```

```
/library/*
```

```
/*/*
```

```
//book
```

The first four examples shown here are all a logical progression of the basic location path covered previously. The last example, however, is something else entirely. The double forward slash (//) refers to descendants of the root node, as well as to the root node itself. For example, //* refers to the root element and every element node in the document.

9.2 CONTEXT NODE

A variation on the previous discussion, //*, is the single period (.), which refers to the context node. Most often used in XSLT to refer to the value of the currently matched node, it works equally well for all node types.

9.3 PARENT NODES

Sometimes it is necessary to obtain the parent node(s) of a particular node or node set. This is accomplished by using a double period (..). The following examples show how it can be used to obtain the parent of the series element (book element).

```
//series/..
//book/series/..
```

9.4 ATTRIBUTE NODES

Attribute nodes are handled in a slightly different manner than the nodes that we have dealt with thus far. To specify an attribute node, prefix it with an "at" sign (@). This distinguishes attribute nodes from element nodes. The following XPath statements obtain a node set consisting of all publisher attributes:

```
//@publisher
//@*
```

9.5 PREDICATES

Predicates are the equivalent to an SQL WHERE clause, basically a way to limit the node set returned by XPath. The basic format is as follows:

```
XPath[condition]
```

Although this isn't very difficult, most mistakes are made in the condition. This is because there is a difference between evaluating XPath in Altova's XMLSPY XPath Evaluator and evaluating XPath in XSLT. I'll give you a hint: "well formed". XMLSPY XPath Evaluator uses the standard programming greater than (>) and less than (<) conditional operators. In XSLT, this would result in the document being not well formed. Table 9-1 lists the conditional operators used in both.

Table 9-1 Conditional Operators Used in XMLSPY XPath Evaluator and XPath in XSLT

Evaluator	XSLT	Description
>	&gt;	Greater than
<	&lt;	Less than
=	=	Equal to
!=	!=	Not equal to

Using the XPath Evaluator, the XPath statement to return all the books published by Del Rey would be as follows:

```
//book[@publisher = 'Del Rey']
```

This statement results in a node set of five books: one by Simak and four by Tolkien. But what if we want only the books that are not part of the *Lord of the Rings* trilogy? In SQL, we use an "and" condition. Because XPath supports both "and" and "or," we do the same:

```
//book[@publisher = 'Del Rey' and series != 'The Lord of the Rings']
```

This results in a single XML book node, Simak's *Way Station*. An alternate, although more verbose, way of coding to obtain the same result shows that multiple predicates can be on a single XPath statement:

```
//book[@publisher = 'Del Rey']/series[. != 'The Lord of the
Rings']/..
```

In addition to being able to obtain nodes and node sets based upon Boolean conditions, it is possible to retrieve a particular instance of a node. For example, let's say that we want the third book in the library, *The Two Towers*. The easiest method of getting it is this:

```
//book[3]
```

This method also can be combined with a Boolean condition to obtain the name of the second book in Tolkien's trilogy:

```
//book[series = 'The Lord of the Rings'][2]
```

Again, the result is *The Two Towers.*

9.6   XPATH FUNCTIONS

In addition to what we have seen so far, XPath provides functions that either operate on or return one of the following four data types:

☞ Boolean
☞ Numeric
☞ Node set
☞ String

9.6.1   Boolean Functions

XPath has four Boolean functions: `true()`, `false()`, `not()`, and `boolean()`. The functions `true()` and `false()` return exactly what you would expect, `true` or `false`. The `not()` takes the Boolean value passed and returns the opposite. This provides yet another roundabout method to find the book *Way Station:*

```
//book[@publisher = 'Del Rey' and not(series = 'The Lord of the
Rings')]
```

The `boolean()` function operates a little differently; it takes the argument and evaluates it, returning either `true` or `false`. If the event of the argument is a node set, only the first node is evaluated; the rest are ignored. Omitting the argument results in the current context node (.) being evaluated, with either `true` or `false` being returned.

9.6.2   Numeric Functions

Six numeric functions exist: `ceiling()`, `count()`, `floor()`, `round()`, `number()`, and `sum()`. Each of the first three functions accepts a single argument and acts upon that single argument. The `ceiling()` function returns the smallest integer that is greater than or equal to the argument. The function `count()` returns the number of nodes in the argument node set. The `floor()` function returns the largest integer that is less than or equal to the argument passed.

The function `round()` returns the integer closest to the argument; if the number is equidistant between two integers, the largest is returned. The `number()` function evaluates the argument, or context node, and returns either the numeric value of the node or NaN (Not a Number). The function `sum()` operates upon the passed node set, first working like the `number()` function and then adding together the individual values and returning the sum.

9.6.3 Node Set Functions

XPath provides five node set functions: `last()`, `position()`, `local-name()`, `name()`, and `namespace-uri()`. The `last()` function returns the number that corresponds to the last node in a node set. For example, this is the XPath statement to find the last book:

```
//book[last()]
```

The `position()` function returns the number that corresponds to the context node. This provides an alternate method of retrieving the same result as the `last()` function by coding either of the following two statements:

```
//book[position() = last()]

//book[position() = 8]
```

The `local-name()` function returns the part of a node name following the colon (`:`). If there is no colon, the function works like the `name()` function, returning the full node name for either the argument or the context node. The `namespace-uri()` function returns the URI used in a namespace declaration, which is the value of the `xmlns` or `xmlns:` attribute.

9.6.4 String Functions

XPath provides a plethora of string functions that can be used either singly or in combination with one another to produce the desired results. These functions are `concat()`, `contains()`, `normalize-space()`, `starts-with()`, `string-length()`, `substring()`, `substring-after()`, `substring-before()`, and `translate()`.

The `concat()` function converts each of the arguments to strings, concatenates them, and then returns the result. The arguments can be literals, nodes, or node sets. However, with node sets, only the first node is evaluated. For example, this produces the string `"Clifford D. Simak, Way Station"`:

```
concat(//author, ', ', //title)
```

The function `contains()` is used to test a string to determine whether it contains another string as a substring. This can be useful when only partial information is available—for example, if you're looking for a book with "Lord" in the title:

```
//title[contains(., 'Lord')]
```

The `normalize-space()` function removes leading and trailing whitespace from a string; in addition, any multioccurrence of whitespace is replaced with a single space. So the string " `Post no bills!` " becomes "`Post no bills!`".

The `starts-with()` function operates in the same manner as the `contains()` function, with the sole exception that only the beginning of a string is tested. So unless the string begins with the substring, the result is `false`.

The `string-length()` function returns the length of the string argument passed, which is particularly useful when testing for elements with or without contents. For example, to test for books that are not part of any series, the following XPath statement could be used:

```
//book[string-length(series) = 0]
```

The next three functions all relate to returning a substring of a string. The `substring()`, `substring-after()` and `substring-before()` functions each return a substring of the `string` argument. The `substring()` function has the following two formats:

```
substring(string, start)

substring(string, start, length)
```

Using the XML document from Listing 9-1, the result of the following XPath would be `Station`:

```
substring(//book[1]/title,5)
```

By specifying the `substring` function's `length` argument in the following manner, the result would be `Stat`:

```
substring(//book[1]/title,5,4)
```

Of course, there is an easier way to get the `Station` results. The `substring-after()` function returns the entire substring immediately following the specified argument substring. Using the `substring-after()` function, it is not necessary to know that the second word starts in position 5; all that is necessary is knowing that it follows a space, as shown in the following example:

```
substring-after(//book[1]/title,' ')
```

The third substring function is `substring-before()`, which returns the entire substring immediately before the argument string.

The final string function is `translate()`, which substitutes characters in the first string argument based upon the characters in the second and third strings. This is the basic format:

```
Translate(string, from-string, to-string)
```

The capabilities of this function lead to several interesting possibilities. For example, let's say that it is necessary to convert a string, such as the author of the third book, to all upper case. This can be accomplished by using the following XPath:

```
translate(//book[3]/author,'qwertyuiopasdfghjklzxcvbnm','QWERTYUIOPAS
DFGHJKLZXCVBNM')
```

Another possible use for `translate` is to remove unwanted characters, such as maybe vowels. The `translate()` function makes this possible. Just specify the characters that you'd like to get rid of in the "from" string, and omit them from the "to" string as shown in the following example:

```
translate(//book[3]/author,'aAeEiIoOuUyY','')
All of a sudden, J.R.R. Tolkien becomes J.R.R. Tlkn.
```

9.7 XPATH EXPRESSIONS

In addition to material already covered, XPath provides some basic mathematical processing. However, it is important to remember that all numbers in XPath are floating-point double precision. In addition, there are special representations for positive and negative infinity, as well as NaN (Not a Number).

XPath also provides the five basic arithmetic operators shown in Table 9-2.

Table 9-2   XPath Arithmetic Operators

Operator	Description
+	Addition
-	Subtraction
*	Multiplication
div	Division
mod	Modula, sometimes referred to as the remainder, or what's left over after division

9.8   XPATH UNIONS

Going back to my original comparison that XPath is to XML what an SQL SELECT is to a relational database, there is yet another similarity: *unions*. In XPath, unions return all nodes in both node sets. This can be quite useful when you're unsure of exactly what you're looking for or working with. For example, let's say that we want either the child elements of the third book node or the attributes. One method would be to use two separate XPath statements. Although this method would work, like most programmers, I'm basically lazy and would rather do it all in one statement by using the union operator (¦), as shown here.

```
//book[3]/* ¦ //book[3]/@*
```

9.9   AXIS

Although it's not usually associated with evil (although cursing is a different story), an axis is a node set starting at a particular node that is based on the relationship between the nodes in an XML document. The basic format for using an axis follows:

```
axis::context-node
```

Table 9-3 describes the properties of the various axes available in XPath.

Table 9-3 XPath Axes

Axis	Description
ancestor	Selects all nodes that are ancestors of the context node, farther up the document tree, in a direct line to the document root node. The resulting node set is in reverse document order—in other words, moving up the tree starting from the document's parent node.
ancestor-or-self	Selects the same nodes as the ancestor axis. However, it starts with the context node instead of the context node's parent.
attribute	Selects all the context node's attributes, if any.
child	Selects all the child nodes of the context node, excluding attributes and namespace nodes.
descendant	Recursively selects all children of the context node and their children until the end of each tree branch.
descendant-or-self	Selects the same nodes as the descendant axis, with the exception of starting with the context node.
following	Selects, in document order, all nodes at any level in the document tree that follow the context node.
following-sibling	Selects, in document order, all nodes at the same level and with the same parent node in the document tree that follow the context node.
namespace	Selects the namespace nodes that are in scope for the context node. If no namespace nodes are in scope, the namespace axis is empty.
parent	Selects the parent node of the context node. If the context node is the root node, the parent axis will be empty.
preceding	Selects all nodes, in reverse document order, excluding ancestor nodes, in the document tree that are before the context node.
preceding-sibling	Selects all nodes, in reverse document order, that are at the same level that have the same parent node as the context node.
self	Selects the context node.

The use of an axis is arguably the most formidable concept for developers new to XPath, who often have difficulty trying to visualize the results of using an axis. Fortunately, tools such as the XPath Evaluator in Altova's XMLSPY make it easier to see the results of specifying a particular axis. Starting with the original XML document from Listing 9-1, the following sections present examples of each of the various axes.

9.9.1   Ancestor Axis Example

XPath Statement

```
//book[3]/ancestor::*
```

Result Node Set

```
library
```

Explanation

Because the context node, the third book node, is a child of the root element, there is only a single ancestor.

9.9.2   ancestor-or-self Axis Example

XPath Statement

```
//book[3]/ancestor-or-self::*
```

Result Node Set

```
book
library
```

Explanation

In addition to the ancestor nodes, the ancestor-or-self axis returns the context node. Also, because the results are in reverse document order, the context node is the first node in the node set, followed by the parent node and so on up the tree.

9.9.3   attribute Axis Example

XPath Statement

```
//book[3]/attribute::*
```

Result Node Set

```
publisher
```

Explanation

Because the context node has only one attribute, it is the only attribute returned in the node set.

9.9.4   child Axis Example

XPath Statement

```
//book[3]/child::*
```

Result Node Set

```
series "The Lord of the Rings"
title "The Two Towers"
author "J.R.R. Tolkien"
```

Explanation

The resulting node set consists of the three child nodes of the context node. I have shown the contents of the individual nodes to distinguish these nodes from similar nodes with different contents.

9.9.5   descendant Axis Example

XPath Statement

```
//book[3]/descendant::*
```

Result Node Set

```
series "The Lord of the Rings"
title "The Two Towers"
author "J.R.R. Tolkien"
```

Explanation

The results shown here are identical to the results from the child axis. This is because of the structure of the XML document. For instance, if any of the child nodes shown here had children of their own, the descendant axis would have returned their children, and so on down the line in document order, whereas the child axis would not.

9.9.6   descendant-or-self Axis Example

XPath Statement

```
//book[3]/descendant-or-self::*
```

Result Node Set

```
book
series "The Lord of the Rings"
title "The Two Towers"
author "J.R.R. Tolkien"
```

Explanation

As with the descendant axis, all child nodes are returned recursively. However, instead of starting with the first child, the context node is the first node in the node set.

9.9.7   following Axis Example

XPath Statement

```
//book[3]/following::*
```

Result Node Set

```
book
series "The Lord of the Rings"
title "The Return of the King"
author "J.R.R. Tolkien"
book
series "Lord Darcy"
title "Too Many Magicians"
author "Randall Garrett"
book
```

```
series "Lord Darcy"
title "Murder and Magic"
author "Randall Garrett"
book
series "Lord Darcy"
title "The Napoli Express"
author "Randall Garrett"
book
series "Lord Darcy"
title "Lord Darcy Investigates"
author "Randall Garrett"
```

Explanation

The resulting node set for the `following` axis is always all the nodes that occur after the context node in document order.

9.9.8   following-sibling Axis Example

XPath Statement

```
//book[3]/following-sibling::*
```

Result Node Set

```
book
book
book
book
book
```

Explanation

These five book nodes retrieved using the `following-sibling` axis are the same nodes that were retrieved by the following axis. The only difference is that the `following-sibling` axis retrieves only those nodes on the same level as the context node and have the same parent as the context node.

9.9.9   namespace Axis Example

XPath Statement

```
//book[3]/namespace::*
```

Result Node Set

```
Empty node set
```

Explanation
Because no namespace was in scope on the context node, the resulting node set is empty. However, if one or more namespaces had been in scope, the resulting node set would have contained those in scope.

9.9.10   parent Axis Example

XPath Statement

```
//book[3]/parent::*
```

Result Node Set

```
library
```

Explanation
The resulting node set will always consist of either an empty node set or a single node. For example, the parent axis of the library element would have retrieved an empty node set.

9.9.11   preceding Axis Example

XPath Statement

```
//book[3]/preceding::*
```

Result Node Set

```
author "J.R.R. Tolkien"
title "The Fellowship of the Ring"
series "The Lord of the Rings"
book
author "Clifford D. Simak"
title "Way Station"
series
book
```

Explanation

The resulting node set of the `preceding` axis is made up of those nodes that occur in the XML document before the context node, in reverse document order.

9.9.12   preceding-sibling Axis Example

XPath Statement

```
//book[3]/preceding-sibling::*
```

Result Node Set

```
book
book
```

Explanation

These book nodes retrieved using the `preceding-sibling` axis are the same nodes that were retrieved by the `preceding` axis. However, the difference is that the `preceding-sibling` axis retrieves only those nodes that are on the same level as the context node and that have the same parent as the context node.

9.9.13   self Axis Example

XPath Statement

```
//book[3]/self::*
```

Result Node Set

```
book
```

Explanation

The `self` axis returns the context node; essentially, the result is the same as if the axis were omitted.

9.10 SUMMARY

The material presented in this chapter completely covers the basic parts of XPath: the various types of paths, context nodes, functions, and axes. As comprehensive as the walkthrough was, it is important to remember that XPath by itself is not an end. It is merely a means to an end. To make XPath shine, it is necessary to use it in conjunction with another tool, such as XLST.

CHAPTER 10

XSLT

The movie *Star Trek: The Wrath of Khan* introduced a device called the Genesis Torpedo that rearranged matter on a subatomic level to produce life-bearing planets. Talk about your mad scientist stuff! eXtensible Stylesheet Language for Transformations (XSLT) is the XML equivalent to Star Trek's Genesis; it rearranges XML at the element level to produce the desired results. However, unlike Genesis, the desired results are not limited to a single type, but rather can be any conceivable XML or text-based format. In addition, instead of the original document being modified, a new document is created in the desired format, which could be identical to the original document or vastly different.

An XSLT document, sometimes referred to as a style sheet, is a well-formed XML document that uses the XSLT namespace (`xmlns:xsl=http://www.w3.org/1999/XSL/Transform`) to describe the rules for transforming the source XML document into the result XML document. XSLT is always used in conjunction with XPath, which specifies the location of various elements within the source document. XSLT, on the other hand, describes the structure of the result document.

Listing 10-1 contains a simple style sheet whose purpose is to simply copy the source XML document to the result XML document. Because no specific node names are used, this style sheet works equally well with all XML documents.

Listing 10-1   Simple Style Sheet to Copy the Source XML Document to the Result XML Document

```
<?xml version="1.0" encoding="UTF-8"?>
<xsl:stylesheet version="1.0"
xmlns:xsl="http://www.w3.org/1999/XSL/Transform">
        <xsl:output method="xml" version="1.0" encoding="UTF-8"/>
```

continues

Listing 10-1   continued

```
<xsl:template match="/">

        <xsl:copy-of select="."/>

    </xsl:template>

</xsl:stylesheet>
```

The XSL style sheet shown in Listing 10-1 works like this. First, the XML declaration describes the version of XML and the character set encoding. The `xsl:stylesheet` element describes the document as a style sheet, and the attributes specify the version of XSLT and the namespace. The `xsl:output` element defines the result document's XML declaration. The `xsl:template` defines a relationship between the source XML document and the result document. For example, the `match` attribute with the / specifies the source document's root node; all child elements of this element will be applied to the root element. Finally, the `xsl:copy-of` specifies to perform a *deep copy* of the context node; in other words, copy the context node and all descendants *recursively*.

This chapter covers the following topics:

☞ Recursive versus iterative style sheets
☞ XPath in the style sheet
☞ Elements
☞ XSLT functions
☞ XSLT concepts
☞ Client-side transformations

10.1 RECURSIVE VERSUS ITERATIVE STYLE SHEETS

One of the things about XSLT is that although the capability exists for *iteration* (looping), it is strongly frowned upon by the development community. Instead, recursive templates are considered the acceptable standard. Although this philosophy requires some changes in the way developers think, it also means that recursive style sheets are often far more compact and not nested nearly as deep as their iterative counterparts. At the very least, recursive style sheets are always far more structured, which can be a major advantage in larger style sheets.

Let's say that our goal is to create an XSLT table and the source XML document shown in Listing 10-2. As a starting point, there are two distinct courses of action: an iterative style sheet (see Listing 10-3) and a recursive style sheet (see Listing 10-4). Each of these two approaches to coding style sheets has its own strengths and weaknesses. For example, the iterative style sheet is about the same length, but it is also nested much deeper than the recursive style sheet.

Listing 10-2   Source XML Document

```
<?xml version="1.0" encoding="UTF-8"?>
<library>
      <book publisher="Del Rey">
            <series/>
            <title>Way Station</title>
            <author>Clifford D. Simak</author>
      </book>
      <book publisher="Del Rey">
            <series>The Lord of the Rings</series>
            <title>The Fellowship of the Ring</title>
            <author>J.R.R. Tolkien</author>
      </book>
      <book publisher="Del Rey">
            <series>The Lord of the Rings</series>
            <title>The Two Towers</title>
            <author>J.R.R. Tolkien</author>
      </book>
      <book publisher="Del Rey">
            <series>The Lord of the Rings</series>
            <title>The Return of the King</title>
            <author>J.R.R. Tolkien</author>
      </book>
      <book publisher="Ace">
            <series>Lord Darcy</series>
            <title>Too Many Magicians</title>
            <author>Randall Garrett</author>
      </book>
      <book publisher="Ace">
            <series>Lord Darcy</series>
            <title>Murder and Magic</title>
            <author>Randall Garrett</author>
      </book>
      <book publisher="Ace">
            <series>Lord Darcy</series>
            <title>The Napoli Express</title>
            <author>Randall Garrett</author>
      </book>
      <book publisher="Ace">
            <series>Lord Darcy</series>
            <title>Lord Darcy Investigates</title>
            <author>Randall Garrett</author>
      </book>
</library>
```

Listing 10-3   Iterative Style Sheet

```xml
<?xml version="1.0" encoding="UTF-8"?>
<xsl:stylesheet version="1.0"
xmlns:xsl="http://www.w3.org/1999/XSL/Transform">
      <xsl:output method="xml" version="1.0" encoding="UTF-8"/>

      <xsl:template match="/">

            <xsl:element name="table">

                  <xsl:for-each select="//book">
                        <xsl:element name="tr">

                              <xsl:for-each select="child::*">
                                    <xsl:element name="td">
                                          <xsl:value-of select="."/>
                                    </xsl:element>
                              </xsl:for-each>

                        </xsl:element>
                  </xsl:for-each>
            </xsl:element>

      </xsl:template>

</xsl:stylesheet>
```

Listing 10-4   Recursive Style Sheet

```xml
<?xml version="1.0" encoding="UTF-8"?>
<xsl:stylesheet version="1.0"
xmlns:xsl="http://www.w3.org/1999/XSL/Transform">
      <xsl:output method="xml" version="1.0" encoding="UTF-8"/>

      <xsl:template match="/">

    \     <xsl:element name="table">
                  <xsl:apply-templates select="//book"/>
            </xsl:element>

      </xsl:template>

      <xsl:template match="*">

            <xsl:if test="count(ancestor::*) = 1">
                  <xsl:element name="tr">
                        <xsl:apply-templates select="child::*"/>
                  </xsl:element>
            </xsl:if>
            <xsl:if test="count(ancestor::*) != 1">
                  <xsl:element name="td">
```

```
                    <xsl:value-of select="."/>
                </xsl:element>
            </xsl:if>

    </xsl:template>

</xsl:stylesheet>
```

The decision to use an iterative design or a recursive design is more a matter of personal taste and comfort than any rule imposed from on high. For example, many developers new to XSLT start by writing iterative style sheets and move to recursive methods only when they become more confident in their abilities. But in the end, the result of the two style sheets is the same as shown in Listing 10-5.

Listing 10-5   Result from Applying Either Style Sheet to the XML in Listing 10-2

```
<?xml version="1.0" encoding="UTF-8"?>
<library>
    <book publisher="Del Rey">
      <series/>
      <title>Way Station</title>
      <author>Clifford D. Simak</author>
    </book>
    <book publisher="Del Rey">
      <series>The Lord of the Rings</series>
      <title>The Fellowship of the Ring</title>
      <author>J.R.R. Tolkien</author>
    </book>
    <book publisher="Del Rey">
      <series>The Lord of the Rings</series>
      <title>The Two Towers</title>
      <author>J.R.R. Tolkien</author>
    </book>
    <book publisher="Del Rey">
      <series>The Lord of the Rings</series>
      <title>The Return of the King</title>
      <author>J.R.R. Tolkien</author>
    </book>
    <book publisher="Ace">
      <series>Lord Darcy</series>
      <title>Too Many Magicians</title>
      <author>Randall Garrett</author>
    </book>
    <book publisher="Ace">
      <series>Lord Darcy</series>
      <title>Murder and Magic</title>
      <author>Randall Garrett</author>
    </book>
```

continues

Listing 10-5 continued

```
    <book publisher="Ace">
      <series>Lord Darcy</series>
      <title>The Napoli Express</title>
      <author>Randall Garrett</author>
    </book>
    <book publisher="Ace">
      <series>Lord Darcy</series>
      <title>Lord Darcy Investigates</title>
      <author>Randall Garrett</author>
    </book>
</library>
```

10.1.1 Scope

If you're in a cubical right now, take a moment and look around; you're the absolute ruler of all that you survey. The desk and its contents all fall under your benevolent influence, as do the coffee cup and its contents. However, all that is beyond the imaginary line that separates your cubical from the corridor is beyond the scope of your influence and belongs to another. This simplistic description of office life is essentially the same as how the concept of scope works in XSLT. In XSLT, scope is applied to both the context node, the current position in the XML document, and the variables.

It is best to think of scope along the same lines as local and global variables in other programming languages. For example, if a variable is defined within an `if` statement, it is accessible only inside that `if` statement. Or if a variable is defined within a function (template in XSLT), it can be used only within that function, not in any subsequent function, unless it is passed as a parameter. Variables defined on the root level are considered global to the entire XSLT document. Also, while we're on the subject of variables, I should describe the toughest issue that new developers have with learning XSLT.

10.1.2 Nonvariable Variables

As with other programming languages, XSLT provides the capability to create variables, which can be a major stumbling block to newcomers. You see, because of the functional nature of XSLT, variables aren't variable, and after they're created, they cannot be assigned a new value within the same scope. This might seem at first to be a problem, but it was intentional because XSLT is not a procedural language, like JavaScript. XSLT variables function more like variables in mathematical functions; you can create them, you can use them, but you can never change them.

This, probably more than any other aspect of XSLT, has caused more developers to run screaming into the night, although I'm not sure, having never conducted any research into the subject. After all, how long can you develop without Jonesing for a fix—er, make that needing a way to alter a variable or something along those lines?

There is, however, a way around this issue; remember what I said about scope? That scope can be both local and global? Imagine, if you will, a recursive template. Yes, the headaches are starting already, but bear with me on this. There is absolutely no reason why a template cannot call itself. Okay, that's really useful information. A template can get around this issue, and it would be even more useful if I were to explain what a template is.

In XSLT, a template is the equivalent to a function in another language, such as PHP or JavaScript. In fact, it isn't all that unusual for a template to have a name and be invoked using that name, just like a function. In addition, templates can accept parameters, just as functions do in other languages. However, there is a major difference between XSLT functions and, say, JavaScript functions.

In JavaScript, functions are required to have names, whereas, in XSLT, templates aren't required to have names. This raises the question, if a template doesn't have a name, then how do you call it? The simple answer is that you don't call it; only named templates can be called. Instead, you apply it. The XSLT `apply-templates` element has an attribute named `select`, which uses XPath to specify which nodes in the source document the template is to be applied to.

10.2   XPath in the Style Sheet

Even though the XSLT elements in the three style sheets shown earlier are unfamiliar, they illustrate that XPath is an indispensable part of the style sheet. The recursive style sheet particularly shows this dependence upon XPath because of the heavy use of `template` and `apply-templates` elements for pattern matching, and the `if` elements for flow control. But because you read the previous chapter on XPath, all this XPath stuff is already old hat. You did read it, didn't you? Skipping ahead to the good parts, eh? For shame, no soup for you!

Before continuing, I'd like to take a moment to explain something to one of my former co-workers who might be reading this (Yeah, right! Like that would ever happen—the last technical book he read was *Curious George Builds a Web Page*) before continuing. First, there is no difference in XPath, regardless of where it is being used. The XPath in Europe is the same as the

XPath in Asia, which is the same as the XPath in North America, and if something on the Mars Rovers use XPath, then that is also the same. It is called a standard, which means that it is standard throughout the solar system. Sorry to those of you who understand the concept of standards; I just needed to exercise (exorcise) that particular demon for personal reasons. Besides, it was getting a little pudgy, and who wants a pudgy demon anyway?

10.3   ELEMENTS

Regardless of whether you consider XSLT to be a markup language, a scripting language, or just a pain in the fanny, it is, first and foremost, a dialect of XML and, therefore, must adhere to all of XML's rules. And I mean all of XML's rules because if it isn't well formed, then end of game. Fortunately, we've been there and done that already, which gives us the opportunity to look at the various XSLT elements available to us. Table 10-1 provides a high-level overview of these elements—not quite an orbital overview, but close. Don't worry; we cover some of these elements in much greater detail shortly.

Table 10-1   XSLT Elements

Element	Attributes	Description
apply-imports		Applies external templates that have been imported using the import element.
apply-templates	select *optional* mode *optional*	Applies templates that were defined locally.
attribute	name namespace *optional*	Specifies an attribute for the preceding element.
attribute-set	name use-attribute-sets *optional*	Defines a named set of attributes that can be used to specify a list of attributes en mass instead of individually.
call-template	name	Used to invoke a named template.
choose		Indicates the beginning of a case structure.
comment		Used to create comments in the output document.
copy	use-attribute-sets *optional*	Copies the current node and namespaces to the output document. However, it does not copy the children of the current node.

Element	Attributes	Description
copy-of	select	Copies the node or nodes specified by the select attribute to the output document.
decimal-format	decimal-separator *optional* digit *optional* grouping-separator *optional* infinity *optional* minus-sign *optional* name *optional* NaN *optional* pattern-separator *optional* per-mille *optional* percent *optional* zero-digit *optional*	Defines the appearance of numbers formatted using the format-number() function.
element	name namespace use-attribute-sets *optional*	Used to create an element in the output document.
fallback		Specifies to the XSL processor alternative code to run in case an XSL element is not supported.
for-each	select	Loops through the node set specified by the select attribute.
if	test	Executes the enclosed XSL when the result of the test is true. It is important to remember that no else clause exists for the if element. In these instances, the choose, when, and otherwise elements should be used.
import	href	Imports an external style sheet, which is the same as including a style sheet.
include	href	Includes an external style sheet, which is the same as importing a style sheet.
key	name match use	Defines a search key that is used to locate specific nodes based upon their value or the value of another node.

continues

Table 10-1   continued

Element	Attributes	Description
message	terminate *optional*	Writes a programmer-defined message to the output document.
namespace-alias	stylesheet-prefix result-prefix	Replaces the namespace specified with the stylesheet-prefix attribute on the input stylesheet with the namespace specified with the result-prefix attribute on the output document.
number	level *optional* count *optional* from *optional* value *optional* format *optional* lang *optional* letter-value *optional* group-separator *optional* grouping-size *optional*	Used to write a formatted number to the output document.
otherwise		Defines the default action for a case structure (choose).
output	method *optional* version *optional* encoding *optional* omit-xml-declaration *optional* standalone *optional* doctype-public *optional* doctype-system *optional* cdata-section-elements *optional* indent *optional* media-type *optional*	Defines the format of the output document.
param	name select *optional*	Used to specify template, stylesheet, and transform input parameters.
preserve-space	elements	Defines the elements for which whitespace is to be preserved on the output document.
processing-instruction	name	Writes an XML processing instruction to the output document.
sort	select *optional* lang *optional* data-type *optional* order *optional* case-order *optional*	Sorts a node set.

Element	Attributes	Description
strip-space	elements	Defines the elements for which whitespace is not to be preserved on the output document.
stylesheet	id *optional* extension-element-prefixes *optional* exclude-result-prefixes *optional* version	Defines the XSL document as a style sheet to the XSLT processor.
template	match *optional* name *optional* priority *optional* mode *optional*	Defines a template, which is essentially an XSL function.
text	disable-output-escaping *optional*	Indicates that the enclosed is text.
transform	id *optional* extension-element-prefixes *optional* exclude-result-prefixes *optional* version	Defines the XSL document as a style sheet to the XSLT processor, identical to the stylesheet element.
value-of	select disable-output-escaping *optional*	Writes the information specified by the select attribute to the output document.
variable	name select *optional*	Defines either a local or global variable to the XSLT processor.
when	test	Defines the individual cases of a case structure (choose).
with-param	name select *optional*	Defines the parameters to a template.

10.3.1 In the Beginning

In the beginning, all your data was painted on the wall of a cave somewhere, and it was good. Depending on the available light, it was human readable, self-describing, colorful, and even pretty. Unfortunately, civilization has advanced to the point that cave paintings just can't express the sheer volume of information available to us today. Enter XML, which, like its distant ancestor, is also human readable, self-describing, and, if you're using an XML editor such as Stylus Studio, both colorful and pretty.

Although it might seem to some people that we've come full circle in our data storage, from cave paintings to XML, there is a distinct advantage to XML. Unlike a cave painting, which pretty much just sits there on the wall looking about the same as it did 40,000 years ago, XML is a bit more portable. With the addition of XSLT, XML is also elastic and flexible. I'm sold on the concept, how about you? Good. The only issue remaining is how to start developing an XSL style sheet.

All XSL style sheets begin with one of two elements, either the stylesheet element or the transform element. They are interchangeable because both do exactly the same thing, although I recommend not using the transform element during months with *r*'s. Wait, maybe that was oysters—I have a tendency to confuse the two.

The next part of the style sheet is the output element, which essentially describes the format of the output. This is where you make the commitment of whether the output document will be XML, HTML, text, or, gasp, even XSLT. Not big on commitment? Not a problem. Just leave out the output element, and the output defaults to XML. Of course, come to think of it, that, too, is a form of commitment.

The next "standard" part of an XSL style sheet is the first template, the one that starts the whole ball rolling. However, before we get there, I should point out that between the first element and the first template is where some really useful elements go. Parameters from the outside world and global variables are just two examples. In fact, let's take a look at Table 10-2, which indicates where elements can be defined in a style sheet and what effect location can have on their behavior.

Table 10-2   XSL Style Sheet Elements and Where They Can Be Defined

Element	Defined Where
apply-imports	Either root or element level
apply-templates	Either root or element level
attribute	Element level
attribute-set	Root level
call-template	Element level
choose	Element level
comment	Either root or element level
copy	Element level
copy-of	Element level
decimal-format	Root level
element	Element level
fallback	Element level
if	Element level
import	Root level
include	Root level

Element	Defined Where
key	Root level
message	Element level
namespace-alias	Root level
number	Root level
otherwise	Element level
output	Root level
preserve-space	Root level
processing-instruction	Root level
sort	Element level
strip-space	Root level
stylesheet	Root level
template	Root level
text	Element level
transform	Root level
value-of	Element level
variable	Element level
when	Element level
with-param	Element level

At last we've come to the first template of the style sheet. Unfortunately, it is kind of anticlimatic because 99 percent of all style sheets start with a template element that looks just like this:

```
<xsl:template match="/">
```

Boring, isn't it? Yes, you can make it more specific and have it look for a particular element that should be in the input document. I don't recommend it, though, because it will only cause problems someday when, for some reason, that specific element is not in the input document. Then comes the inevitable yelling, the finger pointing, and the peasants with pitchforks and torches again. Not a pretty picture.

10.3.2   Templates and How to Use Them

After the initial template, the one that establishes the current location as the root, what are some of the other ways to use templates?

Earlier I stated that templates could have names, although it wasn't required. In XSLT, these named templates fill pretty much the same niche that functions do in a language such as JavaScript or PHP. They can accept parameters and return results. In my opinion, if it looks like a duck and walks like a duck, the odds are, it is a duck. Unless it is a goose, but that is kind of like duckzilla, so it isn't a problem.

Let's take a look at what a typical, although useless, named function looks like. Shown in Listing 10-6, its purpose is to accept two numbers, add them, and return the result.

Listing 10-6   Named Template

```
<xsl:template name="add">
    <xsl:param name="a" />
    <xsl:param name="b" />

    <xsl:value-of select="number($a) + number($b)" />
</xsl:template>
```

Thankfully, this is one of those times when something both seems simple and actually is simple, as long as you remember that dollar signs aren't required at definition but are required when used. However, the same thing can't always be said for templates invoked using XPath—but before we go there, perhaps it would be better to take a look at two more mundane templates. Using the XML shown way back in Listing 10-4, the style sheets shown in Listings 10-7 and 10-8 do exactly the same thing in a slightly different manner.

Listing 10-7   A Pure XSLT Example

```
<?xml version="1.0"?>
<xsl:stylesheet version="1.0"
xmlns:xsl="http://www.w3.org/1999/XSL/Transform">
    <xsl:preserve-space elements="text"/>

    <xsl:template match="/">

      <xsl:element name="div">
        <xsl:apply-templates select="//library"/>
      </xsl:element>

    </xsl:template>

    <xsl:template match="library">

      <xsl:element name="table">
        <xsl:attribute name="width">100%</xsl:attribute>

        <xsl:for-each select="book">
          <xsl:element name="tr">

            <xsl:for-each select="*">
```

```
                    <xsl:element name="td">
                      <xsl:attribute name="width">33%</xsl:attribute>

                      <xsl:value-of select="."/>

                  <xsl:if test="string-length(.) = 0">
                        <xsl:text> </xsl:text>
                      </xsl:if>
                    </xsl:element>
                  </xsl:for-each>
            </xsl:element>
             </xsl:for-each>
            </xsl:element>

        </xsl:template>

</xsl:stylesheet>
```

Listing 10-8 An XSLT/XHTML Hybrid Example

```
<?xml version="1.0"?>
<xsl:stylesheet version="1.0"
xmlns:xsl="http://www.w3.org/1999/XSL/Transform">
      <xsl:preserve-space elements="text"/>

      <xsl:template match="/">

        <xsl:element name="div">
          <xsl:apply-templates select="//library"/>
        </xsl:element>

      </xsl:template>

      <xsl:template match="library">

        <xsl:element name="table">
          <xsl:attribute name="width">100%</xsl:attribute>

          <xsl:for-each select="book">
            <tr>
              <xsl:for-each select="*">
                <td width="33%">
                  <xsl:value-of select="."/>

                  <xsl:if test="string-length(.) = 0">
                    <xsl:text> </xsl:text>
                  </xsl:if>
                </td>
              </xsl:for-each>
            </tr>
          </xsl:for-each>
```

continues

Listing 10-8   continued

```
      </xsl:element>

   </xsl:template>

</xsl:stylesheet>
```

Confused? Don't be. Because XSLT and XHTML are both dialects of XML, there is absolutely nothing wrong with mixing the two. At first glance, the style sheet shown in Listing 10-8 might seem to be a little like a mutt, part this and part that. But as weird as it seems, it is much more common than the purebred solution from Listing 10-7.

Earlier I stated that templates invoked using XPath aren't always simple because, at times, more than one template matches. If you don't expect this, it could, at the very least, be an embarrassment. However, there is a way to specify which template to use when more than one matches the criteria.

The `mode` attribute, which is on both the `template` and `apply-templates` elements, is used to specify which template to use when a particular `select` could result in more than one match. Listing 10-9, a merging of Listings 10-7 and 10-8, has an example of this. The only difference, other than the merging, is the addition of a `mode` attribute for the `mutt` template and a new `apply-templates` element, also with a `mode` attribute.

Listing 10-9   Distinguishing Template Matches Using Mode

```
<?xml version="1.0"?>
<xsl:stylesheet version="1.0"
xmlns:xsl="http://www.w3.org/1999/XSL/Transform">
  <xsl:preserve-space elements="text"/>

  <xsl:template match="/">

    <xsl:element name="div">
      <xsl:apply-templates select="//library" />
      <xsl:apply-templates select="//library" mode="mutt" />
    </xsl:element>

  </xsl:template>

  <xsl:template match="library">

    <xsl:element name="table">
      <xsl:attribute name="width">100%</xsl:attribute>
```

```
        <xsl:for-each select="book">
          <xsl:element name="tr">

             <xsl:for-each select="*">
               <xsl:element name="td">
                 <xsl:attribute name="width">33%</xsl:attribute>

                 <xsl:value-of select="." />

               <xsl:if test="string-length(.) = 0">
                   <xsl:text> </xsl:text>
                 </xsl:if>
               </xsl:element>
             </xsl:for-each>
          </xsl:element>
        </xsl:for-each>
     </xsl:element>

  </xsl:template>

  <xsl:template match="library" mode="mutt">

    <xsl:element name="table">
      <xsl:attribute name="width">100%</xsl:attribute>

      <xsl:for-each select="book">
        <tr>
          <xsl:for-each select="*">
            <td width="33%">
              <xsl:value-of select="." />

              <xsl:if test="string-length(.) = 0">
                  <xsl:text> </xsl:text>
                </xsl:if>
              </td>
            </xsl:for-each>
        </tr>
      </xsl:for-each>
    </xsl:element>

  </xsl:template>

</xsl:stylesheet>
```

The mode attribute provides additional criteria for the match. Instead of
the XPath being the only criteria, the mode is also used. So a simple XPath
match alone is not enough; there also has to be a match to the mode. This
leads to some interesting possibilities, such as when the mode name is
unknown. Just use an asterisk as the mode name and use the mode to indicate
the depth, or something along those lines.

10.3.3   Decisions, Decisions

As in the majority of programming languages, XSLT provides flow control in the way of decision structures. Excluding apply-templates, which can be used for some similar functionality, there is the if element and a case structure, called choose. Basically, it is all easy stuff, but two issues with XSLT decisions can cause many developers problems.

The first of these issues is how to test for greater than and less than, and still keep the document well formed. Fortunately, the previous chapter covered this problem when discussing XPath. The only remaining issue is one that causes quite a number of headaches: a lack of an else for the if element.

Lack of an else might seem like, if not an insurmountable problem, at least an annoying problem. Because of this lack, the choose element is used more often in languages with an else. Listing 10-10 is an example of a workaround for this lack of an else statement.

Listing 10-10   A Workaround

```
<?xml version='1.0'?>
<xsl:stylesheet version="1.0"
xmlns:xsl="http://www.w3.org/1999/XSL/Transform">

  <xsl:template match="/">
    <xsl:variable name="value" select="7" />

    <xsl:element name="div">
      <xsl:choose>
        <xsl:when test="($value mod 2) = 0">Even</xsl:when>
        <xsl:otherwise>Not even</xsl:otherwise>
      </xsl:choose>
    </xsl:element>
  </xsl:template>

</xsl:stylesheet>
```

10.3.4   Sorting Out Looping

XSL style sheets have a built-in mechanism for sorting node sets, which can be rather useful when information needs to be arranged in a specific sequence. As with everything in XSL, sorting is accomplished through the use of an element, which, appropriately, is called sort. Interesting how these things work out, isn't it?

Listings 10-11 and 10-12 both show examples of the use of the sort element, with a couple minor differences. For example, Listing 10-11 uses a for-each element to navigate through the node set, which is sorted into ascending sequence. In Listing 10-12, an `apply-templates` is used, and the node set is sorted into descending sequence.

Listing 10-11 A `for-each` Sort Example

```
<?xml version='1.0'?>
<xsl:stylesheet version="1.0"
xmlns:xsl="http://www.w3.org/1999/XSL/Transform">

  <xsl:template match="/">
    <xsl:element name="table">
      <xsl:attribute name="width">100%</xsl:attribute>

      <xsl:for-each select="//book">
          <xsl:sort select="title" order="ascending"  />

          <xsl:element name="tr">
            <xsl:for-each select="*">
              <xsl:element name="td">
                <xsl:value-of select="." />
              </xsl:element>
            </xsl:for-each>
          </xsl:element>
        </xsl:for-each>
    </xsl:element>

  </xsl:template>

</xsl:stylesheet>
```

Listing 10-12 A `template` `sort` Example

```
<?xml version='1.0'?>
<xsl:stylesheet version="1.0"
xmlns:xsl="http://www.w3.org/1999/XSL/Transform">

  <xsl:template match="/">
    <xsl:element name="table">
      <xsl:attribute name="width">100%</xsl:attribute>

      <xsl:apply-templates select="//book">
        <xsl:sort select="title" order="descending"  />
        </xsl:apply-templates>
       </xsl:element>

  </xsl:template>

  <xsl:template match="*">

    <xsl:element name="tr">
      <xsl:for-each select="*">
        <xsl:element name="td">
```

continues

Listing 10-12   continued

```
            <xsl:value-of select="." />
        </xsl:element>
         </xsl:for-each>
        </xsl:element>

   </xsl:template>

</xsl:stylesheet>
```

10.4 XSLT FUNCTIONS

Unlike XPath, which has a plethora of functions, the number of XSL functions
is significantly lower. Mostly, the reason for this is that the XPath functions
are fully available to supplement the few functions shown in Table 10-3.

Table 10-3   XSL Functions

Function	Description
`Current()`	Returns only the current node in a node set
`document()`	Used to access an XML document other than the source document
`element-available()`	Returns a `true` condition if the passed string is a supported XSL element
`Format-number()`	Returns a formatted numeric string using a number and a pattern as input
`function-available()`	Returns a `true` condition if the passed string is a supported XSL or XPath function
`generate-id(node)`	Returns an ID that is unique to the node passed, regardless of how the node was obtained
`key()`	Returns a node set that was previously indexed using the `key` element
`System-property()`	Returns a value for a specific system property
`unparsed-entity-uri()`	Returns the URI of an unparsed entity

10.5 XSLT CONCEPTS

When developing an XSL style sheet, I usually find myself using only two of
the XSL functions shown earlier: the `key()` function and the `generate-id()`

function, both of which are indispensable when doing something unique to XSL style sheets. I am referring to something called Muenchian grouping.

Muenchian grouping, invented by Steve Muench, the XML Evangelist of the Oracle Corporation, is a method of grouping nodes based upon their values. Although I can describe how it works, it is probably a better idea to take a look at the example of Muenchian grouping shown in Listing 10-13. After that, we take it apart to see how it works.

Listing 10-13   A Muenchian Grouping Example

```
<?xml version="1.0" encoding="UTF-8"?>
<xsl:stylesheet version="1.0"
xmlns:xsl="http://www.w3.org/1999/XSL/Transform">
  <xsl:output method="html" version="1.0" encoding="UTF-8" indent="yes" />
  <xsl:key name="keyBook" match="book" use="series" />

  <xsl:template match="/">

    <xsl:element name="table">
      <xsl:attribute name="width">100%</xsl:attribute>

      <xsl:apply-templates select="//book[1]" mode="header" />
    <xsl:apply-templates select="//book[generate-id(.) = generate-
id(key('keyBook',series)[1])]" />
      <xsl:apply-templates select="//book[string-length(series) =
0]/series" />
  </xsl:element>

  </xsl:template>

<xsl:template match="book">

    <xsl:variable name="key">
      <xsl:value-of select="series" />
    </xsl:variable>

    <xsl:apply-templates select="//series[node() = $key]" />

  </xsl:template>

  <xsl:template match="series">

    <xsl:element name="tr">
      <xsl:apply-templates select="parent::node()/*" mode="cell" />
    </xsl:element>

  </xsl:template>

  <xsl:template match="*" mode="cell">

    <xsl:element name="td">
```

continues

Listing 10-13 continued

```
      <xsl:attribute name="align">left</xsl:attribute>

   <xsl:value-of select="." />
  </xsl:element>

  </xsl:template>

  <xsl:template match="book" mode="header">

  <xsl:element name="tr">
    <xsl:apply-templates select="./*" mode="columnHeader" />
  </xsl:element>

  </xsl:template>

  <xsl:template match="*" mode="columnHeader">

    <xsl:variable
name="lowerCase">qwertyuiopasdfghjklzxcvbnm</xsl:variable>
    <xsl:variable
name="upperCase">QWERTYUIOPASDFGHJKLZXCVBNM</xsl:variable>

    <xsl:element name="th">
      <xsl:attribute name="width">33%</xsl:attribute>

      <xsl:value-of select="translate(name(.),$lowerCase,$upperCase)" />
    </xsl:element>

  </xsl:template>

</xsl:stylesheet>
```

The element that starts the whole ball rolling is the key element, which creates a cross-reference based upon the node specified by the use attribute. Using the series element as the key results in an index consisting of The Lord of the Rings and Lord Darcy, with the book *The Way Station* left out because its series element is null. This cross-reference is accessed using the key function, which accepts two parameters: the name from the key element and the node.

Another function that plays an integral part in Muenchian grouping is the generate-id function. This function, well, generates a unique ID for every node in an XML document every time that the document is processed. So the XPath statement //book[generate-id(.) = generate-id(key('keyBook',series)[1])] locates the first element with each unique key from the cross-reference and applies the matching template. The matching template then uses the unique series to select the matching elements.

It is all pretty basic XSLT and XPath stuff, although it does have a tendency to make grown men whimper like little scared puppies. If it doesn't, here is one that will put someone over the edge: Imagine trying to group based upon multiple criteria, such as author and series. Although it isn't done very often, and you'll probably never have to do it, I'll give you a hint: Concatenate the elements using the `concat` function.

10.6   CLIENT-SIDE TRANSFORMATIONS

Now that we've got an idea of what an XSL style sheet is and what effect it has on XML, I'm thinking that it might be a good idea to see how to apply XSL in the browser. Although browsers that support XSLT all use JavaScript to create the necessary objects, this is yet another one of those instances in which there is Microsoft Internet Explorer and everybody else. Despite this, the flow is essentially the same, regardless of the client's browser.

When setting out to perform client-side transformations, the first tasks are always to obtain the XML and the XSL style sheet. A number of ways exist for doing this, ranging from having the document embedded in the web page, to loading it directly from the web server, to requesting it from a web service. How the document is obtained isn't nearly as important as just obtaining it.

The next task it to create an XSLT processor, pass the style sheet and the XML document, and then get the resulting document and use it. This whole process sounds relatively easy, doesn't it? And my question is loaded, isn't it? The answers to the questions are "yes" and "no." Applying an XSL style sheet in the browser is actually as easy as it sounds.

With client-side transformations, the only "gotcha" is being aware of the browser. ActiveX won't work in Firefox, Flock, Mozilla, or Netscape, and nothing but ActiveX will work in Internet Explorer. Yes, it is an annoyance, but it is nothing that we haven't lived with for the better part of a decade. Besides, this is one of those things that, once coded, can be cloned again and again. In short, it is a nice addition to our bag of tricks.

10.6.1   XSLT in Microsoft Internet Explorer

When working with Internet Explorer, if something isn't part of HTML, or part of CSS, or part of JavaScript, the odds are, it is part of ActiveX. Think of ActiveX as the bilge of Internet Explorer; a lot of stuff is down there, and some of it is scary, but that is another story. In reality, ActiveX is the Internet descendant of Microsoft's original object-based framework, Object Linking and Embedding, or OLE.

ActiveX objects are instantiated using the JavaScript new operator in the following manner:

```
var XSLTemplate = new ActiveXObject('MSXML2.XSLTemplate.3.0');
```

The previous statement is merely the first step in applying an XSL style sheet on the client side using JavaScript. In Internet Explorer, the next step is to specify the XSL style sheet, in the form of an XML document, to the template, like this:

```
XSLTemplate.stylesheet = XSL;
```

The next step is to create an XSLT processor using the instance of the XSL template:

```
var XSLTProcessor = XSLTemplate.createProcessor;
```

Now it is time to specify the XML document to the XSLT processor in the following manner:

```
XSLTProcessor.input = XML;
```

Hang in there; the end is in sight. So far, we've created an XSL template, specified the XSL style sheet, created an XSLT processor, and specified the XML document. This leaves just two steps, the first of which is applying the style sheet:

```
XSLTProcessor.transform();
```

The final step is simply to use the output from the processor, which, incidentally, is text:

```
document.getElementById('example').innerHTML = XSLTProcessor.output;
```

Put together as one routine, the entire sequence of JavaScript is shown in Listing 10-14.

Listing 10-14   Internet Explorer

```
var XSLTemplate = new ActiveXObject('MSXML2.XSLTemplate.3.0');

XSLTemplate.stylesheet = XSL;

var XSLTProcessor = XSLTemplate.createProcessor;

XSLTProcessor.input = XML;

XSLTProcessor.transform();

document.getElementById('example').innerHTML =

XSLTProcessor.output;
```

If you're a big fan of complicated procedures, such as the one necessary with Microsoft Internet Explorer shown earlier, be ready to be disappointed. Unlike Internet Explorer, the other browsers that support XSLT, including open source browsers such as Firefox, Mozilla, and Flock, require a simple three-step process:

1. Create an XSLT processor.
2. Import the style sheet as an XML document.
3. Apply the style sheet and use the resulting XML document or document fragment.

The only oddities, from an Internet Explorer point of view, are the fact that the result is an XML document or document fragment. This means that there are two methods for applying an XSL style sheet: one for documents, transformToDocument, and a second for document fragments, transformToFragment. Listing 10-15 shows how it works using the transformToFragment method.

Listing 10-15   Non-IE

```
var XSLTProcessor = new XSLTProcessor();

XSLTProcessor.importStylesheet(xslt);

document.getElementById('example').appendChild(objXSLTProcessor.transform
ToFragment(xml, document));
```

In my opinion, unless the application is an intranet application, the way to go is to code to use both types of browsers. But that is a personal decision; just remember that sometimes an intranet application doesn't stay an intranet application.

10.7 SUMMARY

XSLT is one of my favorite parts of programming; however, it can be difficult to grasp. To combat this problem, we started at the beginning with iterative and recursive style sheets. Next I covered scope and the issues with nonvariable variables. We then took a little step backward to cover XPath and its relationship to XSLT before rolling up our sleeves and getting down to some serious XSLT.

The basics of templates were discussed, including named templates and the use of the `mode` attribute. Following that, we covered how to handle decisions using `if` and `choose`, along with sorting. The built-in XSLT functions were then described, along with how some of them are used in grouping. Finally, we covered the subject of client-side transformations.

CHAPTER 11

Ajax Using XSLT

"But wait, there's more ...."

I do so feel like someone hawking my wares on a late-night infomercial, but hey, it's true. There is actually more to Ajax than what we've already covered. In fact, we're about to get to one of my favorite parts. I've jokingly referred to the material covered up to this point as "mad scientist stuff," but the material that we're about to cover transcends everything that we've covered up till now. It is called eXtensible Stylesheet Language for Transformations, or XSLT, and I like to think of it as magic. Think of XSLT as the part of a spell that says what to do. The second part of the spell is XPath, which acts as the targeting device for the spell. Tightly intertwined, XSLT and XPath work together to modify or, if you prefer, transform XML.

11.1 XSLT

Transformations are an idea as old as human thought. Primitive societies had werewolves, werebears, and weretigers. The Greeks had warnings against seeing goddesses bathe, unless one was interested in going to parties stag, literally. During the renaissance, there was Shakespeare's *A Midsummer's Night Dream*, in which Bottom was made an Ass of. Today we have Jack Chalker's *Midnight at the Well of Souls* and the Borg from Star Trek. And although the transformations in each of these stories dealt with the physical world and XSLT can affect only XML, they all share many of the same characteristics: Without change, the story can progress no further.

As one who has been working in the programming field for a number of years, I can attest to one thing: About 40 percent of the time, the data is in the wrong format. In ancient times, when great beasts with names such as System 370 or PDP-11 roamed the landscape, data being in the wrong format was a major problem. Programs had to be changed or written from scratch to massage the data to make it usable. Changing programs and creating programs has always been a costly undertaking in any day and age.

Now things are different, as time seems to be speeding up. The great beasts are all either dead or behind glass in museums, where people can stare in awe, never realizing that the old 486 machine that they gave to their kids had more power.

Today much of the information that we deal with is in the form of XML, which, interestingly enough, can be transformed by XSLT in much the same manner as Lon Chaney was by the full moon. Thankfully, however, the XML doesn't get hairy—unless, of course, we want it to.

11.1.1   XML Magic

Here's the quandary: On the client side, we have XML and we want HTML. It's a real pain in the gluteus, isn't it?

Yes, we can write a script to perform the conversion, but it is a time-consuming task accomplished with ill-suited tools. Face it: The majority of scripting languages aren't really built to handle XML. Although it works just fine, when messing around with individual nodes, JavaScript's XML support comes across like a Bose sound system in a Ford Pinto. I'm not saying that it doesn't work—it works just fine, but, unfortunately, six months later it has a tendency to cause questions like, "I wrote this?"

XSLT, as opposed to JavaScript, was designed from the ground up to handle XML. Come to think of it, XSLT is itself a dialect of XML. This has a tendency to lead to some really interesting style sheets when working with XSLT, but that is a topic for another day. Another interesting thing is that although the input has to be XML, nothing says that the output needs to be XML. This means that if you want to transform XML into HTML as opposed to XHTML, by all means do it, but just remember that if you're using SOAP, the package must be well formed.

11.1.2   How Microsoft Shot Itself in the Foot

Back in the old days, during the first browser wars, Microsoft released Internet Explorer version 5.0, the first web browser with XSLT support. It would have been a major victory for Microsoft , if it had not been for one little detail. In their haste, they forgot one little thing about the World Wide Web Consortium's recommendations. You see, recommendations are often vastly different from drafts. In an effort to produce the first browser with XSLT support, Microsoft used a draft as a guide.

For this reason, you sometimes see references to the namespace http:// www.w3.org/TR/WD-xsl instead of http://www.w3.org/1999/XSL/Transform.

It was only with the advent of Microsoft Internet Explorer 6 that Internet Explorer started following the recommendation instead of the draft. Personally, I believe that it is a good idea to ignore the old namespace entirely; I think that Microsoft would like to. And although they're currently considered the third most popular browser, at most, individuals using versions 5.0, 5.01, and 5.5 of Internet Explorer comprise only a fraction of the general population. It is a pretty safe bet that you can ignore these web browsers entirely without alienating anyone but technophobes, the White House, and project leaders who use the term *blink*.

11.1.3 XPath, or I Left It Around Here Someplace

Earlier I stated that XPath was the targeting device for XSLT, which is essentially true. XPath is used to describe the XML node or nodes that we're looking for. As the name suggests, XPath describes the path to the node that we're looking for. For example, let's say that we want the `state_name` node in the XML document shown in Listing 11-1. A number of different ways exist for locating it, some of which are shown in Listing 11-2.

Listing 11-1 A Sample XML Document

```
<states>
     <state>
          <state_abbreviation>AB</state_abbreviation>
          <state_name>Alberta</state_name>
     </state>
     <state>
          <state_abbreviation>AK</state_abbreviation>
          <state_name>Alaska</state_name>
     </state>
     <state>
          <state_abbreviation>AL</state_abbreviation>
          <state_name>Alabama</state_name>
     </state>
     <state>
          <state_abbreviation>AR</state_abbreviation>
          <state_name>Arkansas</state_name>
     </state>
</states>
```

Listing 11-2 Sample XPath

```
/states/state/state_name
/*/*/state_name
/*/*/*[name(.) = 'state_name']
/states/state/*[2]
//state_name
```

Why so many? With XPath, it is possible to describe complete paths, paths with wildcards, and paths based upon its location, or to describe only the node itself. From a high level, such as an orbital view, it works as shown in Table 11-1.

Table 11-1   High-Level View of XPath

XPath Notation	Description
/	Either the root node, in the case of the first slash, or a separator between nodes
//	Anywhere in the document that meets the criteria
*	Wildcard (I know that there is a node here, but I don't know its name)
.	The context node (where we are at this point)
[2]	A predicate stating that the second node is the one we want
states	Qualified node name
state	Qualified node name
state_name	Qualified node name
name()	A function that returns the name of passed node
[name(.) = 'state_name']	A predicate stating that the desired node name is state_name

Alright, that should be enough XPath to get started. Now let's take a gander at the XSLT shown in Listing 11-3, whose purpose is to build an HTML `select` object using the XML from Listing 11-1.

Listing 11-3   Sample XSL Style Sheet

```
<?xml version='1.0'?>
<xsl:stylesheet version="1.0"
xmlns:xsl="http://www.w3.org/1999/XSL/Transform">
     <xsl:output method="html" indent="yes" media-type="text/html"/>

     <xsl:template match="/">

          <select id="myselect" name="myselect">
               <xsl:for-each select="/states/state">
                    <xsl:element name="option">
                         <xsl:attribute name="value">
                              <xsl:value-of
select="state_abbreviation" />
                         </xsl:attribute>
```

```
                              <xsl:value-of select="state_name" />
                      </xsl:element>
              </xsl:for-each>
          </select>

      </xsl:template>

</xsl:stylesheet>
```

Pretty cool, isn't it? At first glance, not only is it nicely indented, but it also has the advantage of being one of the most obscure things that you've ever laid your eyes upon. A second glance reveals some details that you might have missed the first time; for example, the `select` statement looks remarkably like HTML. There is a very good reason for the resemblance: It is HTML. In fact, the `xsl:output` statement even says that it is HTML, and you can take it from me, `xsl:output` statements don't lie.

Upon closer examination, some other details might pop out, such as the `xsl:template` with `match="/"`. From what we covered earlier, the slash means that we're looking for the root node. And while we're examining XPath, you'll find `xsl:for-each` with `select="/states/state"`. Just in case you're wondering, `for-each` means exactly what you think it does: Iterate once for every node that matches the predicate.

Another thing that might jump out is the `xsl:element` node with `name="option"`. This is an alternate method of specifying an output element. The `xsl:attribute` also does exactly what you'd expect from its name; it defines an attribute of the previous `xsl:element`. Finally, the `xsl:value-of` simply copies the node's content from the source document to the output document. In a nutshell, that's pretty much the basics of XSLT and XPath. The next question, of course, is, "So, what does the output HTML look like?" For the answer, check out Listing 11-4.

Listing 11-4   HTML Output

```
<select id="myselect" name="myselect">
  <option value="AB">Alberta</option>
  <option value="AK">Alaska</option>
  <option value="AL">Alabama</option>
  <option value="AR">Arkansas</option>
</select>
```

Later, both in this chapter and in others, you'll find more detailed examples of client-side XSLT.

11.1.4   What I Learned from the Gecko

Back when I was first learning XSLT, I was developing with the bare minimum, a text editor and a copy of Microsoft Internet Explorer version 5.01—and I was happy! Well, at least for about 20 minutes or so, right up to the point I read the World Wide Web Consortium's XSLT recommendation. But we've already covered that, and after I downloaded a copy of Internet Explorer version 6, I was happy again—at least, until I found Mozilla and then Firefox.

My first impression was that there was something wrong with the Gecko XSLT processor, but there was a gnawing doubt. The reason for this was that I'd never personally found an error in a Gecko-based browser, and I had found several in Internet Explorer. So with a critical eye and a hard copy of the recommendation, I began to examine the "bugs" that I had found in the Gecko XSLT processor.

The results came as no surprise to me. Gecko strictly followed the published recommendation, whereas IE seemed somewhat looser around the edges. My problem was that I had developed some bad habits developing in a microcosm and had a tendency to tailor my code to that microcosm. Because of this, I now try out my style sheets in at least two different XSLT processors before I consider them even partially tested.

Let's take a look at how to create an instance of the XSLT processor in Microsoft Internet Explorer and every other web browser on the planet—er, I mean Firefox, yeah, Firefox. Listing 11-5 shows a little cross-browser web page that uses one XML Data Island, the first containing the XML while the XSLT is loaded from the server via the XMLHttpRequest object. This is nothing flashy, merely a "proof of concept." It just creates an HTML select object and plops it on a page.

Listing 11-5   XSLT Cross-Browser Web Page Example

```
<html>
    <head>
            <title>XML Data Island Test</title>
            <style type="text/css">
xml
{
     display: none;
     font-size: 0px
}
            </style>
            <script language="JavaScript">
var _IE = (new RegExp('internet explorer','gi')).test(navigator.appName);
var _XMLHTTP;                                    //
 XMLHttpRequest object
var _objXML;                      // XML DOM document
var _objXSL;                      //
 Stylesheet
```

```
var _objXSLTProcessor;           // XSL Processor
var _xslt = 'stateSelect.xsl'; // Path to style sheet

/*
    Function:    initialize
      Programmer: Edmond Woychowsky
      Purpose:    Perform page initialization.
*/
function initialize() {
  if(_IE) {
    _XMLHTTP = new ActiveXObject('Microsoft.XMLHTTP');

    _objXML =
     new ActiveXObject('MSXML2.FreeThreadedDOMDocument.3.0');
    _objXSL =
    new ActiveXObject('MSXML2.FreeThreadedDOMDocument.3.0');

    _objXML.async = false;
    _objXSL.async = false;

    _objXML.load(document.getElementById('xmlDI').XMLDocument);
  } else {
      var _objParser = new DOMParser();

      _XMLHTTP = new XMLHttpRequest();

      _objXSLTProcessor = new XSLTProcessor();
      _objXML =
_objParser.parseFromString(document.getElementById('xmlDI').innerHTML,
"text/xml");

  }

  _XMLHTTP.onreadystatechange = stateChangeHandler;

  _XMLHTTP.open('GET',_xslt,true);
  _XMLHTTP.send(null);
}

/*
    Function:    stateChangeHandler
      Programmer: Edmond Woychowsky
      Purpose:    Handle the asynchronous response to an
                  XMLHttpRequest, transform the XML Data Island and
                  display the resulting XHTML.
*/
function stateChangeHandler() {
  var strXHTML;

  if(_XMLHTTP.readyState == 4) {
      if(_IE) {
            var _objXSLTemplate =
```

continues

Listing 11-5   continued

```
            new ActiveXObject('MSXML2.XSLTemplate.3.0');

            _objXSL.loadXML(_XMLHTTP.responseText);
            _objXSLTemplate.stylesheet = _objXSL;
            _objXSLTProcessor = _objXSLTemplate.createProcessor;
            _objXSLTProcessor.input = _objXML;

            _objXSLTProcessor.transform();

            strXHTML = _objXSLTProcessor.output;
      } else {
            var _objSerializer = new XMLSerializer();

            _objXSL = _XMLHTTP.responseXML;

            _objXSLTProcessor.importStylesheet(_objXSL);

            strXHTML =
_objSerializer.serializeToString(_objXSLTProcessor.transformToFragment
(_objXML, document));
      }

      document.getElementById('target').innerHTML = strXHTML;
  }
}
            </script>
      </head>
      <body onload="initialize()">
            <xml id="xmlDI">
            <states>
                  <state>
                        <state_abbreviation>AB</state_abbreviation>
                        <state_name>Alberta</state_name>
                  </state>
                  <state>
                        <state_abbreviation>AK</state_abbreviation>
                        <state_name>Alaska</state_name>
                  </state>
                  <state>
                        <state_abbreviation>AL</state_abbreviation>
                        <state_name>Alabama</state_name>
                  </state>
                  <state>
                        <state_abbreviation>AR</state_abbreviation>
                        <state_name>Arkansas</state_name>
                  </state>
            </states>
        </xml>
            <b>XML client-side transformation test</b>
        <div id="target"></div>
      </body>
</html>
```

Alright, now that the proof of concept has been successfully completed, all that remains is to see how it can be applied to our e-commerce website.

A Problem Revisited

Now that we have some of the basics down, let's take a look at how XSLT can be used to provide additional functionality to our e-commerce website. I should point out, however, that when I originally proposed this idea to a client, I was called insane. The comments were that it would be unworkable and that nobody in their right mind would have even suggested it. In my defense, this was the client that used terms such as *blink* and was "looking into" converting all web applications into COBOL so that developers other than the consultants could understand it.

That's enough introductions; without further ado, allow me to describe what I consider the ultimate "mad scientist" website.

Excluding pop-ups, the site would be a single web page, with all communication between the server and the client taking place using the XMLHttpRequest object. Instead of subjecting the visitor to an endless cycle of unloads and reloads, the page would simply request whatever it needed directly. In addition, when a particular XSLT was obtained from the server, the client would cache it, meaning that the next time it was needed, it would already be there. It was within the realm of possibility that eventually the client would have all the XSLT cached on the web browser. The more the visitor did, the better the shopping experience would become.

Needless to say, the website was never created, alas, and my contract was terminated because they felt that resources could be better used supporting their mainframe applications. Personally, I think that they lacked foresight, and if they had pursued the concept to its logical conclusion, they'd now be mentioned in the same breath as Google. Instead, they decided to regress into the future of the 1960s as opposed to the future of the twenty-first century. But I'm hardly an objective observer.

11.2 TABULAR INFORMATION

The previous chapter introduced several JavaScript class constructors in an effort to keep the client-side code manageable. Now is a good time to introduce another, a wrapper around the XSLT processor to handle the browser-specific details involving exactly what is required for XSL transformations. Displaying my usual lack of imagination, the class constructor is named appropriately enough: XSLTProcessor. Table 11-2 shows the properties and methods for this class.

Table 11-2 XSLTProcessor

Name	Parent Class	Type	Description
XSLTProcessor	—	Class	Constructor
importStylesheet	XSLTProcessor	Method	Loads the XSL document for the transformation.
load	XSLTProcessor	Method	Loads the XML document to be transformed.
output	XSLTProcessor	Method	The serialized result of the previous transformation.
readyState	XSLTProcessor	Method	Either the ready state for the XML document or the XSL document, whichever is lower. When they are equal, the appropriate ready state value is returned.
setParameter	XSLTProcessor	Method	Set a parameter for the XSLT processor.
transform	XSLTProcessor	Method	Performs the transformation and returns the serialized result.

With the creation of the XSLTProcessor constructor, the only items remaining are those that are absolutely essential to the website. The essential items are the XSL style sheets themselves, three in total. The first style sheet creates the HTML for the Items page. The purpose of the second style sheet is to create/render the Details page. The final style sheet renders the shopping cart in a slightly different manner than you'd expect. Each of these three items is covered as needed.

11.2.1   Read Only

Please bear with me; what I'm about to say deals only with read-only pages and, to some, might seem to be heresy. When using XSL for read-only pages, data binding isn't necessary; in fact, it is unnecessary overhead. Think about it for a moment: First, the information isn't going to change on the client side. In addition, the transformation process has already taken care of the display of the information. For the aforementioned reasons, it is perfectly acceptable to skip the bind when dealing with read-only information, as the style sheet in Listing 11-6 illustrates.

Listing 11-6   XSL Style Sheet to Produce a Nonbound Table

```xml
<?xml version='1.0'?>
<xsl:stylesheet version="1.0"
xmlns:xsl="http://www.w3.org/1999/XSL/Transform">
      <xsl:output method="html" indent="yes" media-type="text/html"/>

      <xsl:template match="/">
            <xsl:element name="div">
                  <xsl:call-template name="row">
                        <xsl:with-param name="string" select="'Guild
Name:'" />
                        <xsl:with-param name="top" select="'75px'" />
                  </xsl:call-template>
                  <xsl:call-template name="row">
                        <xsl:with-param name="string" select="'Item
Name:'" />
                        <xsl:with-param name="top" select="'92px'" />
                  </xsl:call-template>
                  <xsl:call-template name="row">
                        <xsl:with-param name="string"
select="'Description:'" />
                        <xsl:with-param name="top" select="'110px'" />
                  </xsl:call-template>
                  <xsl:call-template name="row">
                        <xsl:with-param name="string" select="'Price:'" />
                        <xsl:with-param name="top" select="'127px'" />
                  </xsl:call-template>

                  <xsl:call-template name="row">
                        <xsl:with-param name="string"
select="'guild_name'" />
                        <xsl:with-param name="type" select="'data'" />
                        <xsl:with-param name="top" select="'75px'" />
                  </xsl:call-template>
                  <xsl:call-template name="row">
                        <xsl:with-param name="string" select="'item_name'"
/>
                        <xsl:with-param name="type" select="'data'" />
                        <xsl:with-param name="top" select="'92px'" />
                  </xsl:call-template>
                  <xsl:call-template name="row">
                        <xsl:with-param name="string"
select="'item_description'" />
                        <xsl:with-param name="type" select="'data'" />
                        <xsl:with-param name="top" select="'110px'" />
                  </xsl:call-template>
                  <xsl:call-template name="row">
                        <xsl:with-param name="string"
select="'item_price:'" />
                        <xsl:with-param name="type" select="'data'" />
                        <xsl:with-param name="top" select="'127px'" />
                  </xsl:call-template>
```

continues

Listing 11-6   continued

```
            </xsl:element>
      </xsl:template>

      <xsl:template name="row">
            <xsl:param name="dataisland" select="' '" />
            <xsl:param name="string" />
            <xsl:param name="type" select="'header'" />
            <xsl:param name="top" />

            <xsl:variable name="apostrophe">'</xsl:variable>
            <xsl:variable name="nbsp"> </xsl:variable>

            <xsl:element name="div">
                  <xsl:attribute name="class">rowHeader</xsl:attribute>
                  <xsl:attribute name="style">
                        <xsl:choose>
                              <xsl:when test="$type = 'header'">
                                    <xsl:value-of
select="concat($apostrophe,'position: absolute; left: 50px; right: auto%;
bottom: auto; width: 200px; top: ',$top,$apostrophe)" />
                              </xsl:when>
                              <xsl:otherwise>
                                    <xsl:value-of
select="concat($apostrophe,'position: absolute; left: 255px; right: auto%;
bottom: auto; width: 600px; top: ',$top,$apostrophe)" />
                              </xsl:otherwise>
                        </xsl:choose>
                  </xsl:attribute>

                  <xsl:choose>
                        <xsl:when test="$type = 'header'">
                              <xsl:value-of disable-output-escaping="yes"
select="concat($nbsp,$string)" />
                        </xsl:when>
                        <xsl:otherwise>
                              <xsl:attribute name="xmlDI">
                                    <xsl:value-of select="$dataisland" />
                              </xsl:attribute>
                              <xsl:attribute name="xmlNode">
                                    <xsl:value-of select="$string" />
                              </xsl:attribute>
                        </xsl:otherwise>
                  </xsl:choose>
            </xsl:element>
      </xsl:template>
</xsl:stylesheet>
```

This style sheet first creates an HTML Table element with the required attributes to give the site a common look and feel. Next, the column headers are rendered and a template is invoked to create the individual rows, which is the Table element in the source XML document. If there are no Table elements, only the HTML table headers will be produced. The individual cells are produced based upon the node name, and we're done.

Before proceeding any further, however, I want to explain two statements in the style sheet. The first of these is the one that defines the apostrophe variable:

```
<xsl:variable name="apostrophe">'</xsl:variable>
```

The second statement is the one that uses the apostrophe variable:

```
<xsl:value-of select="concat('javascript:pageLoad
(',$apostrophe,'itemsDisplay.xsl',$apostrophe,',
',guild_id,',null)')" />
```

These two statements might seem somewhat odd because if you're even slightly familiar with XSL, you know that there is a perfectly acceptable entity that can be used to render apostrophes. The entity that I refer to is ', which, unfortunately, would cause quite a few headaches if used here. The entity would be treated as if it were, in fact, an apostrophe. The XSLT processor would then consider the previous statement to be equivalent to the following.

```
<xsl:value-of select="concat('javascript:pageLoad
(',',','itemsDisplay.xsl',',',',guild_id,',null)')" />
```

As you can see, this would lead to an error and a nasty error message instead of the page shown in Figure 11-1.

11.2.2 Updateable

Unlike the previous read-only example, binding cannot be ignored when using XSLT to create updateable web pages. Even so, several advantages exist that were unavailable in earlier chapters. For example, there are the funky looping and concatenating strings to build the HTML with the correct number of rows. XSL takes care of those annoying details for us.

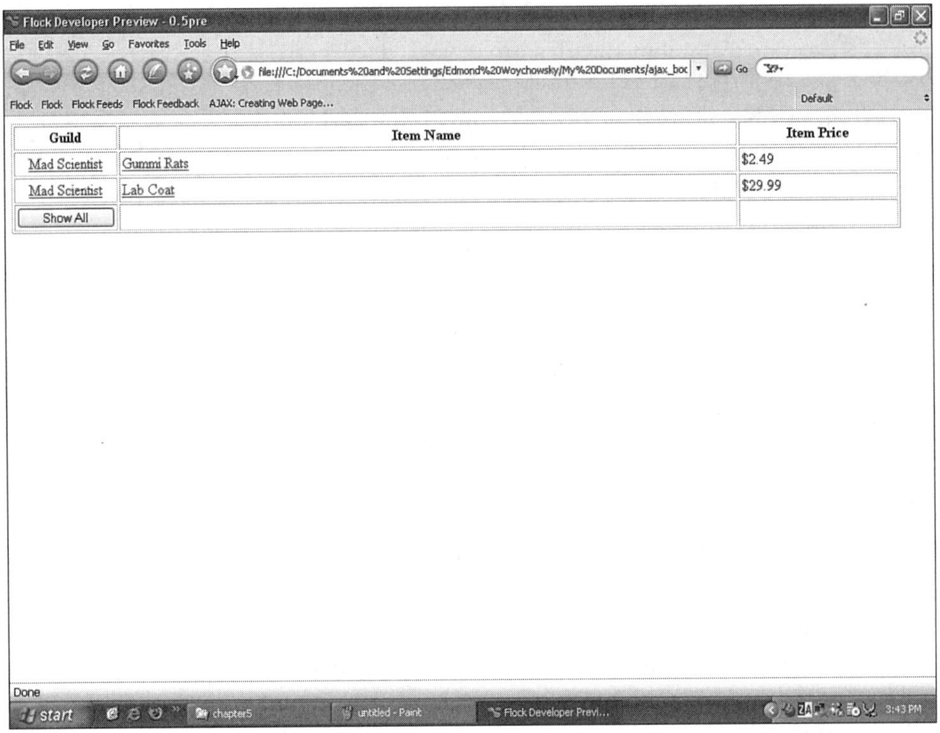

Figure 11-1   The properly rendered page

11.3 ADVANTAGES AND DISADVANTAGES

A number of advantages exist for designing a site that uses client-side XSLT. The first is that it really looks good on the old resumé—strike that. The first is that it becomes possible to design more dynamic websites that can take advantage of the client's machine. In addition, the amount of information can be reduced by caching the XSL style sheets on the client machine. However, if the resources available on the client become something of an issue, there are always alternatives.

The first alternative that comes to mind is to not cache the XSL at all; instead, it could be sent back and forth along with the XML. For large sites, another possibility is to cache only a certain number of pages. This could be handled in sort of a stack: first in, first out.

Concerning caching, one additional idea comes to mind: Forgo the pre-load entirely. Instead, style sheets could be loaded on an as-needed basis. After being loaded, they could then be cached. The interesting thing about this idea is that, from the client's perspective, performance would improve over time— almost as if the site got better with practice. Talk about mad scientist stuff!

Alas, all of this is for naught if the client's browser doesn't support transformations. Not all of them do. I suppose that an alternative should be made available for those that, for some reason, are still running Microsoft Internet Explorer version 3.0. No, I don't mean server-side transformations to accommodate luddites; I'm thinking more along the lines of a link to www.mozilla.org, where they can join everyone else in the twenty-first century.

11.4 SUMMARY

In this chapter, I covered why the idea of performing transformations on the client side is scary, mostly because of the actions of Microsoft. Additionally, I covered the reason why using XSLT on the client side now makes sense, with the advent of Gecko-based browsers and Microsoft Internet Explorer.

CHAPTER 12

Better Living Through Code Reuse

At one time in my career, I was a consultant, or, if you prefer, a hired gun. My job was to ride into town, clean up things, and then ride off into the sunset. It was like being a Wild West hero, just me and my horse—alright, just me and my little blue car. Please believe me when I say that I ride like the late movie star Lee Marvin; have you ever seen *Cat Balloo*? If you haven't, let's just say that my posture in the saddle isn't the best.

The reason that I bring this up is that, like those heroes of old, I lived by my wits, or approximately half of my wits, and what I could carry with me. However, instead of a Colt Dragoon, I carried a laptop loaded with every little tool I had ever written or downloaded. Some of the tools were useful and some of them were not so useful, but nevertheless, it contained everything that I could possibly need, not counting the games. I suppose another way to look at it is that I'm a packrat, but once I code something, I'd rather not code it again.

Of course, it wasn't that I was avoiding coding; actually, I was avoiding the debugging. The act of debugging isn't distasteful, but the act of debugging the same thing again and again gets old really fast. Ever hear the phrase "don't reinvent the wheel"? Well, I wholeheartedly agree with it. Although, maybe if I could make it better ....

The best part of these Ajax tools is that they aren't carved in stone; they are actually more scribbled in crayon. Because of this, they are fluid, meant to be more of a guide than gospel. However, even if you choose not to use these, I recommend that you at least look at them. Most of these functions work pretty much the same.

Why?

The reason is pretty simple. You see, Ajax applications are just like lemonade. In other words, there are a few basic ingredients, as with lemons, sugar, and water. Of course, not all lemonades are created equal. This is mostly because of the amounts of each ingredient and the little extras, such as vodka or checking an object's readyState property.

12.1 REUSE = LAZINESS

I'm not really sure whether it is a character flaw or a skill, but I have a tendency to code some routines twice. The first time is to solve the particular problem at hand; the second time is so that I have a generic solution if the problem crops up somewhere else. Sometimes it does and sometimes it doesn't, but it is nice to be able to accept an assignment and have at least part of the solution coded. It is also a great way to make sure that there is always time to read *User Friendly*.

Unfortunately, when I started my career, this wasn't the case, mostly because I encountered managers who believed in the puritan work ethic: Work constantly until you die, or quit before the age of 33, a burnt-out husk. Basically, the more lines of code, the better, although they sometimes cloaked their philosophy behind the words "I need it so that everyone can understand it" or avoid "mad scientist stuff." However, during the years, this type of manager has largely either died off or retired. I suppose that, on some level, I will miss them, in much the same way as a headache that has gone away. Yes, I will sorely miss the threats of nonpayment for reusing code to create new applications.

"Hello, my name is Ed. I reuse code to death and I am *not* lazy!"

12.1.1 Paid by the Line

Several years ago, as a consultant, I was assigned the responsibility to write client-side JavaScript whose sole purpose was to speed up the client's website. The problem was that they had a vision of what they wanted, but they didn't quite know how to implement it. For example, let's say that a web page consisted of 20 rows in an HTML table, each of which had a `select` created from a database query, and that each `select` had the same options. They saw nothing wrong with executing the same query 20 times and using VBScript 20 times to create the 20 `selects`. Oh, there were two other things: With the exception of looping through the results of the query, there were no loops, and there wasn't even a function that was called 20 times. The code was one straight run. Because it had been written by the lead developer only about six months before and I was only a consultant, I never asked the burning question: Why?

It didn't take me more than a couple of days to figure out the answer. In fact, all it took was one glance at their JavaScript library. The entire library consisted of a single function whose purpose was to determine whether a parameter was numeric, not that it was used anywhere. It was almost like I had stepped through a rift in the fabric of space-time and found myself in an alternate reality. The more I examined the site, the more I kept looking around expecting to see Rod Serling. To give you an idea, it was after Y2K and they were still using HTML FONT tags. There was not a single example of Cascading Style Sheets anywhere. The word *deprecated* didn't exist in their world.

There were classic ASP pages that were in excess of 30,000 lines of mixed script and HTML. I was a stranger in a strange land where developers were paid by the line. It was a new application, not yet in production, so it couldn't have been maintained into incomprehensibility. What else could explain the way that things were?

12.1.2   Paid by the Page

Fortunately, I was paid by the page—alright, actually, it was by the hour, but I had a limited number of hours to produce each page. Couple this with the fact that I'm a hunt-and-peck typist, and you'll quickly understand why I'm a big believer in code reuse. The odd thing was that, with one exception, nobody ever noticed that code was being reused left and right.

On one of my last consulting assignments I met an intern who was fresh out of school yet was one of the sharpest developers I ever met. After working together for about six months, he asked me why it seemed that whenever possible I wrote reusable code that often used reusable code that I had written previously. There was only one way to answer: "I like writing tools to make tools."

A simple enough phrase, "tools to make tools," but what does it mean?

Ask me what I mean, and I'll say that it means that there is an underlying architecture that can be built upon. But to me personally, it goes much deeper than that. Take a moment and look around you; what do you see? You're surrounded by tools—tools that shelter us, tools that entertain us, tools that preserve our images and thoughts beyond our individual lifespan.

Where did these tools that have become so important come from? Somebody created them, another person used them, and yet another person improved them. In essence, the Internet is merely an improvement of a cave painting taken to the nth degree. There's a long history of our species creating "tools to make tools." Therefore, it is only natural to create tools, share those tools, every once in a while wonder who will improve them, and lament the fact that you can't get a good mastodon sandwich anymore.

12.2   JAVASCRIPT OBJECTS

Although it's not an object-oriented language, JavaScript is an object-based language. This means that, although it might not be as powerful as PHP, Ruby, or Java, it is still pretty darn powerful. Add the fact that it is currently the best/only choice available, and you'll quickly understand why objects are important.

Although there are several ways to create objects in JavaScript, I usually use only two. The first method of creating an object in JavaScript is simply a matter of writing a function and assigning it to a variable using the new operator to create an instance, as shown in Listing 12-1.

Listing 12-1   Example `function` Class Constructor

```
function word() {
      var _setCount = 0;              //      Protected variable

      this.theWord;                   //      Public property
      this.setWord = _setWord;        //      Public method setWord
      this.getWord = _getWord;        //      Public method getWord
      this.count = _getSetCount;      //      Public method count

      function _setWord(theWord) {
              //      Public exposed as getWord
            this.theWord = theWord;
            _incrementCount();
      }
      function _getWord() {           //      Public exposed as setWord
            return(this.theWord);
      }
      function _getSetCount() {       //      Public exposed as count
            return(_setCount);
      }
      function _incrementCount() {  //      Private method
            ++_setCount;
      }
}

var myInstance = new word();
```

Now we have an instance of the property word assigned to the variable myInstance, and the only question is, how do we use it? Thankfully, the notation for addressing properties and methods is a relatively standard *instancename.property* or *instancename.method()*. If you're looking at the constructor, the way to distinguish them is that they are all preceded by the this keyword. The way to tell which are properties and which are methods is that methods always are equal to a function. It is important to point out that the parentheses are omitted because including them would cause the method to be invoked as well as exposed.

Although the previous class constructor is essentially useless, it does show the details of how to create a constructor. It has private members, _setCount, and private methods, _incrementCount. Also, as explained previously, it has both public properties, as in theWord, and public methods, as in setWord, getWord, and getSetCount. Of course, an example that is actually useful might not have all of these.

12.2.1   Collections

I might be wrong, but I am of the opinion that the most useful type of data structure that has ever been conceived, excluding the DOM, is perhaps an associative array. If you're unfamiliar with this type of data structure, information is stored in name/value pairs. If you know the name, you can find the value. And the value isn't limited to any particular data type; come to think of it, neither is the name. A good use would be to cache XSL style sheets because they usually don't change very often. After they're cached, it is no longer necessary to bother the web server to get them; all that is necessary is to retrieve them from the cache. However, there is one danger, and that danger is caching information that shouldn't be cached because someone else might change it, as in the results of database queries.

Listing 12-2 is an example of a constructor for a lightweight cache/associative array. The single private property, _cache, is a JavaScript object that is the cache itself. There are three public methods to handle inserting name/value pairs, retrieving values, and purging either selected name/value pairs or the entire contents of the cache.

Listing 12-2   Cache Class Constructor (Associative Array)

```
<!-- <![CDATA[
/*
      Class:    Cache
      Function: Cache
      Purpose:  To act as a client-side cache(associative array).
                Data are stored as name/value pairs.
*/
function Cache() {
  var _cache = new Object();
              // Object to store information
  var _namesArray = new Array();     // Array for names

  this.insert = _insert;             // Method: cache an object
  this.retrieve = _retrieve;         // Method: retrieve object
  this.purge = _purge;               // Method: purge object(s)
  this.names = _names;               // Method: return names

  /*
      Function: _insert
      Method:   insert
      Purpose:  Inserts a name/value pair into the cache.
  */
  function _insert(name,value) {
    _cache[name] = value;            // Cache object

    _namesArray.push(name);          // Store name
  }
```

continues

Listing 12-2   continued

```
/*
    Function: _retrieve
    Method:   retrieve
    Purpose:  Retrieves a value from the cache using a name.
*/
function _retrieve(name) {
  if(typeof(_cache[name]) == 'undefined')
    return(null);                    // Object not cached
  else
    return(_cache[name]);            // Return object
}

/*
    Function: _purge
    Method:   purge
    Purpose:  Purges one or more name/value pairs from
              the cache.
*/
function _purge() {
  if(arguments.length == 0) {
    _cache = new Object();           // Create new cache object
    _namesArray = new Array();       // Create new names array
  } else {
    var singleName;

    _namesArray = new Array();       // Create new names array

    for(var i=0;i < arguments.length;i++)
      _cache[arguments[i]] = null;

    for(singleName in _cache)
      if(_cache[singleName] != null)
        _namesArray.push(singleName);
  }
}

/*
    Function:    _names
    Method:    names
    Purpose:  Returns an array consisting of the names from the
              cache.
*/
function _names() {
  return(_namesArray);
}
}
// ]]> -->
```

As with the previous example, it is necessary to create an instance of the object before using it. Listing 12-3 shows the object being put through its paces, along with the expected results shown in the comments.

Listing 12-3   Listing Head Here

```
var magicWords = new Cache();

magicWords.insert(1,'xyzzy'); // Insert key = 1, value = 'xyzzy'
magicWords.insert(2,'plugh'); // Insert key = 2, value = 'plugh'
magicWords.insert(3,'plover');
// Insert key = 3, value = 'plover'

alert(magicWords.names());        // 1,2,3
alert(magicWords.retrieve(1));    // 'xyzzy'
alert(magicWords.retrieve(2));    // 'plugh'

magicWords.purge(3);
// Purge key/value pair - key = 3

alert(magicWords.retrieve(3));    // null
alert(magicWords.names());        // 1,2

magicWords.purge();               // Purge all key/value pairs

alert(magicWords.retrieve(1));    // null
```

The caching class is pretty straightforward; it is only a wrapper around a JavaScript object that has public methods that allow for changes to the object and retrieval from the object.

12.2.2   XML

Without a doubt, my biggest complaint concerning client-side XML is the lack of a single cross-browser way to create an XML document. This is one of those areas in which cross-browser coding can be a real drag because I have a tendency to create a page using a single browser. Only when I get it working in my browser of choice do I go back and try to make it work for Internet Explorer. In case you are wondering, this makes for some really ugly JavaScript, all sewn together from various mismatched parts. I may be a mad scientist, but there is something to be said for reusability.

That's the reason I cobbled together a few class constructors to neaten things up around the old lab. It's not like I'm using coasters or anything. I'm just trying to make sure that I can understand what I wrote six months from now. They say that the memory is the first thing to go—or is it the hair? Whatever, I can't even remember who "they" are anyway, so it can't be important.

The first of these class constructors is to handle the details involved with using the XMLHttpRequest object. It deals with whether the browser is Microsoft Internet Explorer or any other browser, and then it creates the XMLHTTPRequest object using the syntax appropriate to the specific browser. In addition, it handles readyState changes for asynchronous requests. Unlike the previous example, which was created in much the same manner as a regular JavaScript class, this time a prototype object is created. Although they're not used for these constructors, prototypes offer the advantage of allowing for the possibility of inheritance if it is deemed necessary in the future. Listing 12-4 shows what the constructor looks like.

Listing 12-4   Cross-Browser (Gecko and IE) XMLHttp Class Constructor

```
<!-- <![CDATA[
XMLHttpRequest.prototype = new XMLHttpRequest;
XMLHttpRequest.prototype.constructor = XMLHttpRequest;

/*
      Class:       XMLHttpRequest
      Function:    XMLHttpRequest
      Method:      n/a
      Description: Constructor for this class.
*/
function XMLHttpRequest() {
  try {
    var x = new DOMParser();
    this._IE = false;
  }
  catch(e) { this._IE = true; };
  this._XMLHttp;                        // XMLHttp request object
  this._requestHeader = new Cache();

  if(this._IE)
    this._XMLHttp = new ActiveXObject('Microsoft.XMLHttp');
  else
    this._XMLHttp = new XMLHttpRequest();
}

// Property: GET, POST or HEAD
XMLHttpRequest.prototype.action = 'GET';
                                        // Property: true/false
XMLHttpRequest.prototype.asynchronous = true;
                                        // Property: package to send
XMLHttpRequest.prototype.envelope = null

/*
      Class:       XMLHttpRequest
      Function:    XMLHttpRequest_readyState
      Method:      readyState
      Description: Returns the readyState for the XMLHttpRequest
                   object.
*/
function XMLHttpRequest_readyState() {
  return(this._XMLHttp.readyState);
}
XMLHttpRequest.prototype.readyState = XMLHttpRequest_readyState;
```

```
/*
        Class:         XMLHttpRequest
        Function:      XMLHttpRequest_getResponseHeader
        Method:        getResponseHeader
        Description: Returns a single response header from the last
                     XMLHttpRequest.
*/
function XMLHttpRequest_getResponseHeader(name) {
  return(this._XMLHttp.getResponseHeader(name));
}
XMLHttpRequest.prototype.getResponseHeader =
XMLHttpRequest_getResponseHeader;

/*
        Class:         XMLHttpRequest
        Function:      XMLHttpRequest_getAllResponseHeaders
        Method:        getAllResponseHeaders
        Description: Returns all of the response headers from
                     the last XMLHttpRequest.
*/
function XMLHttpRequest_getAllResponseHeaders() {
  return(this._XMLHttp.getAllResponseHeaders());
}
XMLHttpRequest.prototype.getAllResponseHeaders =
XMLHttpRequest_getAllResponseHeaders;

/*
        Class:         XMLHttpRequest
        Function:      XMLHttpRequest_responseText
        Method:        responseText
        Description: Returns the text response from the last
                     XMLHttpRequest.
*/
function XMLHttpRequest_responseText() {
  return(this._XMLHttp.responseText);
}
XMLHttpRequest.prototype.responseText =
XMLHttpRequest_responseText;

/*
        Class:         XMLHttpRequest
        Function:      XMLHttpRequest_responseXML
        Method:        responseXML
        Description: Returns the XML DOM document response from
                     the last XMLHttpRequest.
*/
function XMLHttpRequest_responseXML() {
  if(this._IE) {
    var xml =
    new ActiveXObject('MSXML2.FreeThreadedDOMDocument.3.0');
```

continues

Listing 12-4   continued

```
    xml.async = true;

    xml.loadXML(this._XMLHttp.responseText);

    return(xml);
  } else
    return(this._XMLHttp.responseXML);
}
XMLHttpRequest.prototype.responseXML =
XMLHttpRequest_responseXML;

/*
      Class:       XMLHttpRequest
      Function:    XMLHttpRequest_stateChangeHandler
      Method:      n/a
      Description: Dummy state change handler for
                   asynchronous requests.
*/
function XMLHttpRequest_stateChangeHandler() { }
XMLHttpRequest.prototype.stateChangeHandler =
XMLHttpRequest_stateChangeHandler;

/*
      Class:       setRequestHeader
      Function:    XMLHttpRequest_setRequestHeader
      Method:      setRequestHeader
      Description: Inserts to the cache of HTTP request headers.
*/
function XMLHttpRequest_setRequestHeader(name,value) {
  this.removeRequestHeader(name);
  this._requestHeader.insert(name,value);
}
XMLHttpRequest.prototype.setRequestHeader =
XMLHttpRequest_setRequestHeader;

/*
      Class:       setRequestHeader
      Function:    XMLHttpRequest_removeRequestHeader
      Method:      n/a
      Description: Removes from the cache of HTTP
                   request headers.
*/
function XMLHttpRequest_removeRequestHeader(name) {
  this._requestHeader.purge(name);
}
XMLHttpRequest.prototype.removeRequestHeader =
XMLHttpRequest_removeRequestHeader;

/*
      Class:       XMLHttpRequest
      Function:    XMLHttpRequest_send
```

```
          Method:      send
          Description: Sends XMLHttpRequest.
*/
function XMLHttpRequest_send() {
  var successful = false;

  if(arguments.length != 0)
    this.envelope = arguments[0];

  switch(this._XMLHttp.readyState) {
    case(4):
    case(0):
      try {
        if(this._IE)
              this._XMLHttp.onreadystatechange =
this.stateChangeHandler;
              else
              this._XMLHttp.stateChangeHandler =
this.XMLHttpRequest_stateChangeHandler;

        this._XMLHttp.open(this.action,this.uri,this.asynchronous);

        var names = this._requestHeader.names();

        for(var i=0;i < names.length;i++)

this._XMLHttp.setRequestHeader(names[i],this._requestHeader.retrieve(names
[i]));

        this._XMLHttp.send(this.envelope);

        successful = true;
      }
      catch(e) { }

      break;
    default:

      break;
  }

  return(successful);
}
XMLHttpRequest.prototype.send = XMLHttpRequest_send;
// ]]> -->
```

The constructor shown does exactly what the handwritten code from the beginning of Chapter 8, "AJAX Using XML and XMLHttpRequest," does. In a nutshell, it sends an XMLHttpRequest to the server, waits for the response, and then acts upon the response. This is not a big deal; just create an instance, and it takes care of everything—unless, of course, you're paid by the line.

Now that we've got a constructor to handle the getting of XML, it might be a good idea to figure out a place to put it. What's needed, as if you didn't already know, is a generic XML document object. It doesn't have to be perfect; it only has to work—and by "work," I mean offer a single set of properties and methods. From the previous chapters, you're already aware that this is written, so let's take a gander at it in Listing 12-5.

Listing 12-5   Cross-Browser XML Document Class Constructor

```
<!-- <![CDATA[
XMLDocument.prototype = new XMLDocument;
XMLDocument.prototype.constructor = XMLDocument;

/*
     Class:      XMLDocument
     Function:   XMLDocument
     Method:     n/a
     Description: Constructor for this class.
*/
function XMLDocument() {
  try {
    var x = new DOMParser();
    this._IE = false;
  }
  catch(e) { this._IE = true; };
  this._XMLHttpRequest = new XMLHttpRequest();
  this._XML;                   // XML DOM document
  this._DOMParser;             // XML DOM parser (Gecko only)
  this._XMLSerializer;         // XML serializer (Gecko only)
  this._state = 0;             // Pseudo readyState

  if(!this._IE) {
    this._DOMParser = new DOMParser();
    this._XMLSerializer = new XMLSerializer();

    this._XML =
    document.implementation.createDocument("", "", null);
  }
}

/*
     Class:      XMLDocument
     Function:   XMLDocument_load
     Method:     load
     Description: Loads the specified XML document.
*/
function XMLDocument_load(xml) {
  var isXMLText = false;
  var isXMLDocument = (typeof(xml) == 'object');

  try {                               // Test for elements
    isXMLText = (new RegExp('<','g')).test(xml);
```

```
      }
      catch(e) { }

      switch(true) {
        case(this._IE && isXMLText):     // Internet Explorer & text
          this._XML =
          new ActiveXObject('MSXML2.FreeThreadedDOMDocument.3.0');

          this._XML.async = true;

          this._XML.loadXML(xml);
          this._state = 4;               // Ready state complete

          break;
        case(!this._IE && isXMLText):    // Not IE & text
          this._XML =
          this._DOMParser.parseFromString(xml,"text/xml");
          this._state = 4;               // Ready state is complete

          break;
        case(this._IE && isXMLDocument):
        // Internet Explorer & XML DOM
          this._XML =
          new ActiveXObject('MSXML2.FreeThreadedDOMDocument.3.0');

          this._XML.async = true;

          try {
            this._XML.loadXML(xml.serialize());
          }
          catch(e) {
            this._XML = xml;
          }

          this._state = 4;               // Ready state complete

          break;
        case(!this._IE && isXMLDocument): // Not IE & XML DOM
          try {
            this._XML = xml.DOMDocument();
          }
          catch(e) {
            this._XML = xml;
          }

          this._state = 4;               // Ready state is complete

          break;
        default:
          this._XMLHttpRequest.uri = xml;

          try {
```

continues

Listing 12-5   continued

```
        this._XMLHttpRequest.send();

        this._state = 1;
      }
      catch(e) {
        if(this._IE) {
          this._XML =
          new ActiveXObject('MSXML2.FreeThreadedDOMDocument.3.0');

          this._XML.async = true;
        } else
          this._XML =
          this._DOMParser.parseFromString(' ','text/xml');

        this._state = 4;                // Error - force complete
      }
  }

  if(this._state == 4)
    this._XMLHttpRequest = new XMLHttpRequest();
}
XMLDocument.prototype.load = XMLDocument_load;

/*
      Class:        XMLDocument
      Function:     XMLDocument_serialize
      Method:       serialize
      Description:  Returns the result of the prior transformation
                    as a serialize XML DOM document (text).
*/
function XMLDocument_serialize() {
  try {
    if(this.readyState() == 4) {

      if(this._XMLHttpRequest.readyState() == 4)
        this.load(this._XMLHttpRequest.responseXML());

      if(this._IE)
        return(this._XML.xml)
      else
        return(this._XMLSerializer.serializeToString(this._XML));
    } else
        return(null);                   // Not loaded
  }
  catch(e) {
    return(null);                       // Invalid document
  }
}
XMLDocument.prototype.serialize = XMLDocument_serialize;

/*
      Class:        XMLDocument
```

```
                  Function:     XMLDocument_DOMDocument
                  Method:       DOMDocument
                  Description:  Returns the result of the prior transformation
                                as a Browser-native XML DOM document.
      */
      function XMLDocument_DOMDocument() {
        try {
          if(this.readyState() == 4) {
            if(this._XMLHttpRequest.readyState() == 4)
              this.load(this._XMLHttpRequest.responseXML());

              return(this._XML);
          } else
            return(null);                         // Document not loaded
        }
        catch(e) {
          return(null);                           // Invalid document
        }
      }
      XMLDocument.prototype.DOMDocument = XMLDocument_DOMDocument;

      /*
            Class:        XMLDocument
            Function:     XMLDocument_readyState
            Method:       readyState
            Description:  Returns the readyState for the XML document.
      */
      function XMLDocument_readyState() {
      if(this._XMLHttpRequest.readyState() == 0)
        return(4);
      else
        return(this._XMLHttpRequest.readyState());
      }
      XMLDocument.prototype.readyState = XMLDocument_readyState;

      /*
            Class:        XMLDocument
            Function:     XMLHttpRequest_setRequestHeader
            Method:       n/a
            Description:  Inserts to the cache of HTTP request headers.
      */
      function XMLDocument_setRequestHeader(name,value) {
          this._XMLHttpRequest.setRequestHeader(name,value);
      }
      XMLDocument.prototype.setRequestHeader =
      XMLDocument_setRequestHeader;

      /*
            Class:        XMLDocument
            Function:     XMLDocument_getResponseHeader
            Method:       getResponseHeader
            Description:  Returns a single response header from the last
```

continues

Listing 12-5   continued

```
                XMLHttpRequest.
*/
function XMLDocument_getResponseHeader(name) {
  return(this._XMLHttpRequest.getResponseHeader(name));
}
XMLDocument.prototype.getResponseHeader =
XMLDocument_getResponseHeader;

/*
     Class:       XMLDocument
     Function:    XMLDocument_getAllResponseHeaders
     Method:      getAllResponseHeaders
     Description: Returns all of the response headers from
                  the last XMLHttpRequest.
*/
function XMLDocument_getAllResponseHeaders() {
  return(this._XMLHttpRequest.getAllResponseHeaders());
}
XMLDocument.prototype.getAllResponseHeaders =
XMLDocument_getAllResponseHeaders;

/*
     Class:       XMLDocument
     Function:    XMLDocument_setEnvelope
     Method:      setEnvelope
     Description: Sets the envelope for an XMLHttpRequest.
*/
function XMLDocument_setEnvelope(value) {
  this._XMLHttpRequest.envelope = value;
  this._XMLHttpRequest.action = 'POST';
}
XMLDocument.prototype.setEnvelope = XMLDocument_setEnvelope;

/*
     Class:       XMLDocument
     Function:    XMLDocument_selectNodes
     Method:      selectNodes
     Description: Returns an array of XMLDocument based upon
                  an XPath statement.
*/
function XMLDocument_selectNodes(xpath) {
  var results;
  var resultArray = new Array();      // XML Document result array

  if(this.readyState() == 4)
    if(this._XMLHttpRequest.readyState() == 4)
      this.load(this._XMLHttpRequest.responseXML());

  if(_IE) {
    results = this._XML.selectNodes(xpath);
```

```
      for(var i=0;i < results.length;i++) {
        resultArray.push(new XMLDocument());
        resultArray[i].load(results[i].xml);
      }
    } else {                          // XPath evaluator
      var evaluator = new XPathEvaluator();
      var resolver =
 evaluator.createNSResolver(this._XML.documentElement);
      var result;                    // Single XPath result
      var xml;
      var i = 0;                      // Counter

      results =
 evaluator.evaluate(xpath,this._XML,resolver,XPathResult.ANY_TYPE,null);

      while(result = results.iterateNext()) {
        xml = document.implementation.createDocument(""," ",null);

        xml.appendChild(xml.importNode(result,true));
        resultArray.push(new XMLDocument());
        resultArray[i].load(this._XMLSerializer.serializeToString(xml));

        ++i;
      }
    }

  return(resultArray);
}
XMLDocument.prototype.selectNodes = XMLDocument_selectNodes;

/*
      Class:       XMLDocument
      Function:    XMLDocument_selectSingleNode
      Method:      selectSingleNode
      Description: Returns a single XML document based upon an
                   XPath statement.
*/
function XMLDocument_selectSingleNode(xpath) {
  return(this.selectNodes(xpath)[0]);
}
XMLDocument.prototype.selectSingleNode =
XMLDocument_selectSingleNode;
// ]]> -->
```

Now that there is a generic constructor for XML documents and a constructor for the XSLT Request object, the next task is to ask the nice web service for an XML document. To do this, a quick and easy way of producing a SOAP envelope is required. In writing this constructor, I learned something about SOAP that I hadn't realized in the past: SOAP is, in some ways, like a car. With a car, there is a base model, and, regardless of the options, the base model remains the same. Oh, sure, some cars have better sound systems and some have bigger engines, but underneath all the little extras, the cars are essentially the same. Take my car, for example; with the exception of the dirt and the dent on the hood from a flower pot, when you get past the options, it is just like the other car from that model year.

This same approach was used when writing the SOAPEnvelope constructor. A basic template serves as a starting point, and all of the other options are then added on. These options consist of things such as the operator, content, and namespace—all required, but very often different from request to request. Listing 12-6 shows the inner workings of this constructor.

Listing 12-6 Cross-Browser SOAPEnvelope Class Constructor That Uses Regular Expressions

```
<!-- <![CDATA[
SOAPEnvelope.prototype = new SOAPEnvelope;
SOAPEnvelope.prototype.constructor = SOAPEnvelope;

/*
        Class:       SOAPEnvelope
        Function:    SOAPEnvelope
        Method:      n/a
        Description: Constructor for this class.
*/
<!-- <![CDATA[
function SOAPEnvelope() {
   this._template = '<?xml version="1.0" encoding="utf-8"?>';

   this._template += '<soap:Envelope
xmlns:xsi="http://www.w3.org/2001/XMLSchema-instance"
xmlns:xsd="http://www.w3.org/2001/XMLSchema"
xmlns:soap="http://schemas.xmlsoap.org/soap/envelope/">';
   this._template += '<soap:Body>';
   this._template += '<_operator xmlns="_namespace">';
   this._template += '_package';
   this._template += '</_operator>';
   this._template += '</soap:Body>';
   this._template += '</soap:Envelope>';
}

SOAPEnvelope.prototype.operator = null;
SOAPEnvelope.prototype.namespace = 'http://tempuri.org/';
SOAPEnvelope.prototype.content = null;

/*
        Class:       SOAPEnvelope
        Function:    SOAPEnvelope_envelope
        Method:      envelope
        Description: Returns the readyState for the XMLHttpRequest
                     object.
*/
```

```
function SOAPEnvelope_envelope() {
  var work;

  work = this._template.replace(/_operator/g,this.operator);
  work = work.replace(/_namespace/g,this.namespace);
  work = work.replace(/_package/g,this.content);

  return(work);
}
SOAPEnvelope.prototype.envelope = SOAPEnvelope_envelope;
// ]]> -->
```

12.2.3   XSLT

The final constructor that was used in the examples was the XSLTProcessor constructor, which serves as the poster child for code reuse. It has two instances of XMLDocument objects, one for the XML document and one for the XSL style sheet. It also serves fairly well to show some of the difference between Gecko-based browsers such as Firefox, Mozilla, and Netscape, and Microsoft Internet Explorer.

These differences range from Internet Explorer needing a template to create a processor to something as simple as Firefox needing a serializer to obtain the text representation of an XML document. Listing 12-7 shows the constructor for the XSLTProcessor.

Listing 12-7   Cross-Browser XSLTProcessor Class, Used for Transformations

```
<!-- <![CDATA[
XsltProcessor.prototype = new XsltProcessor;
XsltProcessor.prototype.constructor = XsltProcessor;

/*
      Class:       XsltProcessor
      Function:    XsltProcessor
      Method:      n/a
      Description: Constructor for this class.
*/
function XsltProcessor() {
  try {
    var x = new DOMParser();
    this._IE = false;
  }
  catch(e) { this._IE = true; };
  this._xsl = new XMLDocument(); // Input XSL style sheet
  this._xml = new XMLDocument(); // Input XML document
  this._output;                  // Output (text)
```

continues

Listing 12-7   continued

```
  this._XMLSerializer;            // XML serializer (Gecko only)
  this._XSLTemplate;              // XSLT template (IE only)
  this._XsltProcessor;            // XSLT processor

  if(!this._IE)
    this._XMLSerializer = new XMLSerializer();
}

/*
      Class:       XsltProcessor
      Function:    XsltProcessor_initialize
      Method:      _initialize
      Description: Initializes/re-initializes the XSLT processor.
*/
function XsltProcessor_initialize() {
  if(this._IE) {
    this._XSLTemplate =
    new ActiveXObject('MSXML2.XSLTemplate.3.0');

    this._XSLTemplate.stylesheet = this._xsl.DOMDocument();

    this._XsltProcessor = this._XSLTemplate.createProcessor;
  } else
    this._XsltProcessor = new XSLTProcessor();
}
XsltProcessor.prototype._initialize = XsltProcessor_initialize;

/*
      Class:       XsltProcessor
      Function:    XsltProcessor_setParameter
      Method:      setParameter
      Description: Inserts an XSLT parameter to the parameter
                   cache.
*/
function XsltProcessor_setParameter(name,value) {
  try {
    if(this._IE)
      this._XsltProcessor.addParameter(name,value);
    else
      this._XsltProcessor.setParameter(null,name,value);
  }
  catch(e) {
    this._initialize();
    this.setParameter(name,value);
  }
}
XsltProcessor.prototype.setParameter =
XsltProcessor_setParameter;

/*
      Class:       XsltProcessor
      Function:    XsltProcessor_load
```

```
      Method:      load
      Description: Loads the XML document to be transformed.
*/
function XsltProcessor_load(xml) {
  try {
    this._xml.load(xml);
  }
  catch(e) {
    this._initialize();
  }
}
XsltProcessor.prototype.load = XsltProcessor_load;

/*
      Class:       XsltProcessor
      Function:    XsltProcessor_importStylesheet
      Method:      importStylesheet
      Description: Loads the XSL style sheet for the
                   transformation.
*/
function XsltProcessor_importStylesheet(xsl) {
  try {
    this._xsl.load(xsl);
  }
  catch(e) {
    this._initialize();
  }
}
XsltProcessor.prototype.importStylesheet =
XsltProcessor_importStylesheet;

/*
      Class:       XsltProcessor
      Function:    XsltProcessor_readyState
      Method:      readyState
      Description: Returns the readyState for a combination of
                   the XML document and the XSL style sheet.
*/
function XsltProcessor_readyState() {
  switch(true) {
    case((this._xsl.readyState() == 0) && (this._xsl.readyState() == 0)):
      return(this._xsl.readyState());

      break;
    case((this._xsl.readyState() > 0) && (this._xsl.readyState() < 4)):
      return(this._xsl.readyState());

      break;
    case((this._xml.readyState() > 0) && (this._xml.readyState() < 4)):
      return(this._xml.readyState());

      break;
```

continues

Listing 12-7   continued

```
    default:
      return(4);

      break;
  }
}
XsltProcessor.prototype.readyState = XsltProcessor_readyState;

/*
      Class:       XsltProcessor
      Function:    XsltProcessor_transform
      Method:      transform
      Description: Performs the XSL transformation using the
                   supplied XML document and XSL style sheet.
                   Returns the result as an XML document.
*/
function XsltProcessor_transform() {
  if(this._IE) {
    this._XsltProcessor.input = this._xml.DOMDocument();

    this._XsltProcessor.transform();

    this._output = this._XsltProcessor.output;
  } else {
    this._XsltProcessor.importStylesheet(this._xsl.DOMDocument());

    this._output =
this._XMLSerializer.serializeToString(this._XsltProcessor.transformToDocum
ent(this._xml.DOMDocument(),document));
  }

  this._initialize();

  return(this._output);
}
XsltProcessor.prototype.transform = XsltProcessor_transform;

/*
      Class:       XsltProcessor
      Function:    XsltProcessor_serialize
      Method:      serialize
      Description: Returns the result of the prior transformation
                   as a serialize XML document (text).
*/
function XsltProcessor_serialize() {
  return(this._output);
}
XsltProcessor.prototype.serialize = XsltProcessor_serialize;
// ]]> -->
```

12.2.4   Serialization Without Berries

One common item that you'll notice throughout each of the previous constructors is that serialization plays a big part in handling XML. Several reasons account for this, the first being that XML was designed to be human readable, and humans read text, not binary. For example, when was the last time you heard, "ASCII 65, uppercase 'A'"? I'm the one who was called a mad scientist, and I don't deal with that stuff, so I can't imagine the more mundane members of humanity doing things like that.

The second reason for serialization is the underlying architecture of the web, the Hypertext Transfer Protocol, or HTTP, for short. The HTML, XHTML, JavaScript, CSS, XML, and XSL travel back and forth from the server to the client as text. Without serialization, all of the "X-stuff," as an old supervisor of mine put it, wouldn't be going anywhere.

Another reason for serialization is that, unlike an XML object, very little overhead is associated with text. An XML DOM document requires between three and ten times the memory of the equivalent text document. This overhead could cause some issues in the client's browser on older machines. Of course, the issue of overhead has to be weighted against parsing the text to load a document.

My final reason for serialization is that it is just so easy to load an XML document from a text document. In Microsoft Internet Explorer, it is simply a matter of using the `loadXML` method. With Firefox, a little more work is necessary, but not too much. Just use the `DOMParser`'s `parseFromString` method and reconstituted XML, just like freeze-dried coffee or freeze-dried minions.

12.3   GENERIC XSLT

Whenever I'm creating an XSL style sheet, unless I'm very, very careful, my style sheets are basically a one-trick pony. Yeah, they do that one trick well, but as I said before, I'm paid by the page, not by the line. Maybe this is the reason the style sheets that I create are—hmm, how to put it nicely?—weird. Yes, that's the word, *weird*.

It isn't that they don't work—they work perfectly well. It is more along the lines that I use a lot of relative positioning. Although this approach might seem somewhat dangerous, there are several ways to decrease the danger to tolerable levels. More simply put, take cautions to prevent the style sheets from blowing up and taking the web page out with them. One of these methods is to always make sure that the XML document has the same basic structure, `/root/row/node`. This makes it far less likely that you will encounter any surprises.

Remember back to Chapter 9, "XPath," to the brief introduction to XPath with all the slashes and asterisks? Well, the asterisks are wildcards, used when the node name is unknown. This means that `/*/*/*` is the equivalent to `/root/row/node`—at least, when we want all the nodes that are the second descendant of the root node.

12.3.1 Forms

As long as the structure of the XML document is known, it isn't very difficult to create generic XSL style sheets. Knowing the names of the individual nodes isn't important, either, although, for the extremely lazy, like myself, the names can be important when creating either labels or column headers. To show what I mean, it is necessary to introduce two XSLT functions.

The first of these functions is the `name` function. It provides the name of the node passed, which, in these cases, is the context node ".". It returns the actual node name, so if the node name is `item_price`, then `item_price` is returned. Yes, I am aware that a label or header with `item_price` isn't much better than no label at all, which is where the second function, `translate`, comes in.

The `translate` function, well, translates. It replaces one character with another, so instead of having a label or a header of `item_price`, it can be ITEM PRICE. For me, the latter is a lot more like what I expect when visiting a website. Accepting three parameters—the source string, the from string, and the to string—it returns a string consisting of one-for-one replacements of characters.

I should cover a couple things before we use the `translate` function. The first of these is that in instances when the from string doesn't contain a particular character, that character is copied unchanged. The second thing is that it is a good idea to verify that characters in the from string and characters in the to string are in the same position in their respective strings. Or, more simply stated, using a from string of `qwerty` and a to string of `wertyu` will result in a Caesar Cipher. And although a Caesar Cipher might have been state-of-the-art in 40 B.C., I'm reasonably sure that it isn't the result that you've hoped for.

With that out of the way, let's take a look at Listing 12-8, which is an XSL style sheet that creates a basic form.

Listing 12-8   Generic XSL Style Sheet to Produce an HTML Table

```
<?xml version='1.0'?>
<xsl:stylesheet version="1.0"
xmlns:xsl="http://www.w3.org/1999/XSL/Transform">
      <xsl:output method="html" indent="yes" media-type="text/html"/>

      <xsl:template match="/">

          <xsl:element name="table">
```

```
                <xsl:apply-templates select="/*/*/*" />
        </xsl:element>

    </xsl:template>

    <xsl:template match="*">

        <xsl:element name="tr">
            <xsl:element name="td">
                <xsl:value-of
select="translate(name(.),'qwertyuiopasdfghjklzxcvbnm_','QWERTYUIOPASDFGHJ
KLZXCVBNM ')" />
            </xsl:element>
            <xsl:element name="td">
                <xsl:element name="input">
                    <xsl:attribute
name="type">text</xsl:attribute>
                    <xsl:attribute name="name">
                        <xsl:value-of select="name(.)" />
                    </xsl:attribute>
                    <xsl:attribute name="value">
                        <xsl:value-of select="." />
                    </xsl:attribute>
                </xsl:element>
            </xsl:element>
        </xsl:element>

    </xsl:template>

</xsl:stylesheet>
```

This is nothing fancy, but it is a proof of concept that can be taken further to show that it is, in fact, possible to create a generic XSL style sheet that produces HTML forms. Although it is rather simple—primitive, even—it is easy to imagine some possibilities, such as specifying input types via parameters.

12.3.2   Tabular

Applying a generic XSL style sheet to tabular information isn't very different from applying it to create a form. Really only a couple differences arise when working with tabular information instead of a form. The first difference is that, instead of labels at the side, they're column headers on the top. All that is required to do this is to create two templates; the first deals with creating a table row, and the second creates a table header. Other than that, the only real difference is the addition of a predicate, [1], to ensure that the header is created only once. We then have an XSL style sheet that looks like the one in Listing 12-9.

Listing 12-9   Generic XSL Style Sheet to Produce an HTML Table with Headers Based upon the Node Name

```xml
<?xml version='1.0'?>
<xsl:stylesheet version="1.0"
xmlns:xsl="http://www.w3.org/1999/XSL/Transform">
      <xsl:output method="html" indent="yes" media-type="text/html"/>

      <xsl:template match="/">
            <xsl:element name="table">
                  <xsl:apply-templates select="/*/*[1]" mode="header" />
                  <xsl:apply-templates select="/*/*" mode="row" />
            </xsl:element>
      </xsl:template>

      <xsl:template match="*" mode="header">
            <xsl:element name="tr">
                  <xsl:apply-templates select="./*" mode="column" />
            </xsl:element>
      </xsl:template>

      <xsl:template match="*" mode="row">
            <xsl:element name="tr">
                  <xsl:apply-templates select="./*" mode="node" />
            </xsl:element>
      </xsl:template>

      <xsl:template match="*" mode="column">
            <xsl:element name="th">
                  <xsl:value-of
select="translate(name(.),'qwertyuiopasdfghjklzxcvbnm_','QWERTYUIOPASDFGHJ
KLZXCVBNM ')" />
            </xsl:element>
      </xsl:template>

      <xsl:template match="*" mode="node">
            <xsl:element name="td">
                  <xsl:value-of select="." />
            </xsl:element>
      </xsl:template>

</xsl:stylesheet>
```

Of course, the examples shown here are rather simple, and there are a number of ways to improve them. One of these ways to dress up the generic style sheets is to write the header template with xsl:when to output more meaningful headers. Another possibility is to use Cascading Style Sheets to give a more polished look and feel. Finally, right-justifying numbers wouldn't hurt.

12.4 SUMMARY

The advantages of code reuse are obvious; large pieces of code need only be designed, coded, tested, and documented once. Whether it is a class constructor, a function, or an XSL style sheet, if at least part of a solution is already written, you're that much closer to delivery of the final application.

Another issue is that developers can be insulated from the ins and outs of the various web browsers. No longer is there a sharp learning curve ahead or the feeling of hopelessness associated with trying to make something work in Internet Explorer while trying not to break it in Firefox. I have to admit that at times I've fixed a web page in one browser only to find that in the other browser it was fixed in the same way that the vet fixed my cat, Moreta.

The important thing to remember is that if you can complete three web pages in the time that it takes for Igor to complete one, who do you think will be shown the door the next time that the layoff fairy pays a visit?

Unfortunately, some development shops still cling to the outmoded idea that the better programmer writes more lines of code. Thankfully, this idea is going the way of the three-martini lunch. Gin, yuck! When you get down to it, the biggest possible problem is that if one of the constructors has a bug, every page that uses that constructor either directly or indirectly has the same bug.

CHAPTER 13

Traveling with Ruby on Rails

Mention the subject of Ajax, and within five minutes somebody will bring up Ruby on Rails. Just as with Ajax, Ruby on Rails has become a winning phrase in corporate buzzword bingo. It is kind of sad that both topics have been relegated to buzzwords, with managers wielding them interchangeably, like they're some kind of weapons. Unfortunately, managers are just as likely to hurt themselves as somebody else, which just goes to show that it is a good idea to know what the tools are before attempting to use them.

In this chapter, we cover some of the history of Ruby on Rails, followed by what it is and how to install it on a system running Windows XP. From there, we examine how to start developing, using Ruby on Rails, and how to solve a simple problem using it.

Unfortunately, it is beyond the scope of this book to do more than introduce Ruby on Rails. There is actually a logical reason for this, beyond the fact that I'm more of a JavaScript guy than a Ruby guy. The reason for this is college.

Huh?

When I was in college, some students, well, complained about how the professors taught. The problem is that the professors didn't give them the code required for every assignment. We were taught, for example, how to create a data structure, but not the particular data structure for Question 6 on the midterm. The professors pointed us in a direction and expected us to reach the destination on our own. Gee, the nerve of those professors—they pointed us in a particular direction and expected us to find the way ourselves.

Seriously, this is merely an example, not the answer to Question 6. So if you choose to seriously examine Ruby on Rails, allow me to point the way.

13.1 WHAT IS RUBY ON RAILS?

A single word in the English language, in my opinion, sums up what Ruby on Rails is: *synergy.* Just in case you're unaware of the meaning of the word *synergy,* it roughly means that the whole is greater than the sum of its parts. Need a few examples of synergy? How about chocolate and peanut butter? Individually, either ingredient is good, but put them together and, well, yum!

With Ruby on Rails, instead of chocolate and peanut butter, there is Ruby and Rails. This realization leads me to two additional questions. The first is "Beyond being a deep-red corundum crystal, just what is Ruby?" There is, after all one thing that I am certain of, and it is that Ruby is a language and not a mineral, although it is possible to create a laser using a ruby, and lasers are the meat and potatoes of most mad scientists.

13.1.1   Ruby

The Ruby that is referred to in this chapter is an object-oriented programming language created by Yukihiro Matsumoto of Japan in 1993. In Japan, not surprisingly, Ruby quickly became quite popular, with home-field advantage and all that kind of stuff. However, because of its price tag of zero (it is, after all, an open source language), Ruby began to catch on outside of Japan. Yes, against all odds, Ruby become something of a phenomenon.

Although some might consider it odd that an open source language from a land far away from our little piece of the universe planted the seed of the idea of Ajax, I do not. I, for one, am open to ideas, regardless of the source. Alright, I'm a little more open to the ideas that relate to food, but, then, I'm one of those developers who eats anything that doesn't try to eat me first.

The interesting thing is that, even with people like me, mad scientists without enough time who like sushi and green tea ice cream, Ruby's popularity was growing only slowly—faster than a bonsai tree, but slower than Godzilla, Pokemon, or Yu-gi-oh. Fortunately, something changed back in 2004. No, radiation was not involved, but what happened is that Ruby got Rails.

13.1.2   Ruby on Rails

The word *Rails* is rather interesting; it brings up connotations of a sleek, silent, fast electric train moving into the future. That's a pretty nice connotation, especially when tied to web development, which, in my opinion, more often resembles a runaway steam train with no brakes on a downgrade, going into a hairpin curve during a snowstorm on Monday. In short, the average project is an accident waiting to happen. The accident might never happen, but the potential is there regardless. Rails is a full-stack programming framework implemented in Ruby whose purpose is to smooth the development of web applications.

Created by a Danish college student, David Heinemeier Hansson, Rails is open source and is based upon two simple principles. The first is that fewer lines of code equal fewer coding errors. This is a sensible idea because smaller, tighter code requires less time to write and debug. This remaining time could then be put toward testing or toward the inevitable feature creep that rises like a monster from a slab.

The second principle of Rails is configuration. Unlike many environments, Rails doesn't use configuration files. Instead, Rails uses information in application code itself to determine its configuration. This eliminates the "Doh!" factor that occurs whenever an application is moved to another environment, even when the environment is merely another developer's laptop. Although I can't speak for anyone else, I do know from personal experience that configuration files are one of those things that fall through the cracks about 20 percent of the time.

13.2 INSTALLATION

This entire preamble leads to the two important questions of where to get Ruby and where to get Rails. That's easy. A simple Google search for "ruby rails" is enough to answer both questions simultaneously. I do recommend a single search instead of individual searches, unless, of course, you are also interested in jewelry and traveling by train.

The process of installing Ruby is dependent upon which operating system your machine is running. For wimps like me who happen to be running Windows XP Professional, listening to Jethro Tull, and writing a book, installation is simply a matter of downloading an .exe and double-clicking it to get the ball rolling. It installs just like the shrink-wrapped software that you purchase, minus the autorun CD and price tag, as Figures 13-1 and 13-2 show.

If the lack of an autorun CD makes you nervous, then, by all means, create your own autorun CD. However, if the lack of a price tag makes you nervous, I recommend that you buy a second copy of this book and give it to a friend as a gift. In this manner, you've got a bill and you've also given the nice people at Prentice Hall a reason to send me a check. In short, everyone is happy all around.

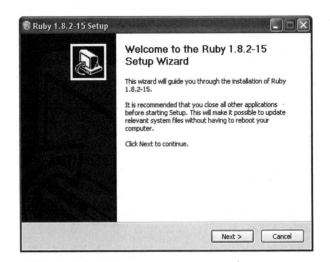

Figure 13-1   Windows installation wizard

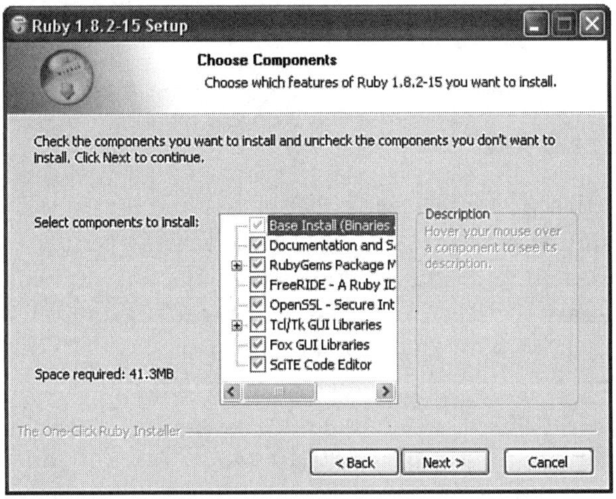

Figure 13-2   Choosing components in the Windows wizard

In a Windows environment, the installation of Ruby on Rails requires a couple additional steps. The first of these steps is to install Rails itself. If you have an Internet connection, this is just a single line; it is at the command prompt, but, nevertheless, it is a single line (see Figure 13-3).

However, if you are a real web developer and not a quiche-eating Windows user, installation will be a little more complex. Don't worry, it isn't a "Windows is superior" thing—in fact, it is more of a "Windows has training wheels" thing. Now that I've thoroughly confused you, the fact is that the

RubyGems package manager is part of the Windows installer, which isn't the case with Linux. However, because Linux isn't a stagnant environment, I recommend checking the Ruby website for the latest installation procedures.

Now that you've (hopefully), installed Ruby and Rails, it is time to kick the steel wheels (ouch) and take it out for a little spin. Woo-hoo!

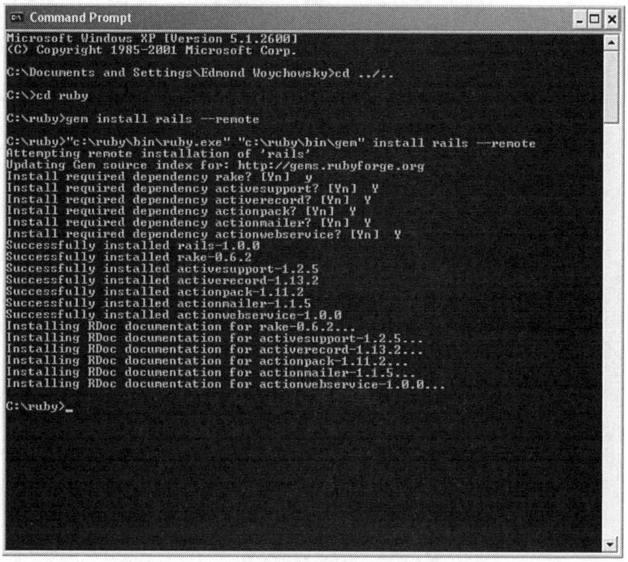

Figure 13-3   Installing Rails at the command prompt

13.3 A LITTLE RUBY ON RAILS WARM-UP

As stated previously, Ruby is the object-oriented programming language, and Rails is the framework used to develop applications. Let's say, for example, that I want to create a mad scientist application using Ruby on Rails. The steps would be something like the following:

1. If it doesn't exist, create a folder/directory to hold each of my Ruby on Rails applications. In this example, I created a folder called `rails` on my C: drive.

2. Using the command prompt, enter `cd rails`. This changes the current directory to `C:\rails`.

3. Create an empty web application by running the command `rails madscientist`, as shown in Figure 13-4.

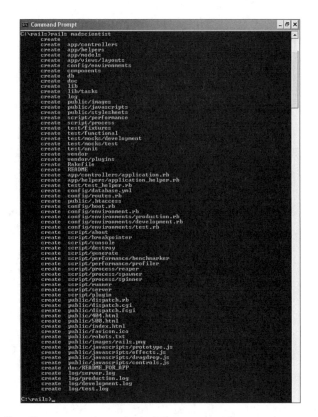

Figure 13-4   Creating an empty project at the command prompt

4. Start the web server WEBrick, which is included with Ruby, as shown in Figure 13-5.

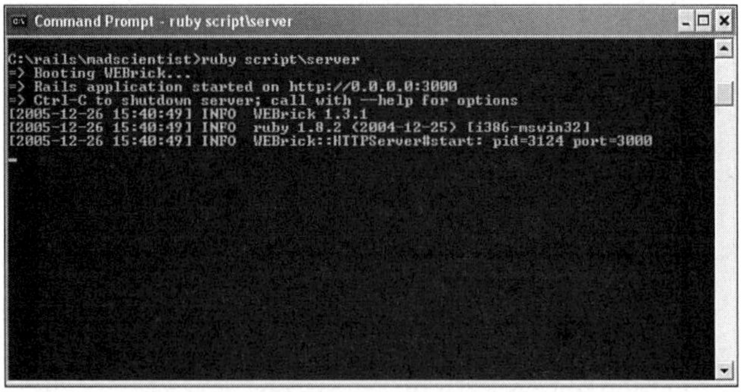

Figure 13-5   Starting the WEBrick web server at the command prompt

5. Check out what is out on the web server in the browser of your choice (see Figure 13-6).

Figure 13-6   The default start page

Not very impressive, is it?

6. Now is a good time to type Ctrl+C in the command prompt window to shut down WEBrick, as shown in Figure 13-7, before falling back and regrouping.

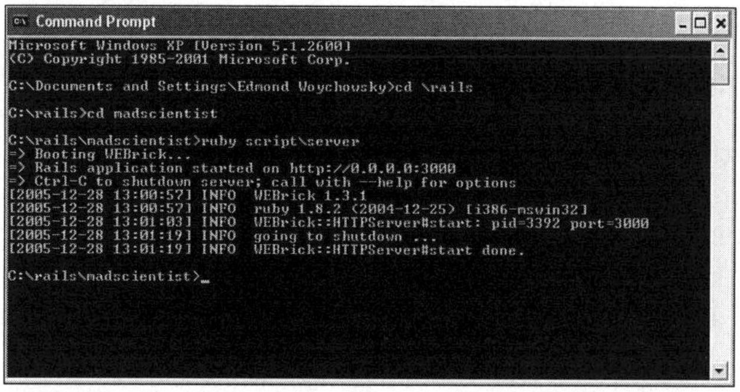

Figure 13-7   Shutting down the WEBrick web server at the command prompt

Well, we're only partway there; in fact, we should consider ourselves lucky that there is anything at all to show. Satisfied? Neither am I, so to progress further, we need to understand where things go in a Rails application.

The `rails madscientist` command created a number of folders and files that perform various functions. Take, for example, the `database.yml` file in the `config` folder; its purpose is to provide the application with details regarding the database to be used by the application. This is an example of the Rails "place for everything and everything in its place" approach. Personally, I wish this idea was more widespread. It would have gotten me out of some embarrassing moments in the past.

Another folder that is of interest is the `public` folder. Along with its three child folders, `images`, `javascripts`, and `stylesheets`, it provides a standard location for stashing the aforementioned. In most other environments, locating these types of files is more akin to a treasure hunt than web development.

The final folders that I'll cover are the `app` folder, along with the child folders called: `controllers`, `helpers`, `models`, and `views`. Still feel like you're in the dark? Give me a moment to illuminate. The first directory, `controllers`, contains classes that handle web requests from the visitor. The `helpers` directory holds helper classes, which are used by other classes, such as controller classes. Model classes, contained in the `models` subdirectory, are used to wrap the data stored in a database. Personally, I think that this is where application development can get really messy and often goes wrong. Finally, there is the `views` subdirectory, which holds the views. Views are the templates that are converted to HTML and returned to the visitor's web browsers.

Although at first glance it might seem that the application is spread around a bit, that really isn't the case. Instead of the normal "I know it is around here somewhere" approach usually associated with web development, Rails provides a consistent location for each class. If only this approach could be applied to the real world, I would spend a lot less time looking for my watch.

13.4 A PROBLEM REVISITED

Now that I've got some kind of idea (yeah, right) of what I'm doing with Ruby on Rails, the next question is how to use it in an application. The first task is to identify exactly what I want to do. For example, let's say that I want to display the items contained in the item table. The first necessary task is to generate a data model using the command console, as shown in Figure 13-8.

Figure 13-8   Generating a data model at the command prompt

The next step is to update the `database.yml` in the `config` directory to use the MySQL database from the previous chapters. The following is a snippet of the necessary code.

```
development:
  adapter: mysql
  host: localhost
  database: ajax
  username: root
  password: wyvern
```

These are the subsequent steps:

1. Generate a controller for the item data model (see Figure 13-9).

Figure 13-9   Generating a controller for the data model at the command prompt

2. Add a single line to the generated controller (See Listing 13-1).

Listing 13-1

```
class ItemController < ApplicationController
  scaffold :item
end
```

3. Fire up WEBrick to see what happens (see Figure 13-10).

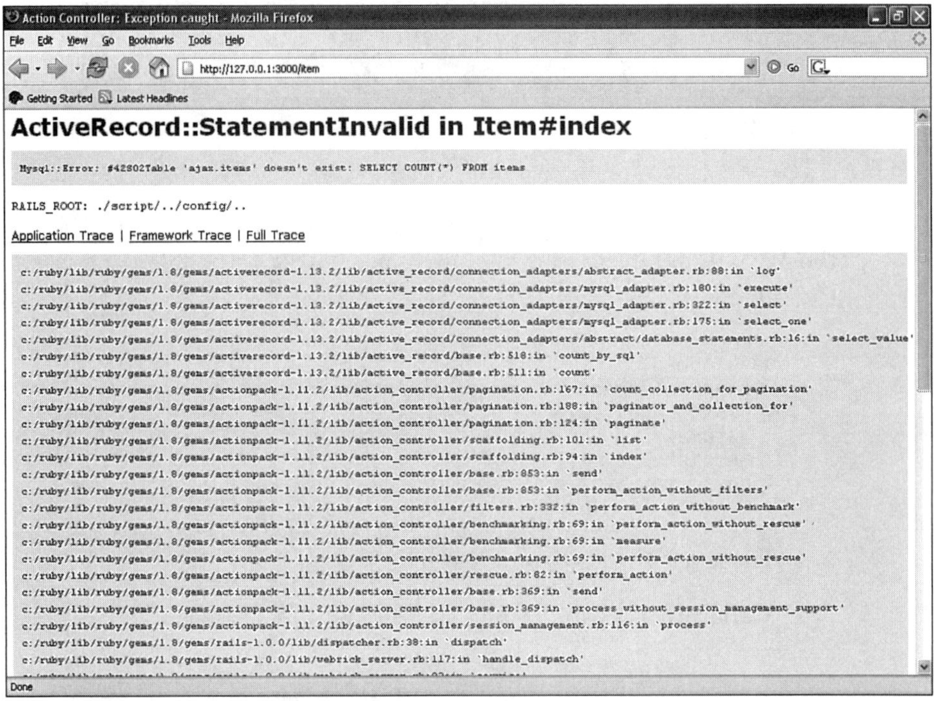

Figure 13-10   A "Doh!" moment accessing a database

Hmm, not exactly what I expected. It seems that Rails changed the table name item to items. Not good. Being among the lazy, I decided to go into the MySQL Query Browser and change the table name from item to items (see Figure 13-11) and try again (see Figure 13-12).

That is a little closer to what I am looking for. The trick is that, by default, Rails generates a query assuming that item is the row and items is the table. This isn't a big deal; it is just something to keep in mind when creating tables and using the defaults.

But what if you don't want to use the stuff generated by default, and where does Ajax fit into things?

Figure 13-11   Changing the database name in MySQL

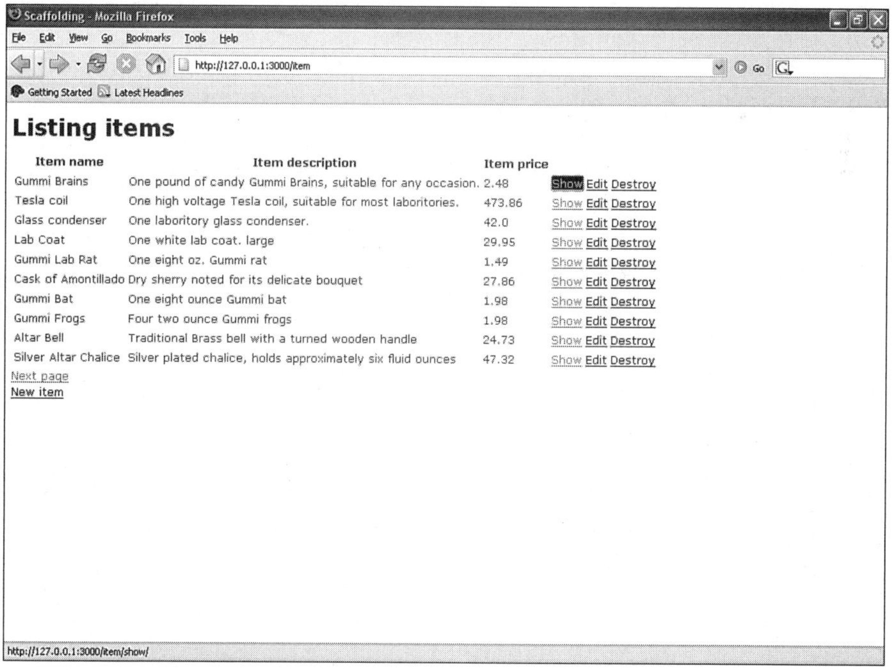

Figure 13-12   A working example

The answer to the first question is simple enough: Just generate a scaffold, as Figure 13-13 shows.

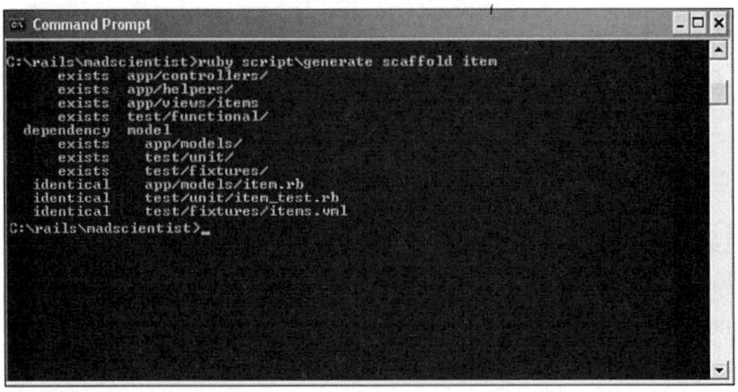

Figure 13-13   Generating a scaffold at the command prompt

It is then necessary to add the logic to the controller, the view, the layout, and the various templates.

This leaves only one question unanswered: Ajax? Remember the javascripts folder under the public folder? Well, in there is a file named prototypes.js that has all the logic required for asynchronous JavaScript and XML in Ruby on Rails. If you're interested, I'll offer a hint: Look at the xml_http_request? method. There's a lot to it, and I recommend playing.

13.5 WHITHER AJAX?

Considering the number of goodies built into the Rails API, finding exactly where the Ajax functionality is hidden could take a little work. However, because I'm really crumby at keeping secrets, I'll spill the beans; everything that we're interested in is in the JavaScriptHelper module, as Table 13-1 shows.

Table 13-1   JavaScriptHelper Methods

Method	Description
define_javascript_functions()	Includes all the JavaScriptHelper's JavaScript functions in the page.
draggable_element (element_id, options = {})	Makes the element with the corresponding ID draggable.
drop_receiving_element (element_id, options = {})	Forces the dropping (drag and drop) of an element. Also makes an Ajax call.

Method	Description
`escape_javascript(javascript)`	Escapes the provided JavaScript.
`evaluate_remote_response()`	Creates a JavaScript function that can evaluate a document returned from the server.
`form_remote_tag(options = {})`	Creates an HTML form that will be submitted using the `XMLHttpRequest` object.
`javascript_tag(content)`	Creates a JavaScript HTML tag/end tag that contains the provided content.
`link_to_function(name, function, html_options = {})`	Creates a hyperlink that links to a client-side JavaScript function.
`link_to_remote(name, options = {}, html_options = {})`	Creates a hyperlink that links to the server via an asynchronous `XMLHttpRequest` request.
`observe_field(field_id, options = {})`	Watches a field with the provided ID for user changes.
`observe_form(form_id, options = {})`	Watches the form with the provided ID for user changes.
`periodically_call_remote (options = {})`	Calls a provided URL whenever the interval elapses. If no interval is provided, a default of 10 seconds is used.
`remote_function(options)`	Returns a JavaScript snippet necessary for a remote function.
`sortable_element(element_id, options = {})`	Alters the HTML element with the corresponding `element_id` so that the element is sortable via an Ajax call.
`submit_to_remote(name, value, options = {})`	Displays a button that submits a form using the `XMLHttpRequest` object asynchronously.
`update_element_function (element_id, options = {}, &block)`	Updates the browser's DOM using the passed arguments.
`visual_effect(name, element_id = false, js_options = {})`	Returns JavaScript code that uses Ajax callbacks for visual effects.

Because I find myself in pretty much the same situation as one of the professors when I went to college—at least, as far as Ruby on Rails is concerned—I'm putting off an example of Ajax using Ruby on Rails until Chapter 14, "Traveling Farther with Ruby." The reason for this is that I'm a little out of my comfort zone here; like the professor, I'm essentially taking a class during the day and teaching it at night.

13.6 SUMMARY

In this chapter, we covered some of the history of Ruby on Rails, including the fact that Ruby on Rails is separated into Ruby and Rails. From there, we covered the process of installing Ruby and then installing Rails and viewing the default page. Then we covered how to create an empty project and fire up the included WEBrick web server and access a MySQL database, albeit with a little difficulty. In essence, the purpose of this chapter is to point the reader in the right direction when in search of an environment that supports Ajax.

CHAPTER 14

Traveling Farther with Ruby

If you're one of those developers who has never ventured outside the world of shrink-wrapped software, you've probably never heard of Ruby, the programming language I introduced in Chapter 13, "Traveling with Ruby on Rails," not the gem. As I noted in the last chapter Ruby, the language, is an object-oriented language that was created by Yukihiro Matsumoto of Japan and released into the wild in 1995. Ruby has many advantages over other programming languages that fill the same niche.

The first of these advantages is that Ruby is interpreted instead of compiled. On the surface, this might sound like a disadvantage, but it really isn't. Because I'm currently running only Windows XP, at times there has been a binary version of a program that only works on another operating system, such as Linux. However, with a scripted language such as Ruby, as long as I've installed it, I am good to go. Now all I need is to find a Ruby version of Hunt the Wumpus, and I'm all set.

Like Godzilla, it has expanded beyond its humble roots as a glimmer in its creator's eye to become something of a cult phenomenon. Oh, I mean *cult* in the good sense—no chanting or wearing funny clothes like those strange people who get dressed up to go to Renaissance festivals.

Seriously, Ruby is an object-oriented language that has capabilities and features that today's fast-paced development environment needs. And did I mention that Ruby is open source? Yes, when you get past the cost of the hardware, all that's required is the cost of an Internet connection and the time that it takes to download and install. I'd do the math for you, but fractions are not really my strong suit.

Instead, you can take a closer look at Ruby's data types while I take off the sword belt. Because there are unwritten rules that grapefruit must be served in halves and all introductions to programming languages must start with data types, we start there.

The layout of this chapter goes pretty much like this:

☞ Data types

☞ Operators

☞ Flow-control statements

☞ Threads

☞ Ajax

There is that word again, *Ajax*. You knew that it would pop up again somewhere. There is, however, a minor difference; basically, we take a quick look at the generated code to see how it works. I don't know about you, but I've always paid attention to the man behind the curtain.

14.1 DATA TYPES

Data types in Ruby aren't the data types that you're used to from the more traditional languages, such as C, COBOL, or Pascal. Because Ruby is purely object-oriented, you won't even find the primitive data types available in Java, for instance. In Ruby, you see, all data types are based upon classes.

This doesn't mean that there is no such thing as an integer or a string in Ruby; it means only that they are instances of the Integer and String classes. To some, this "everything is a class" approach might sound like overkill, but it also makes a lot of sense. Personally, I think it would be easier to code without having to change gears all the time. Just put my mind in OOP gear and go. This leaves the question, go where? I'm thinking of an island.

14.1.1 Numeric

"I am not a number, I'm a free man!" is the somewhat well-known quote from the British television series *The Prisoner*. I really don't see what Number Six was complaining about—it could have been worse. He could, for example, have had a job that he hated in a nuclear power plant, like Number Five did. Number Six does, however, share something in common with Homer—er, Number Five. You see, they were both integers.

Integer, with a capital *I*, is the base class from which all things integer are derived. Examples of classes derived from Integer are Bignum and Fixnum. Although each has its own characteristics, they both inherit from the Integer base class, whose properties and methods appear in Table 14-1.

Table 14-1   `Integer` Properties and Methods

Method	Class	Description
chr	Integer	Returns a string containing the character equivalent to the number value.
downto	Integer	Iterates a block of code.
integer?	Integer	Returns `true`.
next	Integer	Increments the value by 1.
size	Bignum	Returns the number of bytes used to store the value.
size	Fixnum	Returns the number of bytes used to store the value.
step	Integer	Increments the value to an ending value in increments of a set value.
succ	Integer	Increments the value by 1. Essentially, the same as the next method.
times	Integer	Executes a block of code a preset number of times.
to_f	Bignum	Converts the value to a float. When the value is too large to be contained in a float, infinity is returned.
to_f	Fixnum	Converts the value to a float.
to_i	Bignum	Returns a `Bignum`.
to_i	Fixnum	Returns a `Bignum`.
to_s	Bignum	Returns a `String`.
to_s	Fixnum	Returns a `String`.
upto	Integer	Executes a block of code, incrementing the value by 1 until the indicated value is reached.

However, with the exception of those poor souls trapped on the island, there is more to life than integers; there's floating point, called Float in Ruby. In case you've forgotten, floating-point numbers are those numbers with fractions, like when the statisticians say that the average American family has 2.6 children. The number 2.6 is a floating-point number and, depending on my mood, is either of my two half-brothers.

As with the `Integer` class, the `Float` class has a number of properties and methods, which are described in Table 14-2.

Table 14-2   `Float` Properties and Methods

Method	Description
ceil	Returns the closest integer, either equal to or greater than the float's value.
finite?	A Boolean indicating whether the value is a valid floating-point number.
floor	Returns the largest integer that is less than or equal to the value.

continues

Table 14-2   continued

Method	Description
infinite?	Returns true or false, indicating whether the value is infinite.
nan?	Returns true or false, indicating whether the value is Not A Number.
round	Rounds the value to the nearest integer.
to_f	Returns a Float.
to_i	Converts the value to an integer.
to_s	Returns a String.

14.1.2   String

For people who program in more than one language, there is a major advantage to strings being instances of the String class. Think of it as one-stop shopping; if something needs to be done, there's a really good chance that there is a method to do it. In fact, there are so many that I recommend going to the Ruby home page (www.ruby-lang.org/en/) to see them all.

14.1.3   Boolean

In programming, there are always two possible answers to any question: true and false. Maybe that is why there are two classes, Trueclass and Falseclass. Actually, with the dynamic nature of variables in Ruby, that is the truth. The Trueclass represents a logically true value, and the Falseclass represents a logically false class.

14.1.4   Objects

Possibly because of the total lack of primitives, the built-in objects in Ruby are incredibly rich and varied. There are objects for hashing, objects for file access, and even an object for arrays. In many instances, if you can imagine it, an object probably already is available for what is necessary, as the following list of built-in classes shows:

Array	FalseClass
Bignum	File::Stat
Binding	File
Class	Fixnum
Continuation	Float
Dir	Hash
Exception	Integer

IO	Regexp
MatchData	String
Method	Struct
Module	Struct::Tms
NilClass	ThreadGroup
Numeric	Thread
Object	Time
Proc	TrueClass
Range	

With all those built-in properties and methods, it might be a little while before it is necessary to write an object of our own, but it might be a good idea to give it a try. Let's say, for example, that we want to add a math class that would have two methods: add and subtract. Through diligent work and clean living, we would create the code shown in Listing 14-1.

Listing 14-1   myMath Class

```
class MyMath
  def add(a, b)
    puts a + b
  end

  def subtract(a, b)
    puts a - b
  end
end

m = MyMath.new
m.add(1, 1)
m.subtract(4,2)
```

That's all there is to creating and using a class in Ruby. Unfortunately, I was evil and skipped ahead a little by using variables and operators. Thinking about it, this is a little like a college class I had. After an unusually difficult test, the professor announced that no one got Question 10 correct, and perhaps the reason was that he had forgotten to teach that. Hmm ....

14.2 VARIABLES

Ruby supports a couple different types of variables, instance variables and class variables. Instead of making you guess whether their names actually mean what they say, I'll just come out and say it. The names mean what they say. Instance variables are created for each instance of the class. With class variables, on the other hand, all instances of the class share one variable. Although instance variables are common, class variables are somewhat less so. This does not mean that they aren't as useful; in fact, many times there is simply no substitute for a class variable.

The only question concerning variables is how to distinguish between instance variables and class variables. Are there little signs hanging off them that say "instance variable" and "class variable"? In a word, yes.

Instance variables and class variables are distinguished by the prefix. Instance variables are prefixed by a single @, whereas class variables are prefixed by two @. So @Bob is an instance variable, and @@Paul is a class variable.

Now that we have someplace to put our information, let's do something to it.

14.3 OPERATORS

Regardless of the language, there is usually some commonality. There's addition, subtraction, multiplication, division, and assignment. In some languages, including Ruby and JavaScript, the addition operator does double duty as the concatenation operator. This means that examples such as the following are pretty much the same, regardless of the language:

```
X = 1 + 1
X = 1 - 1
X = 1 * 1
X = 1 / 1
```

However, occasionally will you see something a little out of the ordinary, usually in languages that borrow some of their syntax from C. In Ruby, they're called multiple assignments; I like to think of them as less typing. Consider, for a moment, the following line of code:

```
X = X + 5
```

All that it does is increment the variable X by 5, so wouldn't it be easier to type this instead?

```
X += 5
```

Yeah, all that I'm saving is two keystrokes, the second X and a space, but it adds up. Imagine for a moment the variable name was my last name, Woychowsky instead of X. Having to type it only once would greatly extend the life of the W key. The same shortcut is available for subtraction, multiplication, and division.

14.4 FLOW-CONTROL STATEMENTS

In any type of nontrivial program, flow control is possibly the most important factor in programming. Without some kind of flow control in programming languages, computers would essentially be very expensive desktop ornaments. Come to think of it, when you got past the forwarding of every e-mail received each day to his team, I once had a manager whose computer was a very expensive desktop ornament. He actually once forwarded the same message 14 times before realizing that he had somehow been added to his address list for the team. But I'm wandering, so let's get back to flow control, starting with conditions.

14.4.1 Conditions

In your average run-of-the-mill language, there is the `if` statement, and that is pretty much all there is to it. Ruby has an `if` that looks something like this:

```
if x == 1
   b = 2
end
```

Pretty easy. Let's add a layer of complexity with an `else`:

```
if x == 1
   b = 2
else
   b = 3
end
```

In Ruby, it is also possible to take it to a higher degree of complexity by using the `elsif` statement:

```
if x == 1
   b = 2
elsif x == 2
   b = 4
else
   b = 3
end
```

Before I forget, for the purpose of clarity, Ruby permits the addition of a `then` to the `if` statement:

```
if x == 1 then
   b = 2
end
```

Remember all the way back to Chapter 4, "JavaScript"? Remember conditional operators? Well, they're back! In fact, here is an example:

```
b = (x == 1 ? 2 : 3)
```

A few years ago, I grew a goatee, which I have since shaved off. At the time, my reason for growing it was strictly personal and strange. You see, I wanted to pass myself off as the evil Ed from a parallel dimension. My plan for work domination failed, but it gave me the opportunity to appreciate the evil things from parallel dimensions. For example, did you know that Ruby has an evil `if` called `unless`?

The `unless` statement executes the code within only when the condition is false. If this doesn't fit the textbook, or, at least *Star Trek*, example of something from a parallel dimension, I don't know what does.

14.4.2 Looping

Some days I feel like I'm going around in circles, usually in the morning while I'm getting ready for work. The problem probably stems from a deep-seated need for coffee to get moving in the morning. This wasn't always the case, but back in high school, I worked in a pancake house and got hooked. The free coffee just seemed to help—that is, until I drank fifteen 20-ounce cups in the course of a day. I could have threaded a sewing machine needle while the machine was running. It hasn't been that bad in a while, but my morning ritual still requires coffee, as Ruby, shown in Listing 14-2, illustrates.

Listing 14-2   My Morning in Ruby: `while` Loop

```
cupsofcoffee = 0

while cupsofcoffee < 4
  puts "hurry..."
  cupsofcoffee += 1
end
```

The great thing about describing one's morning programmatically is that there are always alternative ways of expressing one's self. For example, some mornings the blanket monster is holding me back and I just can't seem to get moving until there is a certain level of coffee in my system. Mornings like these are better expressed by the code shown in Listing 14-3.

Listing 14-3   My Morning in Ruby: `until` Loop

```
cupsofcoffee = 0

until cupsofcoffee >= 4
  puts "hurry..."
  cupsofcoffee += 1
end
```

A while back, I used to have one of those coffee pots that had a timer. On those mornings when I had programmed it the night before, coffee was already going. Ah, a set number of cups of coffee just waiting for cream and sugar. I suppose Listing 14-4 best sums it up.

Listing 14-4   My Morning in Ruby: `for/in` Loop

```
puts "for-in loop"
for x in ["hurry...", "hurry...", "hurry...", "hurry..."]
      puts x
end
```

Nowadays, I have one of those coffee makers that takes a Pod. Just drop in the Pod and hit the button, and 90 seconds later there's coffee. This takes making coffee from being an art to being more of a science, a feeling that is best conveyed by the example shown in Listing 14-5.

Listing 14-5   My Morning in Ruby: `for/in` Loop

```
puts "Iterators"
1.step(4,1) do |x|
  puts "hurry..."
end
```

14.5 THREADS

Ruby has a feature that every language should have: the capability to multithread. Personally, I'm fond of forking a thread whenever something that I'm about to do is time consuming. For instance, any kind of input/output operation or attempt to obtain information from another server deserves another thread.

In Ruby, threads are compatible across all platforms, which is quite an accomplishment. However, I recommend further reading on the subject of multithreading. From personal experience, I know that multithreading is truly a dark art and is not meant to be undertaken lightly.

14.6 AJAX

All this discussion of Ruby leaves us with only one question: Where the (fill-in-the-blank) does Ajax fit in? Well, remember Rails from Chapter 13? That is where Ajax fits in, but for me to prove it, we have to generate another controller (see Figure 14-1).

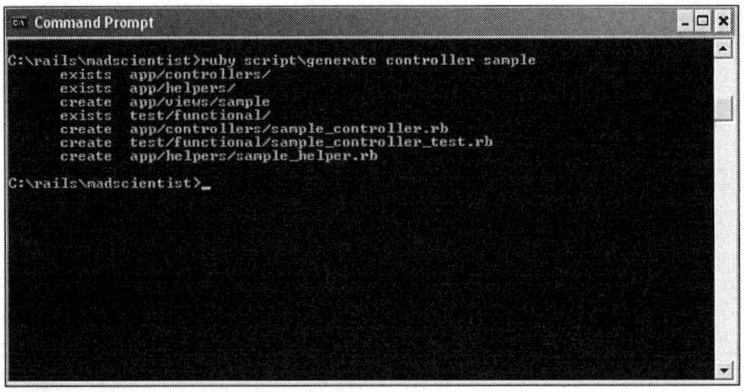

Figure 14-1   Generating a controller

We're interested in two files: `sample_controller.rb` under `madscientist\` `app\controllers`, and `index.rhtml` under `madscientist\app\views\sample`. The first file is the Ruby application controller that defines the sample class. This class, shown in Listing 14-6, will do all our server-side dirty work. The purpose of the second file (see Listing 14-7), on the other hand, is to handle the client-side part of the Ajax demo.

Listing 14-6 `controller.rb`

```ruby
class SampleController < ApplicationController
  def index
  end

  def echo_data
    render_text "<i>" + params[:textinformation] + "</i>"
  end
end
```

Listing 14-7 `index.rhtml`

```
<html>
  <head>
    <title>link_to_remote Demo</title>
    <%= javascript_include_tag "prototype" %>
  </head>
  <body>
    <%= form_remote_tag(:update => "form", :url => { :action => :echo_data
}) %>
      Text
      <%= text_field_tag :textinformation %>
      <%= submit_tag "Echo" %>
      <%= end_form_tag %>
    <br />
    <div id="form">
    </div>
  </body>
</html>
```

After these two files have been modified, in the case of `controller.rb`, or created, as `index.rhtml` needs to be, we're ready to start WEBrick (see Figure 14-2) and bring up the page (see Figure 14-3).

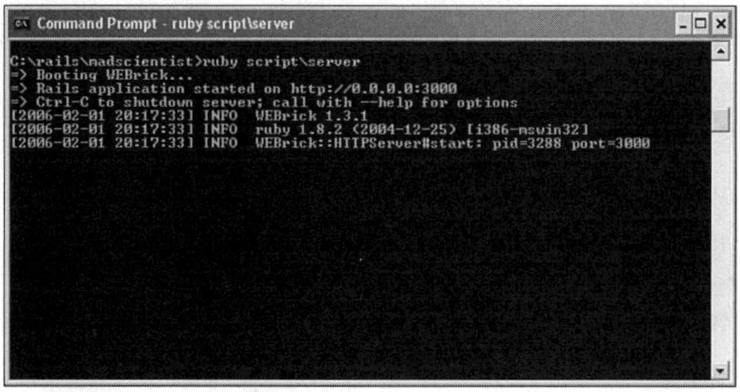

Figure 14-2 WEBrick

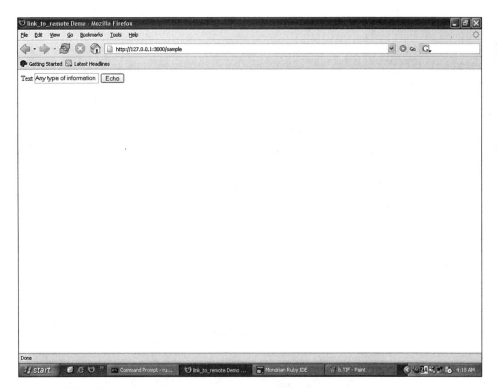

Figure 14-3   Generated page

This leaves just trying out the page, whose sole purpose is to echo back from the server anything entered in the text box when the button is clicked. Figure 14-4 shows the result.

Because I'm one of those people who needs to know how something works, I've included Listing 14-8 showing the generated HTML.

Listing 14-8   Generated HTML

```
    <html>
  <head>
    <title>link_to_remote Demo</title>
    <script src="/javascripts/prototype.js"
type="text/javascript"></script>
  </head>
  <body>
    <form action="/sample/echo_data" method="post" onsubmit="new
Ajax.Updater('form', '/sample/echo_data', {asynchronous:true,
evalScripts:true, parameters:Form.serialize(this)}); return false;">
    Text
    <input id="textinformation" name="textinformation" type="text" />
```

```
        <input name="commit" type="submit" value="Echo" />
      </form>
        <br />
      <div id="form"></div>
    </body>
</html>
```

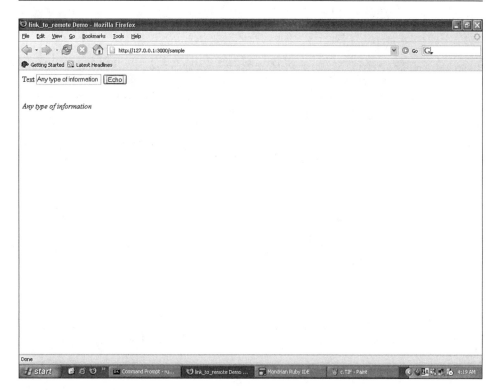

Figure 14-4 Echoed text

Interesting isn't it? The source from `index.rhtml` transmogrifies into some pretty neat HTML, with all the Ajax goodies built right in. The j a v a s c r i p t _ include_tag includes `prototype.js`, in which resides all the necessary client-side JavaScript, while the rest of the tags describe an HTML form. Personally, I am beginning to feel like I have found the Promised Land, and I'm not leaving. In roughly 24 lines of code, we've got a simple Ajax application. Of course, there is more to it than that; this example only touches upon some of the features available in the Rails API. But Ruby on Rails shows some definite promise.

14.7 SUMMARY

In this chapter, we lightly touched upon the Ruby programming language, a subject that could take an entire book in itself. We pointed out the fact that Ruby has no primitives and that all variables are, in fact, objects. The numeric objects were covered in some detail, and we lightly touched upon strings and Booleans. An example of creating a custom class was shown to illustrate just how easy it actually is.

We discussed operators, including the more unusual multiple assignment operators, before we covered loops of various types. Next, we touched upon the possibility of using threads in Ruby. Finally, the chapter closed with an example of how Ruby on Rails can be used to create an Ajax application with very little typing.

CHAPTER 15

The Essential Cross-Browser HTML DOM

Whether or not the average web developer is aware of it, it is out there, unseen and unnoticed, but nevertheless out there. Allow me to explain before you decide that I've popped a gasket and need to be taken to a nice soft room, the kind with padded walls. I am referring to the HTML Document Object Model—yes, that often ignored application programming interface that can be both a blessing and a curse.

Yes, the average web developer uses the HTML DOM only to the extent that is absolutely necessary to perform the job, and no further. The reasons for this are many, ranging from the fact that in the early days of web browsers, everybody did their own thing, to the fact that client-side code is often considered unreliable because some people are using web browsers that belong more fittingly in a museum than in a computer that was manufactured in the twenty-first century.

I suppose that this could be considered a major issue, the idea that web applications need to work on every browser released since the beginning of time. You might consider me something of a snob for saying this, but why should everyone who is willing to advance beyond the mid-1990s be penalized? You don't see electrical power being looked down upon because some groups don't approve of it. Regardless of the reason for ignoring the HTML DOM, unless they're fond of web applications that behave like mainframe applications from the 1970s, people will have to either get with the program or be left behind.

This chapter is organized along the following lines:

☞ Interfaces
☞ Document
☞ Frames
☞ Collections

15.1 INTERFACES

The HTML Document Object Model is an application programming interface (API) that defines the structure of an HTML document in the browser. In addition, it defines how that document can be accessed and manipulated through the use of JavaScript, sometimes embedded within the very same HTML document that is being manipulated.

This sounds a little scary doesn't it? The idea that a JavaScript routine could essentially modify the very fabric of its own universe can be terrifying. Just one oops, and it is over—it modified itself right out of existence. For all intents and purposes, as far as the browser was concerned, it would have never existed. Fortunately, this takes a little work to accomplish, and only the JavaScript function and possibly the associated page would cease to exist. Believe me, if this wasn't the case, I would have winked out long ago.

Table 15-1 shows the various HTML Document Object Model interfaces available through JavaScript. I would like to point out that the majority of these interfaces correspond to actual HTML elements. Yes, name an HTML element, and there is a corresponding interface; remember, though, that just because an interface exists for a deprecated element, you don't have to use it. It is still deprecated.

Table 15-1   HTML Document Object Model Interfaces Available Through JavaScript

Interface Name	Description
HTMLCollection	A collection of HTML nodes
HTMLDocument	The root element of the HTML document
HTMLElement	The base class for all HTML elements
HTMLHtmlElement	Corresponds to the html element
HTMLHeadElement	Corresponds to the head element
HTMLLinkElement	Corresponds to the link element
HTMLTitleElement	Corresponds to the title element
HTMLMetaElement	Corresponds to the meta element
HTMLBaseElement	Corresponds to the base element
HTMLIsIndexElement	Corresponds to the isindex element
HTMLStyleElement	Corresponds to the style element
HTMLBodyElement	Corresponds to the body element
HTMLFormElement	Corresponds to the form element
HTMLSelectElement	Corresponds to the select element.
HTMLOptGroupElement	Corresponds to the option group element
HTMLOptionElement	Corresponds to the option element
HTMLInputElement	Corresponds to the input element

Interface Name	Description
HTMLTextAreaElement	Corresponds to the text area element
HTMLButtonElement	Corresponds to the button element
HTMLLabelElement	Corresponds to the label element
HTMLFieldSetElement	Corresponds to the field set element
HTMLLegendElement	Corresponds to the legend element
HTMLUListElement	Corresponds to the unordered list element
HTMLOListElement	Corresponds to the ordered list element
HTMLDListElement	Corresponds to the dash list element
HTMLDirectoryElement	Corresponds to the directory element
HTMLMenuElement	Corresponds to the menu element
HTMLLIElement	Corresponds to the list element
HTMLBlockquoteElement	Corresponds to the block quote element
HTMLDivElement	Corresponds to the div element
HTMLParagraphElement	Corresponds to the paragraph element
HTMLHeadingElement	Corresponds to the heading elements
HTMLQuoteElement	Corresponds to the quote element
HTMLPreElement	Corresponds to the preformatted element
HTMLBRElement	Corresponds to the break element
HTMLBaseFontElement	Corresponds to the base font element
HTMLFontElement	Corresponds to the font element
HTMLHRElement	Corresponds to the horizontal rule element
HTMLModElement	Corresponds to the modification elements
HTMLAnchorElement	Corresponds to the anchor element
HTMLImageElement	Corresponds to the image element
HTMLObjectElement	Corresponds to the object element
HTMLParamElement	Corresponds to the parameter element
HTMLAppletElement	Corresponds to the applet element
HTMLMapElement	Corresponds to the map element
HTMLAreaElement	Corresponds to the area element
HTMLScriptElement	Corresponds to the script element
HTMLTableElement	Corresponds to the table element
HTMLTableCaptionElement	Corresponds to the table caption element
HTMLTableColElement	Corresponds to the table column element
HTMLTableSectionElement	Corresponds to the table section element
HTMLTableRowElement	Corresponds to the table row element
HTMLTableCellElement	Corresponds to the table cell element
HTMLFrameSetElement	Corresponds to the frame set element
HTMLFrameElement	Corresponds to the frame element
HTMLIFrameElement	Corresponds to the iframe element

15.1.1   Window

Although it's not officially part of the HTML Document Object Model, the window object is the big kahuna, the big cheese, or, in web development terms, top of the hierarchy. Many web developers don't realize it, but all HTML documents are actually children of the window object. This means that it is as valid to code window.document as it is to code document. You will probably see only the latter as opposed to the former, but I think it's a good idea to point out the possibility of the former, if only to avoid those Homer Simpson moments: Doh!

15.2 DOCUMENT

Alright, now we are officially dealing with the HTML Document Object Model in all its hierarchical glory. The only question is, what does the word *hierarchical* mean in reference to the HTML DOM?

To me, it means that I envision the structure as a tree, but not the binary kind or the kind growing outside. It has a single root and branches (elements), and sometimes those branches have branches (more elements). In my mind, the only difference from the growing kind of tree is that the root is at the top, but since I'm in Pennsylvania, I think of trees in China and everything is alright. If you happen to be in China, just envision trees in Pennsylvania, and you'll be fine. Ex-mainframe programmers should think IMS DB to get themselves through this section.

Seriously, as weird as it sounds, the concept of hierarchical data has been around for a long time. Consider the HTML document shown in Listing 15-1 for a moment.

Listing 15-1   An HTML Document

```
<html>
  <head>
    <title>Test</title>
    <script language="JavaScript"></script>
  </head>
  <body>
    <h1>Test 1</h1>
    <h2>Test 2</h2>
    <h3>Test 3</h3>
  </body>
</html>
```

This document could alternatively be depicted graphically as shown in Figure 15-1.

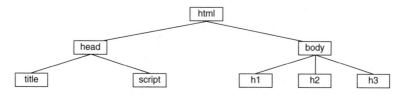

Figure 15-1 Graphic depiction of HTML document in Listing 15-1

See, it's hierarchical. There is a single root, the html element, which has two children, the head and body elements. The head and body elements are siblings because they both share the same parent. The head element has two children, and the title and script elements and the body element have three children: the H1, H2, and H3 elements. The title and script elements are siblings, and the H1, H2, and H3 elements are siblings, but the two groups of elements are not siblings because they have different parents.

So far, this has pretty much been an intellectual exercise, so how excited can someone get about a picture? Um, I mean, a picture that doesn't come with a rating!

What I mean is, maybe it would help if there were a convenient table that covered the various properties and methods available through the document interface. Fortunately, Igor has put together Table 15-2 to give you some idea of what is available.

Table 15-2 HTML DOM Properties/Methods

Property/Method	Description
anchors	A collection consisting of the anchors in the current document.
applets	A collection consisting of the applets in the current document.
attributes	A collection consisting of the attributes for the current node.
body	The body element of the page.
childNodes	A nodeset consisting of the child nodes of the current node. Please note that the nodeset can be empty.
cookie	A collection consisting of the cookies associated with the current document.
doctype	The Document Type Declaration associated with this XML document.
documentElement	The document's root element.
domain	The server's domain name.
firstChild	The first child node of the current node.

continues

Table 15-2 continued

Property/Method	Description
forms	A collection consisting of the forms in the current document.
frames	A collection consisting of the frames in the current document.
images	A collection consisting of the images in the current document.
implementation	The DOMImplementation for this document.
lastChild	The last child of the current node.
links	A collection consisting of the links in the current document.
nextSibling	The next child of the current node's parent.
nodeName	The name of the node.
nodeType	The type of the node.
nodeValue	The value of the node.
ownerDocument	The Document associated with the current element.
parentNode	The parent of the current node.
previousSibling	The previous child of the current node's parent.
referrer	The URI of the page that linked to this page.
title	The title of the HTML document.
URL	The current page's URL.
appendChild(new)	Appends the new child node as the last child.
cloneNode(deep)	Duplicates the specified node. The Boolean parameter deep is used to indicate a deep copy, whether or not the children should be copied.
close()	Closes the document stream and also causes the document to be rendered.
createAttribute(name)	Creates an attribute.
createCDATASection(data)	Creates a CDATASection node using the data provided.
createComment(data)	Creates a comment node using the data provided.
createDocumentFragment()	Creates an empty document fragment.
createElement(tagName)	Creates the specified element.
createEntityReference(name)	Creates an EntityReference.
createProcessingInstruction (target,data)	Creates a ProcessingInstruction node.
createTextNode(data)	Creates a Text element using the **data** provided.

Property/Method	Description
getElementById(elementId)	Returns a single element based upon that element's id attribute. When there is more than one element with the same id, only the first is returned.
getElementByName(elementName)	Returns a collection of elements based upon the element's name.
getElementsByTagName(tagname)	Returns a nodeset consisting of elements with matching tag names.
hasChildNodes()	Returns true if child nodes exist and false if child nodes do not exist.
insertBefore(new,reference)	Inserts the new child node before the reference child node.
open()	Opens the document stream for writing.
removeChild(old)	Removes the old child node.
replaceChild(new,old)	Replaces the old child node with the new child node.
write()	Writes a text string to the document.
writeln()	Writes a text string to the document and appends a newline character.

Before moving on, I want to remind you that the document is hierarchical. This means that each element has properties and methods of its own. Rather than go crazy trying to create some kind of uber table with every possible property and method for the interfaces shown in Table 15-1, I decided to create Table 15-3. Table 15-3 covers the properties and methods common to the various elements.

Table 15-3 Properties/Methods Common to the Various HTML DOM Interfaces

Property/Method	Description
attributes	A collection consisting of the attributes for the current node.
childNodes	A nodeset consisting of the child nodes of the current node. Please note that the nodeset can be empty.
className	The element's class attribute.
dir	The element's text direction.
firstChild	The first child node of the current node.
id	The element's identifier.
lang	The element's language code.
lastChild	The last child of the current node.

continues

Table 15-3   continued

Property/Method	Description
nextSibling	The next child of the current node's parent.
nodeName	The name of the node.
nodeType	The type of the node. See Table 15-2 for accepted values.
nodeValue	The value of the node.
ownerDocument	The document associated with the current element.
parentNode	The parent of the current node.
previousSibling	The previous child of the current node's parent.
tagName	The tag name of the element.
title	The element's title.
appendChild(new)	Appends the new child node as the last child.
cloneNode(deep)	Duplicates the specified node. The Boolean parameter deep is used to indicate a deep copy, whether or not the children should be copied.
getAttribute(name)	Returns the value of an attribute based upon name.
getAttributeNode(name)	Retrieves an Attr node by name.
getElementsByTagName(tagname)	Returns a nodeset consisting of elements with matching tag names.
hasChildNodes()	Returns true if child nodes exist and false if child nodes do not exist.
insertBefore(new,reference)	Inserts the new child node before the reference child node.
normalize()	Normalizes the specified element and children of the specified element.
removeAttribute(name)	Removes an attribute by name.
removeAttributeNode(name)	Removes an Attr node by name.
removeChild(old)	Removes the old child node.
replaceChild(new,old)	Replaces the old child node with the new child node.
setAttribute(name,value)	Creates an attribute and sets its value.
setAttributeNode(name)	Adds an Attr node by name.

I want to add a little hint on how to find some of the remaining properties or methods for the various interfaces. Basically, it goes like this: If it is a property or method of the element, there is a really good chance that it is also a property or method of the interface. It might sound strange that this has to be mentioned, but I've found that everyone has a blind spot concerning something in their career. In case you were wondering, mine is peasants with pitchforks and torches.

15.3 FRAMES

From an HTML Document Object Model point of view, frames are rather odd creatures because they are essentially HTML documents within HTML documents. Consider for a moment the fact that it is possible to have more than one document at a time. For example, the following is perfectly legal:

```
document.frames[1].document.body
```

It refers to the body of the document in the frame with an index of 1. This has a tendency to throw off quite a number of people, probably because it is a "wheels within wheels" kind of relationship, a bit tough to grasp the first time around. There is also the added complexity that if the script is executing in a frame itself, it could quite be playing with either the parent document or a sibling document, or even the child of a sibling. The important thing to remember is that anything that can be done with the current document can also be done with another document.

15.4 COLLECTIONS

As you probably noticed in Table 15-1, there is an interface whose sole purpose is to deal with collections. Add to this the various collections defined in Tables 15-2 and 15-3, and it becomes apparent very quickly that somebody really likes collections. Who can blame them?

Collections make for very compact code that can be stepped through in a sequential manner. Table 15-4 details the single property and two methods available through the collection interface.

Table 15-4 The Property and the Methods Available Through the Collection Interface

Property/Method	Description
length	The number of items in the collection
item()	Retrieves an individual item from a collection based upon that item's index
namedItem()	Retrieves an individual item from a collection based upon that item's identifier

15.5 SUMMARY

This chapter is by no means a complete explanation of the HTML Document Object Model, but it was never intended to be. Rather than be an encyclopedic rendition of the HTML DOM, its purpose is to be more of an overview, with the good parts underlined. I'd like to think that there is a slight possibility that I hit the mark, but then, maybe I'm delusional.

CHAPTER 16

Other Items of Interest

Although I do have a rather loose grip on reality, my grip isn't so loose that I think that the information contained within these pages is the be all and end all concerning asynchronous JavaScript and XML. Ajax is nearly unique in having both the excitement associated with a new topic and the maturity that is associated with only a well-established technique. In fact, the last topic that I can think of that had the same dual nature was NASA's Apollo program. On one hand, the idea of sending people to the Moon and returning them safely to Earth was the stuff of science fiction. On the other hand, humanity has been playing with rockets for centuries, occasionally with disastrous results.

Come to think of it, Ajax and the Apollo program have a great deal in common. On one hand, the idea of web applications that have the look and feel of Linux and Windows applications is the stuff of science fiction. On the other hand, humanity has been creating web applications for the last several years, occasionally with disastrous results. Hmm, there seems to be some kind of pattern going on here.

In this chapter, I address some technologies that are complementary to Ajax, one that is similar or is a kind of proprietary approach to Ajax, and then finish with some further/final thoughts on browsers. Essentially, the purpose of this chapter is not only to sum up everything that has been covered in this book, but also to provide a starting point on where to look for other possible ways of doing things. For example, about two months ago, I spoke with a developer who did Ajax. However, his technique was to use a Java applet for communications instead of the `XMLHttpRequest` object. What I am trying to convey is that there are multiple answers to every question, all of them equally correct. So here are some of the answers, with my personal opinions sprinkled about.

16.1 SARISSA

Although it's officially only an open source cross-browser JavaScript XML library, Sarissa is one of those libraries whose capabilities extend far beyond the basic XML support that I expected. This is a rare occurrence in today's world, where we can all remember being disappointed by movies, jobs, and most members of Congress. Sarissa wraps the browser's native XML application programming interfaces with common interfaces. This makes life much easier for the client-side developer than it would otherwise be.

Unlike my home-grown library, which supports only Microsoft Internet Explorer and Gecko-based browsers such as Firefox, Flock, Mozilla, and Netscape, Sarissa supports a wide range of browsers on multiple platforms. This serves as a really good example of what a number of dedicated developers can accomplish when they put their minds to it, as opposed to the lone mad scientist or even the bloated corporation. Sarissa supports, at least partially, the following web browsers:

☞ Firefox
☞ Konqueror (KDE 3.3)
☞ Microsoft Internet Explorer (MSXML 3.0)
☞ Mozilla
☞ Opera
☞ Safari

That's quite an impressive list of web browsers; I don't even have a machine capable of running Safari. I normally just press my nose to the window of the Apple Store and wish. Come to think of it, I usually do that with most stores that sell computers, including online ones. Well, at least now my wife knows how the monitor on her computer got the nose prints on it and who the nose prints belong to.

16.1.1 A Brief Overview of Sarissa

Table 16-1 briefly examines the goodies available in Sarissa, which read like a Who's Who of Ajax features.

Table 16-1   Sarissa Features

Action	Description
DOM Document Object (create)	Creates a new instance of an XML DOM document
DOM Document Object (load)	Loads an XML DOM document from either a remote source, such as the server, or a string either synchronously or asynchronously
Parse	Parses an XML DOM document for errors
Serialize	Serializes an XML DOM document to a text string
XMLHttpRequest	Communicates with the web server via the XMLHttpRequest object
XPath	Provides the capability to apply an XPath statement with JavaScript

The overall syntax for Sarissa is both logical and consistent. By *logical,* I mean that if a particular parameter is necessary for a certain object, it is there. The consistency that I'm referring to is the capability to write a script once and be able to run it on any of the supported web browsers, without having to monkey around with the code too much. What a concept!

To see what I mean, let's take a look at how to create an XML DOM document using Sarissa:

```
var myXMLDocument = Sarissa.getDomDocument();
```

Relatively simple and painless, isn't it?

Loading the XML document from a remote source is only slightly more complex, unless you're indecisive, in which case you've got real problems in deciding between synchronous and asynchronous. Never mind, I'll go out on a limb and show how it is done synchronously in Listing 16-1 and asynchronously in Listing 16-2.

Listing 16-1   Loading Synchronously

```
var myXMLDocument = Sarissa.getDomDocument();

myXMLDocument.async = false;
myXMLDocument.load("duckzilla.xml");
```

Listing 16-2   Loading Asynchronously

```
var myXMLDocument = Sarissa.getDomDocument();

myXMLDocument.async = true;
myXMLDocument.onreadystatechange = readyStateHandler;
myXMLDocument.load("duckzilla.xml");

function readyStateHandler() {
  if(myXMLDocument.readyState == 4)
    alert('Loaded.');
}
```

But what if the XML isn't remote? Say, for example, that it is already on the page in a JavaScript string. In that case, Listing 16-3 is the example for you.

Listing 16-3   Loading an XML Document Already on the Page

```
var myXMLDocument = Sarissa.getDomDocument();
var myDOMParser = new DOMParser();
var myXMLString = '<xyzzy>plugh</xyzzy>';

myXMLDocument = myDOMParser.parseFromString(myXMLString,'text/xml');
```

Alright, now through one means or another, we have an XML document loaded. This leaves only the question of what to do with it. That's a minor detail; it isn't like it's leftover Thanksgiving turkey or anything like that. We are not going to run out of ideas. Nobody has ever considered making XML enchiladas or XML stroganoff. XML gives us two possible options; we can either transform it or send it somewhere.

We start with the option to transform it because I consider myself something of an XSLT geek, especially when performing dangerous acts such as client-side transformations. I'm always up for playing with anything that could possibly make my job easier, and it doesn't get much easier than this. There are only a couple simple rules to remember when using XSLT with Sarissa: The XML is an XML document, and the XSL style sheet is also an XML document. That's all there is to it, and Listing 16-4 presents an example.

Listing 16-4   XSLT with Sarissa

```
var myXMLDocument = Sarissa.getDomDocument();
var myXSLDocument = Sarissa.getDomDocument();
var myXSLTProcessor = new XSLTProcessor();
var myXMLTransformed;

// Synchronous load of XML document
```

```
myXMLDocument.async = false;
myXMLDocument.load("jeckle.xml");

// Synchronous load of XSL stylesheet
myXSLDocument.async = false;
myXSLDocument.load("hyde.xsl");

// Import stylesheet
myXSLTProcessor.importStylesheet(myXSLDocument);

// Add a parameter 'take' value 'formula'
myXSLTProcessor.setParameter(null, 'take', 'formula');

// Transform, result in myXMLTransformed
myXMLTransformed = myXSLTProcessor.transformToDocument(myXMLDocument);
```

With XSLT out of the way, this leaves Sarissa's implementation of the XMLHttpRequest object as the last piece that I cover here. This implementation of the XMLHttpRequest object offers no surprises, unless you've jumped ahead to this chapter just to read about Sarissa. If this is the case, allow me to explain that XMLHttpRequest is available in two distinct flavors: synchronous and asynchronous. Synchronous is the one that waits quietly in line for its response, and asynchronous is the one that does other things and expects a callback with periodic updates. Listing 16-5 shows an example of a synchronous request, and Listing 16-6 shows an asynchronous request.

Listing 16-5 Synchronous Request

```
var myXMLHttpRequest = new XMLHttpRequest();

myXMLHttpRequest.open('GET','manticore.xml',false);
myXMLHttpRequest.send(null);
```

Listing 16-6 Asynchronous Request

```
var myXMLHttpRequest = new XMLHttpRequest();

myXMLHttpRequest.open('GET','ELP.xml',true);

myXMLHttpRequest.onreadystatechange = function() {
  if(myXMLHHttpRequest.readyState == 4)
    alert('Done.');
}

myXMLHttpRequest.send(null);
```

If you're interested in using Sarissa for an Ajax application or any web application of your own, I heartily recommend it. The source code for Sarissa is available for download from SourceForge.net, whose URL is, coincidentally, www.sourceforge.net. If you're unfamiliar with SourceForge.net, I recommend that you put aside an afternoon, and about 30 blank CDs, and peruse their selections of open source goodies. In addition to a vast array of software, there is, amazingly enough, documentation to go along with the software. It, like Sarissa, is well worth the time.

16.2 JSON AND JSON-RPC

There's definitely a Greek theme with many of the names involved with using the XMLHttpRequest object. First there is Ajax itself, a legendary hero, followed by Microsoft's version called ATLAS, one of the Titans. Finally, there is JSON, pronounced "Jason," which stands for JavaScript Object Notation.

16.2.1 JavaScript Object Notation

Although I am by no means an expert on the subject, JavaScript Object Notation (JSON) works as a kind of replacement for XML. This might sound a little weird, but it makes perfect sense when viewed from a cross-browser point of view. The reason for this is that more web browsers support JavaScript than XML. This is just another way to distribute applications to as many people as possible.

JSON appears to work something along the lines of children's building blocks. With blocks, a few basic shapes are used in conjunction with imagination to create complex structures. The same can be said of JSON: A few basic "shapes" are used in conjunction with imagination to create complex structures. The only difference is that whereas children's blocks result in physical structures, JSON results in logical structures.

Let's take a look at the two basic data structures (blocks) that are used to create more complex structures in JSON. The first of these basic data structures is the name-value pair, which really isn't anything that we have not already seen in earlier chapters. Just think along the lines of a JavaScript collection or associative array, and you'll be fine.

The second basic data structure in JSON has the formidable description of "an ordered list of values." Ooh, sounds scary. In fact, it sounds a lot scarier than its actual name, array. Say "an ordered list of values," and people will pay attention; say "array," and unless you're talking about an array of missile silos, nobody cares.

These structures, in turn, are used to create somewhat more complex structures. The first of these more complex structures is an object; such objects consist of an unordered list of name-value pairs, with the following syntax for an empty object:

```
object_name { }
```

Of course, an empty object isn't very useful, so it is necessary to add members as string-value pairs. Of course, sometimes saying nothing is enough.

That is a high-level (as in, orbital) view of the concepts behind JSON. All we need to look at now is the actual syntax. After all, because the information going back and forth from the web server and the web browser has to be text, an internal representation of a JavaScript array would probably cause some problems when trying to send it to and fro.

16.3 ATLAS

ATLAS is Microsoft's answer to Ajax. Talk about a group that suffers from the "not invented here" syndrome. For those of you who are unfamiliar with this syndrome, it goes something along the lines of this:

1. If we didn't invent it, then it is evil.
2. If we can sell a knock-off, then the original is evil and ours is innovative.
3. In a product this innovative, there are bound to be some bugs, but we're not at fault.

The first time that I encountered this syndrome was in a computer terminal that was manufactured by the company I worked at. It had a detached keyboard that must have weighed 20 kilos or so, but it was considered superior to those terminals with keyboards that could be placed on one's lap, which is, in my opinion, the purpose of a detached keyboard.

Over the years, I've encountered the syndrome in various locations, usually associated with some kind of kludge. Usually it was a software kludge, either a homegrown procedure or utility that might have filled some kind of need, probably back during the Pliocene. Nevertheless, whatever it was, it was created locally and was, therefore, better than anything from any other source.

Of course, there is an alternative reason for Microsoft creating ATLAS beyond the "not invented here" syndrome. Perhaps Microsoft intends to either Balkanize the technology by creating incompatible alternatives or attempt to seize control by having their own flavor. There is, however, the additional possibility that they have allowed themselves to be blindsided again. Personally, I am most fond of the last possibility because it is kind of reassuring to think that the company that some consider to be "The Evil Empire" has once again missed the bus.

16.3.1   A Picture of ATLAS

Unfortunately, to use Microsoft's ATLAS technologies, it is necessary to have a machine running Windows and a copy of Visual Studio 2005. Although my laptop does run Windows XP Professional, I don't have a copy of Visual Studio 2005, and with a price tag of $549 for the Professional version, it isn't something that I will be purchasing in the near future. After all, $549 will buy a large number of seasons of *Stargate SG1,* Gummi Lab Rats, and turkey club sandwiches. For mad scientists, it is all a matter of priorities.

16.4   The World Wide Web Consortium

As I stated earlier, the World Wide Web Consortium is, in most instances, the source of all things Web related. For this reason, I recommend that you occasionally visit its website, www.w3.org, to peruse the home page and see if there is anything new. In fact, this is one of those great spots to determine which skill to learn next. After all, unless we keep our skills current, or even a little more than current, it is quite possible that we could go the way of the dinosaur—or, at least, the way of the majority of American steel workers.

The World Wide Web Consortium is also one of those websites, like SourceForge, where it is possible to find some free goodies. However, unlike SourceForge, most people think of only documentation when they think of the World Wide Web Consortium. Fortunately, there is much more to the World Wide Web Consortium than a mere collection of HTML pages and PDF files. Many people don't realize that, in addition to the all the documents describing various technologies, there are quite often documents describing support for those various technologies—such as which web browsers support CSS Level 1, information that can be of some use when shopping for a new web browser.

16.5   Web Browsers

The scary part about this section is that I had to actually look to see which web browsers are installed on my Toshiba notebook. Over the last several months, my collection has grown beyond my usual two browsers to include the following (in alphabetical order):

☞ Firefox (www.mozilla.org)

☞ Flock (www.flock.com)

☞ Microsoft Internet Explorer (www.microsoft.com)

☞ Netscape (http://browser.netscape.com)

☞ Opera (www.opera.com)

In addition to adding browsers beyond the original two, several Firefox upgrades were installed during the same timeframe.

All in all, I discovered several interesting things about these browsers and myself. The first is that, as annoying as Microsoft Internet Explorer is, it pales in comparison to Opera. Opera is closed as tight as an oyster. In addition, some versions of Opera lie, claiming to be Microsoft Internet Explorer. This wouldn't be a problem if it behaved the same way as Microsoft Internet Explorer, but, unfortunately, it doesn't. In the end, I was forced to abandon Opera.

Of the remaining browsers, Firefox, Flock, and Netscape are all based upon Gecko, which means that if something works in one, it should work in all. In fact, I wasn't surprised to find this to be the case. Talk about consistency!

However, I want to point out one item concerning these browsers. Because they are open source, they have a tendency to change more often than Microsoft Internet Explorer—but, then, years change more often than Microsoft Internet Explorer. This could be an issue in testing to keep in mind.

Finally, there is Microsoft Internet Explorer, which, at this time, is still the number one web browser in use. Unlike the other browsers, unless you're running Windows or have an Apple computer, you're pretty much hosed if you want to run Internet Explorer. But there's always Firefox or Flock or Netscape.

16.6 SUMMARY

This chapter served as something of a wrap-up for the entire book—a weird wrap-up because, although Ajax has been around for several years, it is still evolving. Examples of this are Sarissa, JSON, and Microsoft's ATLAS, different approaches to solving what is basically the same problem. I also made mention of both the World Wide Web Consortium and SourceForge, with the former being useful for documentation and the latter being useful for development tools. For those of us whose spouses insist upon wasting money on the mortgage instead of development tools, those SourceForge tools come in handy. Finally, I gave the web addresses for the web browsers available at the time of this writing.

Symbols

A

G

N

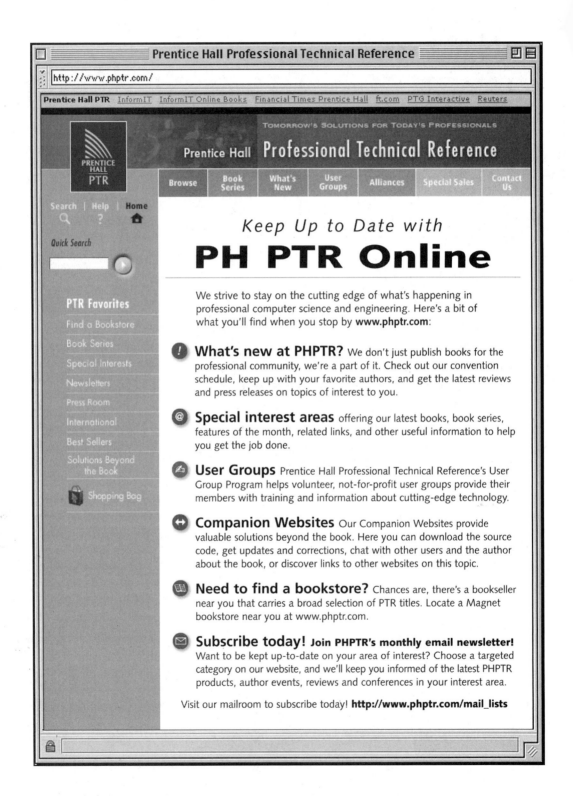

Prentice Hall Professional Technical Reference

http://www.phptr.com/

TOMORROW'S SOLUTIONS FOR TODAY'S PROFESSIONALS

Prentice Hall **Professional Technical Reference**

| Browse | Book Series | What's New | User Groups | Alliances | Special Sales | Contact Us |

Search | Help | Home

Quick Search

PTR Favorites

Find a Bookstore

Book Series

Special Interests

Newsletters

Press Room

International

Best Sellers

Solutions Beyond the Book

Shopping Bag

Keep Up to Date with
PH PTR Online

We strive to stay on the cutting edge of what's happening in professional computer science and engineering. Here's a bit of what you'll find when you stop by **www.phptr.com**:

What's new at PHPTR? We don't just publish books for the professional community, we're a part of it. Check out our convention schedule, keep up with your favorite authors, and get the latest reviews and press releases on topics of interest to you.

Special interest areas offering our latest books, book series, features of the month, related links, and other useful information to help you get the job done.

User Groups Prentice Hall Professional Technical Reference's User Group Program helps volunteer, not-for-profit user groups provide their members with training and information about cutting-edge technology.

Companion Websites Our Companion Websites provide valuable solutions beyond the book. Here you can download the source code, get updates and corrections, chat with other users and the author about the book, or discover links to other websites on this topic.

Need to find a bookstore? Chances are, there's a bookseller near you that carries a broad selection of PTR titles. Locate a Magnet bookstore near you at www.phptr.com.

Subscribe today! **Join PHPTR's monthly email newsletter!** Want to be kept up-to-date on your area of interest? Choose a targeted category on our website, and we'll keep you informed of the latest PHPTR products, author events, reviews and conferences in your interest area.

Visit our mailroom to subscribe today! **http://www.phptr.com/mail_lists**